# NORTHERN
# Mythology

13-Digit ISBN: 978-1-64643-461-9
10-Digit ISBN: 1-64643-461-7

This book may be ordered by mail from the publisher. Please include $5.99 for
postage and handling. Please support your local bookseller first!

Books published by Cider Mill Press Book Publishers are available at special
discounts for bulk purchases in the United States by corporations, institutions,
and other organizations. For more information, please contact the publisher.

Cider Mill Press Book Publishers
"Where good books are ready for press"
501 Nelson Place
Nashville, Tennessee 37214

cidermillpress.com

Typography: Noort, Neutraface 2 Display


Printed in Malaysia

23 24 25 26 27 OFF 5 4 3 2 1

First Edition

# NORTHERN
# Mythology

## TALES FROM NORSE, FINNISH & SÁMI TRADITIONS

### TIM RAYBORN

Illustrations by JO PARRY

CIDER MILL PRESS

BOOK PUBLISHERS

# Contents

# Introduction

When asked about Scandinavian myth, history, and culture, you might imagine violent, marauding Vikings sailing in their longships, or perhaps you think of fjords, the northern lights, reindeer, and Arctic landscapes. You probably know Marvel's *Thor* movies, and maybe you've watched the *Vikings* television show. You've no doubt heard of Thor, Loki, and Odin. If you have children, you might even know of the Sámi, who play a prominent role in Disney's *Frozen II*.

But do you know the Old Norse stories of the skiing huntress Skadi, the gossipy squirrel Ratatoskr, or Mimir, a literal talking head? What about the fantastic adventures of the Finnish wizard Väinämöinen, the dark goddess Louhi, or the handsome but arrogant Lemminkäinen in the lands of Kalevala and Pohjola? And beyond Disney's animated portrayal, what do you really know about the indigenous Sámi, a semi-nomadic people who have endured great hardships and attempts to eradicate their beliefs and culture over the past several centuries?

These wonderful northern myths and legends deserve a much wider audience. This book will help with that!

While the modern world still looks back to Greek and Roman myths for inspiration and insight, the mythologies of Northern Europe have not been so influential. Though some Norse gods have found their way into the modern world, the Finnish tales are all but unknown outside of academic circles and to those interested in world mythology. And after centuries of persecution and discrimination, the Sámi are emerging onto the world stage while holding on to many traditional beliefs that have survived against all odds.

But beyond superhero reimaginings and historical fiction, most people don't know much about ancient Scandinavian myth, history, and culture. And that's a shame, because these gods, people, and stories are endlessly fascinating in their own right. They can still inspire us with tales of epic adventures, magical transformations, and gods behaving badly.

The northern myths have long enticed specialists and enthusiasts with their haunting imagery, their familiar-but-not stories, and even tales that are downright strange, which just makes them all the more interesting. The people who preserved and believed in them lived in vibrant societies with their own unique characteristics, values, flaws, and wisdom.

Here you will find an introduction to the wonderful but often unfamiliar myths of three cultures, which probably influenced each other at various times throughout their histories. These tales are funny, sad, violent, vulgar, heart-breaking, and often odd, taking the reader to worlds unknown and to landscapes undreamed of. They are populated with all manner of weird and wonderful beings, gods, spirits, heroes, and magical items.

And yet, these stories from long ago offer us familiar dilemmas, not so different from those we face in the twenty-first century: questions about friendship, loyalty, family, the purpose of life, the purpose of death, our place in the universe, and much more. These myths can be gateways to unique new worlds that allow us to understand our own just a bit more.

So, enjoy this book however you'd like. Read it all the way through or dip into entries as you please. And take a trip back to a time of snow and ice, of war and bloodshed, but also of warmth and good company, love and loss, humor and laughter, good food and drink, and adventures of all kinds, from the mundane to the outrageous. The hall is open, the fires are roaring, the mead is poured, and your journey awaits!

# Norse Gods, Goddesses & Myths

The Norse myths are undoubtedly the best known stories in this book. Many of them were detailed in medieval Icelandic writings by those who no longer believed in them, but who still wanted to preserve them from oblivion. The Icelandic works known as the *Poetic Edda* and the *Prose Edda* have saved many amazing tales from being lost forever, even if these writers did sometimes overlay the myths with Christian biases or perhaps even make up their own versions of stories.

The old gods of Scandinavia continue to offer endless fascination to legions of admirers today. Odin, Thor, and Loki have become household names in the modern world, thanks to the popularity of recent television series and Marvel movies. Shows such as *Vikings* and *The Last Kingdom* have further popularized the Viking Age and its people. Whole musical genres of trance, folk, and dark ambient bands (such as Wardruna, Heilung, Kjell Braaten, and others) and heavy metal bands (including Týr, Enslaved, Amon Amarth, and many more) derive their inspiration from the mythologies of Northern Europe. Modern incarnations of religions devoted to the Norse deities are represented by several names, including heathenry (a good general term), Ásatrúarfélagið (the Asatru Fellowship, an official state religion in Iceland), various organizations in Scandinavia, the United States, and beyond, or even just Norse paganism. These new-but-old faiths are growing in popularity all the time, with tens, if not hundreds of thousands, of practitioners around the globe. The Vikings and their world appear to be coming back with a vengeance!

And yet, for all the information we do possess about these remarkable gods and the hardy people that worshiped them, there is much that is frustratingly incomplete: casual mentions of otherwise unknown gods with the briefest descriptions, allusions to lost stories that must have been well known at the time, contradictory tales, confusion over names and identities, and much more. Scholars have worked hard to piece together these tattered threads of tradition to come up with something coherent. And of course, it's entirely likely that there was no one "true" tradition, and that the same gods were revered in many different ways across different regions of the northern world. Who can say if Odin or Thor was honored the same way in Iceland as in England, or in Sweden as in Russia? We simply don't know.

Many of the stories that do survive probably had very distinct versions in different times and areas, and a number of them were certainly colored by the beliefs of the Christians who later wrote them down. We have no idea how many stories and myths we've lost forever because some scribe decided that they were unimportant or (more likely) offensive.

The surviving tales themselves are often full of contradictions. Sometimes one god is related to another, but then in a separate version of the myth, they're not, or perhaps they're connected in a different way. Some stories give details about certain events that other versions leave out completely. Some myths tell us that one god performed a feat, while another version names a different god taking the same action. All these conflicts show that there was no one, unified way of looking at these gods and the religious practices that grew up around them. There was no single holy scripture, no "Nordic pope," and nothing demanding conformity or doctrinal consistency. Rather, Norse culture had a large collection of gods and spirits whose worship varied over time. Certain key details about a given god (such as Odin having one eye) might carry over from region to region, but it was likely that groups of people envisioned their own versions of these gods, adapting them to their unique environments and situations. So, this book will have a lot of "might have been," "we're not exactly sure," "it seems that," and "this is yet another conflicting account." You have been warned.

A majority of the stories we do have come from medieval Iceland, and we are exceptionally lucky to have them at all. Two of our main sources, the *Poetic Edda* and the *Prose Edda*, were both written in Iceland on either side of the year 1200. The *Poetic Edda*, as the name suggests, is a collection of longer, epic poems that tell about the gods and the jötnar (the "giants"), and their adventures, their wishes, wins, and losses. A significant number of poems are devoted to the Germanic tales of Sigurd, Fafnir the dragon, Attila the Hun, and many others, known to the modern world from the *Ring of the Nibelung* and in Wagner's operas. These stories originated outside of Scandinavia but found their way into northern myths to sit alongside the tales of the Norse gods. Because of their different nature and the vast amount of space needed to do justice to them, this book will not discuss them, and will focus on the stories about the Norse gods only.

The second work, the *Prose Edda*, was composed in the thirteenth century by Snorri Sturluson, an Icelandic poet, lawyer, political leader, and historian who grew up in Iceland but spent time in Norway before returning to Iceland to write the *Prose Edda* and other important works beginning in the 1220s. He was murdered in 1241, the victim of men who were agents of the king of Norway. Political and territorial disputes were common in Iceland and farther abroad, and Snorri fell victim to them.

The *Prose Edda* gives us much additional information about the gods, often only hinted at in the *Poetic Edda*. Snorri quotes verses from the poetic collection to support his own work, so he clearly knew it well. The problem, of course, is how reliable is Snorri or the compilers of the *Prose Edda*? These are works by Christian writers, setting down these myths roughly 200 years after the "official" conversion of Iceland to Christianity (in the year 1000). And while it took several centuries for devotion to the old gods to be completely eradicated, can we trust that these writers are bringing us texts and information without inserting their own biases and opinions? No, we cannot, but these are the stories we have, so we need to work with them and try to tease out what might be original and what might be later invention. There are undoubtedly more than a few Christian inserts into these tales, and we will look at some of them in more detail later.

To make things even more complicated, the manuscripts that survive are later copies, produced after Snorri and his colleagues wrote them. Fortunately, the writers of the *Eddas* likely recorded their material from those Icelanders who still knew the old songs and poems. There might well have been an element of national pride in holding on to these remarkable myths as a part of the cultural heritage. Still, we have to approach them with at least some caution.

Ultimately, we can never know what mixture of politics, religious beliefs, and personal opinion motivated the Icelandic (and other) scribes and scholars to preserve these tales. We can only be glad that they exist in some form, imperfect though they might be. How much they were colored by Icelandic culture and its landscape is another question that we can't answer fully. Some of the descriptions, especially of the end of the world (Ragnarök), seem very much influenced by Iceland's volcanic landscape, its lava and smoke, its steam and ash. It's possible that the fiery fate of Ragnarök was unknown in other parts of Viking Age Scandinavia, especially as it related to death and the potential end of all things. But this imagery would have sat well with Icelandic Christians who saw similarities between their geologically active island home and the terrible descriptions of Revelation and other apocalyptic accounts.

Beyond the Icelandic works, we have other sources for the Norse gods that are less specific, or at least less concerned about any kind of accuracy in relaying the myths to us. A Danish writer, Saxo Grammaticus (c. 1150–c. 1220) wrote his *Gesta Danorum*, a history of Denmark that contains bits and pieces of old myths and legends woven throughout. In his version, the gods are eu-hemerized, in other words, represented as real human beings who came to be worshiped by some of their ignorant followers (Saxo was a devout Christian). To be fair, Snorri does this as well, but he relayed the myths in a more straightforward way, where-as Saxo just jumbled up everything according to whatever he felt like doing! Even so, some of his accounts hint at alternate ver-sions of the Icelandic myths that might be part of a separate set of beliefs and traditions in certain Scandinavian locations. We'll look at a few of those later.

The eleventh-century chronicler Adam of Bremen wrote about some of the customs of the pagan Norse, and while he gave details that could be accurate (as well as some intriguing alternate versions of myths), we also have to take some of his claims with a large grain of salt, since he most certainly wanted to portray the pagan Scandinavians as barbaric and in desperate need of Christian salvation.

There are also images and inscriptions on old rocks and stones that illustrate scenes from a few of the tales in the *Eddas*, indicating that some of these myths might be very old, probably even predating the era we call the Viking Age (late eighth centu-ry to the mid-eleventh century).

The gods and other supernatural entities play roles in the Ice-landic sagas, quasi-historical accounts about the brave people who settled Iceland, Greenland, and Vinland (in North America). These people also had many adventures in lands far to the east and south of their Scandinavian homeland. Such accounts of-ten reinforce some of the tales presented here, while also adding their own elements. The sagas give us some insight into how the gods might have been worshiped and what kind of pagan prac-tices were in use, though again, we need to be cautious about taking too much at face value, entertaining as these stories are.

The poetry of the Viking Age was composed and recited (be-ing spoken and perhaps sung) by special poets known as skalds. These artists were not usually literate, but instead composed lengthy works orally and held them in their impressive memories. They took care to accurately pass down their poems through the generations, until such time as someone took enough interest to write them down. Sadly, this means that countless skaldic poems were lost forever over the centuries, but again, we are fortunate to have the ones that we do. Skaldic poetry overlaps with the *Poetic Edda*, but there are many poems that survive in other sources. Some of these also mention the gods and might allude to different versions of myths or even hint at stories that haven't survived, offering a tantalizing glimpse into a wider mythic world. The poets of the time were fond of using kennings, which are compound expressions with a metaphorical meaning. Instead of saying "the sea," they might use a term like "the whale road," or when referring to fire, they'd say, "the bane of wood." Some kennings are obscure and require a decent knowledge of Norse lore and language to understand. We still use kennings in modern times when we say things like "fender bender" for a car accident, or "bookworm" for someone who enjoys reading. They add color and vividness to a language.

For the sake of clarity, this section will largely focus on the material in both *Eddas* but will also draw useful information from some of these other sources to try to paint a fuller picture of the often murky world of Norse myth, with all of its confusions and contradictions.

But what of the Norse world itself? We tend to think of Viking/Norse cultures as hyper-masculine, warrior based, with stratified class and gender roles, and this was often true. And yet, many myths have a notable current of gender and sexual subversion, where gender roles are mixed or swapped, and where not everyone and everything is what they seem. Why would Odin the Allfather—the god of battle and death—learn Seidr, a Norse magic associated with the goddess Freya, when it was more often the work of women and possibly even seen as shameful for men to practice? Small statues from archaeological sites sometimes depict Odin and other male figures in what seem to be women's clothing. Loki switches sex more than once to give birth to strange creatures. He also accuses Freya of having sex with everyone at a feast gathering; does he mean gods only, or perhaps goddesses as well? Why does Heimdall lie with both wives and husbands when siring the social classes of Nordic society? Was Njord the sea god originally a goddess? Was Skadi the winter goddess originally a god? Is it possible that some viewed (possibly negatively) practitioners of Seidr as a third gender, a trait assigned to certain Siberian shamans? Some of these questions will be explored in the following pages, even though we can only answer them with educated guesses.

In addition to questions of identity and sexuality, several of these gods have disabilities: Odin is famously missing an eye, Tyr's right hand was bitten off by the wolf, Heimdall might have left one ear in the Well of Mimir at one root of the World Tree, while Odin's son, Hod, is blind. These descriptions turn on the head the idea that gods must always represent perfection. But in a society that valued warriors, some people probably were missing limbs or other body parts that they'd lost in battle, who nevertheless survived and lived to tell about their exploits. It's perhaps natural that this situation would be reflected in their gods. A verse from the *Hávamál*, the sayings of Odin, says:

The lame can ride a horse,

The handless man can drive cattle,

The deaf one can fight and prevail,

To be blind is better than to burn on a pyre:

There is nothing the dead can do.

There was a place for the disadvantaged in Norse society, if they could contribute something, and this is reflected in their gods, as well.

The Norse gods and their ways are very different from the Christian religion that replaced them. They are not always kind, wise, loving, or forgiving (though neither were Christians, for that matter!). These gods often engage in all-too-human behaviors: they argue and fight, lie and deceive, can be petty and greedy, have affairs, and indulge in good food and drink, sometimes to excess (they're known to get drunk and hurl insults). But they are also honorable, protective, devoted to one another and their families, committed to their oaths, generous, and hospitable. They are very much a reflection of the peoples that worshiped them. They have much to teach us about humanity's good and bad qualities, and their strange, beguiling stories can still capture our imaginations across a thousand years and more.

It's worth mentioning something here about the words "myth" and "mythology." We tend to think of a myth as a synonym for "lie" and perhaps mythology as a synonym for "fiction." But myth is a richer and more meaningful word, deriving from the Greek word mythos, meaning word, speech, story, conversation, and more. Myths reflect the cultural identity of a people and tell us much about them. A mythic story is not so much about being true or false, but rather what it conveys to those that encounter it. As a somewhat famous saying from Joseph Campbell goes, "A myth is something that has never happened, but is happening all the time." It's not about locating a story in history and trying to find out what "really" happened, as those Christians who made the Norse gods into humans attempted to do. Instead, it's about learning from the imagery and symbolism and seeing what resonates with us now. This is why many see the Greek myths as so timeless and relevant, thousands of years later. The Norse myths are no less rich in content and meaning for those who dare to explore their strange and beautiful settings and inhabitants.

So herein is a mythical array of the weird and the wonderful, the touching and the brutal, the joyous and the heartbreaking, as envisioned by the Scandinavians of more than 1,000 years ago. These gods reflect the fullness of human experience and emotions, and they were well suited as deities and patrons to the peoples of the north, people who lived in harsh landscapes, but nevertheless triumphed and set out to explore and settle in the wider world, often far beyond the boundaries of their homelands. They took their gods with them, and now we can enjoy their tales anew.

A few notes before we begin. Some of the tales in this section have been condensed or simplified to aid in easier reading, but the key points are there. They are based primarily on the *Poetic Edda* and *Prose Edda*, along with a few other works. Each entry lists the main source(s) for the myth under the title.

Each myth includes a background discussion at the end that offers further insight into what the stories and symbolism might mean, based on different current scholars' readings and takes, as well as the author's own. Any or none of these opinions might be true! Often there are several scholarly debates about deeper meanings, but that fact just makes these tales all the more fascinating. None of these opinions are meant to be the last word, and research is always ongoing.

Throughout this section, there are alternate spellings given for some names. These are there to show how the words originally looked in medieval manuscripts and scholarly editions. For ease of reading, most names have been modernized: Óðinn becomes Odin, Þórr is Thor, Skaði changes to Skadi, and so on. Occasionally a minor character might have only the Old Norse spelling if they don't appear too often, just to give the flavor for their original names. But the myths will be easier to read with modernized spellings, rather than expecting readers to wrap their minds around Old Norse and Icelandic ones.

# THE AESIR AND THE VANIR

According to usual interpretations, Norse mythology has two sets of gods, the Aesir and the Vanir. The Aesir are generally more action-oriented and representative of civilization, while the Vanir tend to be associated with nature, love, magic, and fertility. Some scholars think that this unlikely combination was the result of two cultures mixing at some point.

The Vanir might have been the gods of a people who came to Scandinavia, perhaps from the east, who were separate from the Sámi, who lived in the far north. Meanwhile, the Aesir were probably "imported" by the Germanic peoples who migrated into the Scandinavian regions over several centuries, beginning in prehistoric times all the way up to the year 100 CE or so. But this is only one theory.

Indeed, the mythology tells of an Aesir-Vanir war, wherein the two groups of gods battled each other over the ages, eventually settled into a truce, and then became allies. They never again went to war, though there was sometimes tension between them.

Today, this story seems like a mythical retelling of actual conflicts between two groups of people with two distinct sets of gods, who eventually put aside their differences and agreed to live together. In a mythic parallel, as the Aesir and Vanir settled their differences and struck up an eventual friendship, the tales of their adventures could begin in earnest.

And while the named Vanir gods were far fewer in number (many probably don't survive, or were never written down), two of them, Freya and Freyr, were among the most important of all the gods in Scandinavia. These two never lost that importance, such that Freyr, for example, was noted as one of the chief gods worshiped in Sweden, alongside Odin and Thor. Reverence for Freya would continue for many centuries in Scandinavian folk belief, despite attempts to stamp out such ancient devotions.

All of this would seem to be pretty straightforward, but some scholars have recently questioned just how common these collections of gods were to all the Norse people. They have suggested that the idea of the "gods of Asgard" who lived together or near each other and regularly gathered for feasting and council under the rule of Odin is anachronistic. This idea resembles the Greek concept of Olympus and its gods, rather than any actual Nordic beliefs of the time. To be sure, there are stories of the gods meeting and taking council, and even of small god "team-ups" (especially Loki, who sticks his nose into everything, as tricksters often do!), but by and large, there is little to indicate that all the gods were believed to live in one place and that all of them were worshiped by all people throughout Scandinavia.

As we'll see, there are many conflicting tales about the gods, their deeds, and their characteristics that suggest multiple contradictory myths believed by different groups of people in different places. It's entirely possible that localized groups only worshiped one god primarily, and maybe would turn to a few others in times of need or under special circumstances. The skaldic poetry that survives was composed for educated, wealthy people who had a very different perspective on the cosmos than most others or the common people. So, it's difficult, if not impossible, to discover just what the everyday men and women of Viking Age Scandinavia believed and who they worshiped. There was no one "religion" as we would think of it, but rather a collection of smaller cults devoted to particular gods. By the way, "cults" here does not refer to brainwashing or secretive organizations that fleece their followers out of money; that's a modern definition. A cult was simply originally a small(ish) group of people who held to a certain set of beliefs and practices, devoted to a given god. Christianity was once a cult in the greater Roman Empire.

Such cults would have been spread all around Scandinavia, maybe being no larger than regional, or even limited to a collection of settlements. For example, the people of one area might be devoted to Thor, while another nearby group might worship Freyr. This doesn't mean that they didn't believe in each other's gods or that they were hostile to each other. They simply focused on the god or gods that were most important to them and their communities and didn't concern themselves as much with the others, much less conceive of the idea that they all lived in some celestial realm and interacted with each other on a daily basis. It's true that the large temple in Uppsala seems to have been dedicated to Freyr, Odin, and Thor, though this location was a meeting place for travelers from all over, and not just Scandinavia, but also from regions much farther away. It would have made sense to accommodate different gods and beliefs. Think of how Jerusalem (and other cities) has synagogues, churches, and mosques, to which believers of these different religions flock.

There is evidence that Odin, while certainly known in earlier centuries, really came into prominence as a possible "Allfather" of the gods in about the fifth or sixth century, and that before then, that role might have been given to Tyr or even Thor, and maybe still was in certain locations. The idea of the war god seems to have become more important at this time, with leaders wanting to gather around one or two deities and possibly claim descent from them to enhance their power. (This claim of divine kingship became common a few centuries later.) Since much of what we know about the Norse gods was written down in Iceland in the early thirteenth century, we can simply never know all the variations and small details that might have been a part of daily spiritual life, both among the would-be kings and their followers, and certainly among farmers and thralls (slaves).

Is it possible that some Norse people didn't even know about many of the other major gods, much less considered them to be a part of some big family or pantheon? That's a reasonable assumption. Maybe some people only ever knew and honored Thor, and so saw him as the creator god, while others assigned this role to Odin and made Thor subordinate, or never knew him at all. Snorri and the Icelandic poets liked to lump them all together, but we'll probably never know if this practice was common throughout mainland Scandinavia, or a later Icelandic belief or a poetic invention.

Indeed, there are only a handful of surviving stories that have large numbers of gods in them, and it's possible that they never met in believers' minds otherwise. They might have been gods from completely different belief systems or religions, combined later into a coherent whole.

Other scholars have gone even further and suggested that there might not have been a division between Aesir and Vanir at all. They argue that both were names for gods, and the word "Vanir" might simply have been used when it was more poetically appropriate, such as for alliterations. This isn't a widely accepted theory—at least not yet—but it does show that the final word on these gods has yet to be told.

Even though this might sound complicated, it doesn't radically change how we can approach the gods in a general sense. These stories are still here for us to enjoy and explore their deeper meanings. There is no doubt that this collection of myths and gods does come from the general Scandinavian region, so the Norse gods have every right to be presented together as a whole, even if they were thought of differently over 1,000 years ago. With that in mind, let us first delve into the wonderful biographies of these colorful and remarkable deities, with all their virtues and failings, good characteristics and bad. They give us a fascinating view into the spiritual lives of the pagan Norse peoples, and there is much they can still teach us and inspire us with today.

## ODIN (ÓÐINN)

Any discussion of the Norse gods must begin with Odin, of course. Odin is the Allfather, the chief deity of the Norse gods, a descendant of the primal beings and one of the creators of the worlds and of humanity, along with his two brothers, Vili and Vé, or Hoenir and Lodur, depending on which source you trust for their names. Odin is one of the major players in many of the most important Norse myths. He is famous for having only one eye, having sacrificed the other to obtain wisdom from the Well of Mimir. He is also the one who collects the runes after hanging on the World Tree as a sacrifice to himself for nine nights (more on both sacrifices later). Odin can be said to "rule" over the gods, but not as a king or a dictator; the other gods are frequently in conflict with him and can defy him for their own purposes. Even his own wife, Frigg, grows tired of some of his nonsense from time to time!

Odin is on an endless quest of knowledge and wisdom, sometimes to the point of becoming obsessive about it. The goddess Freya taught him the magic of Seidr, even though its practice was often seen as shameful for men to pursue in Norse culture. Loki would later insult him for it in a quarrel with all the gods that would mark him an outcast. But a god is not a man, and Odin can do as he wishes!

While Odin is married to the goddess Frigg and has children with her (Baldr and Hod), he is a rampant philanderer and is said to have had affairs with multiple goddesses and jötnar ("giants"), resulting in a number of offspring. In this way, he resembles Zeus, who also couldn't keep his hands to himself. Even the mighty god Thor is the son of Odin and the jötunn (giantess) Jord, not of Frigg. What Frigg thinks of his behavior is never revealed, though we can imagine her as being a long-suffering wife like Hera, but one who stands up to her husband when she needs to and takes her own lovers (Odin's brothers) when it suits her.

Odin is an old god, worshiped by the Germanic tribes in the Roman era as Wotan, and later by the pagan Anglo-Saxons in England as Woden. It is from this latter name that we get our English day-name of Wednesday (Wōdnesdæg, "Woden's Day"), one of four days of the week named for the Anglo-Saxon versions of the same gods (we'll get to the other gods so honored in their own entries). The name ultimately comes from a proto-Germanic word, *Wōðanaz, meaning something like "Master of the

Possessed" or "Lord of Frenzy." This name in turn comes from the proto-Indo-European *wod-eno: "mad," "raging," or perhaps "inspired." All these meanings point to Odin's nature: a god associated with battle and frenzy, trance states, and even being possessed by battle lust. In the Viking Age, he was undoubtedly called upon for battle-favor, and it seems that the infamous warriors known as the berserkers were devoted to him. They might have worked themselves up into a killing frenzy, perhaps in an altered state, before entering the fight.

We don't have many physical descriptions of the Norse gods, but Odin is usually depicted as having one eye and possibly an impressive beard and a broad-brimmed hat. He wanders the worlds on foot and on horseback, ever seeking new knowledge.

He is a god associated with battle and death. Warriors worshiped him in the hopes that they would be called after death in battle to sit in his great hall Valhǫll, better known as Valhalla, the "Hall of the Slain." These warriors, known as the Einherjar, or the "Army of One," will fight each other daily and feast nightly until they are called upon to fight against the enemies of the gods at Ragnarök. But this honor might come at a terrible price, for Odin is said to be rather wily, and can remove his favor from some of his preferred warriors to bring about their deaths in battle and thus join him in his hall sooner than they might have expected or wanted. The life of a Viking or a Norse warrior of any kind was always fraught with peril and uncertainty, and the god they worshiped could be just as unpredictable, though this didn't diminish the Allfather's popularity among them.

Odin's eight-legged horse, Sleipnir ("The Slipper"), was birthed by Loki in a strange story of shapeshifting, and later he gives the steed to Odin as a gift. On Sleipnir, Odin can ride through the many realms. He also has the services of two ravens, Hugin ("Thought") and Munin ("Memory" or "Mind"). These names might only date from the Viking Age, but war figures accompanied by two birds (usually ravens) are found in earlier Germanic imagery, suggesting that the idea of Odin and his ravens might be very old. Some see them as projections of Odin's own consciousness, or perhaps remnants of an older spiritual practice that might have come from the east. Each day, Odin sends them out into the worlds to learn new information. He waits for them to return, but worries that they might not. He especially worries that Munin won't come back. We're not sure why he worries about one raven more than the other.

Two wolves—Geri and Freki—complete Odin's menagerie. Their names both mean "Greedy" and perhaps "Ravenous" or even "Gluttonous," which might refer to their appetites. The poem *Grímnismál* tells us that Odin feeds them, while he himself lives only on wine. This odd detail might be just for dramatic effect. Odin, like the other gods, seems to eat the fruit (probably apples) that the goddess Idunn provides, which keeps them all young. Unless Odin is drinking apple wine, of course!

Speaking of wolves, Odin's fate is to be devoured by the wolf Fenrir at the end of the world, Ragnarök, and to be avenged by his son, Vidar (Víðarr). Odin knows this, and he comes to realize that no matter what he does, this destiny cannot be changed. So, he will ride out on that fateful day, understanding that it will be his last.

And while Odin is a god of battle, he is also a god of poetry, eloquence, and inspiration. He goes to great lengths to capture the mead of poetry and bring it back not only to the other gods, but also to human poets who will receive inspiration from it. And as a master of wisdom, he is always interested in engaging in battles of wits, rather than battles of arms. In one moment, he can seem to be paternal and caring, and in another cruel, devious, and callous.

For all of Odin's importance, it's possible that he was not always the chief god among the Germanic peoples. The god Tyr seems to have held that prime spot early on, with Wotan/Odin replacing him at some point, probably slowly over time. And it's also likely that there were some areas of Scandinavia where Odin was not seen as the chief deity, and took second place to other gods like Freyr, or even Thor, especially in parts of what is now modern Sweden. Many Scandinavian kings in the eighth and ninth centuries probably wanted a single god around which to have their warriors focus, and Odin was an excellent choice. These people weren't monotheists by any means, but they likely gave their devotion to only a handful of gods at a time, or perhaps to just one, and probably not to a whole "pantheon" of Norse gods. For them, Odin was the perfect choice.

## THOR (ÞÓRR)

Of all the Norse gods, Thor, the "god of thunder," is probably the most famous of all. This was true long before Marvel Comics came along with its own blond-haired version and the Marvel movies made Chris Hemsworth, who plays him, a household name.

Thor is the son of Odin and Jord, the Earth. And yet, Thor and his wife, Sif, might also represent an old sky and Earth myth. There could have been several versions of Thor's relationship to the land, of which these two happen to survive. Curiously, Jord is herself a jötunn, so it seems a bit strange that so much of Thor's activity is bound up in fighting and slaying the jötnar. There's no indication that he has a bad relationship with his mother, so his role might be seen as the one who pushes back the chaos that always surrounds and threatens to overwhelm everything. But even he eventually succumbs to that chaos at Ragnarök.

Thor was very popular in Viking Age Scandinavia and beyond, being honored in Germany as Donar and in Anglo-Saxon England as Thunor, lending his name to Thursday (þunresdæg, or "Thunor's Day"). Gods of the sky—as well as thunder and lightning—are fairly common in Indo-European myth: Indra in India, Perkunas in the Baltics, the Finnish Ukko, the Slavic god Perun, and the Celtic god Taranis. There is almost certainly an ancient connection between some of them, even if they developed differently in various cultures.

The Germanic tribes venerated Thor during the Roman period, and it seems that Roman writers believed that he was Hercules; they also wrote that Odin was Mercury. Romans often affixed their own gods' names onto those of their neighbors, and some Romans probably believed that they were even the same deities just known by different names. In any case, Germanic worship of Thor has a long history. Indeed, the Christian writer Adam of Bremen recorded that at the great temple of Uppsala (in modern Sweden), Thor's statue was in the center, flanked on either side by Odin and Freyr. That Odin wasn't at the center clearly shows that there was never one single hierarchy or pantheon in which every god had a designated place. Adam also tells us that the people were so fond of Thor that in the year 1030 they lynched an Englishman who had come to preach Christian conversion to them and had defaced an image of Thor.

Thor's popularity continued after "official" Christianization in Scandinavia and Iceland, and he was still invoked for help and protection, just as the goddess Freya would also linger in the minds of the people long after the authorities wanted her forgotten. While kings and princes saw political advantage in becoming Christian and aligning themselves with Catholic Rome and mainland European powers, everyday people were less willing to give up their traditional beliefs and continued to hold them in secret.

Throughout the *Eddas*, Thor goes forth on many adventures, usually getting into fights of some kind. He is seen as hot tempered, impatient, and perhaps not the sharpest tool in the shed since he's easily deceived in various tales. Generally, he's good and well meaning. He is not only a mighty warrior who slays jötnar and monsters, but as a thunder and sky god, farmers and others looked to him for favorable weather: rain for crops, calm weather for a sea journey, mild weather for other outdoor undertakings, and so on. Thor seems to have an especially strong connection

with mortals, as opposed to some other gods who are more aloof. This would explain his popularity as a god of the people.

Descriptions of the Norse gods are often frustratingly sparse, which might have had to do with how the people themselves visualized (or rather didn't *consistently* visualize) their deities. While Thor has long been depicted with red hair and a red beard, another description in the *Prose Edda* describes him as having hair that is fairer and more beautiful than gold. Freya is likewise often thought of as having golden, strawberry blonde, or red hair, so the overlap between these colors seems common. Some descriptions of gold call it "red gold," so there might be a connection here, or an indication that these colors were somewhat interchangeable. In any case, the red-haired Thor was a common image in the Viking Age and beyond.

His famed hammer, Mjolnir, is his most prized possession. He also owns a pair of gauntlets (Járngreipr) that he used to wield the hammer, and a special belt (Megingjörð) that amplifies his strength. With these, he slays many mighty foes. Pendants depicting a stylized version of Thor's hammer have been found in large numbers across the northern world in archaeological excavations, probably proving how popular he was. Some scholars have suggested that these small hammers might have begun to appear in greater numbers in the later pagan Viking Age, as a way of heathens pushing back against the Christian cross that was starting to make its appearance on church buildings and around people's necks. But archaeological finds of small hammers pre-date the presence of Christianity in the north, so the symbol is obviously very old. Curiously, it is the only tool of the Norse gods that seems to have been made into an everyday adornment. No miniature spears of Odin or ships of Freyr, for example, have been found. This might be evidence for Thor's enduring popularity for several centuries. As such, Mjolnir has become a symbol of overall faith for many modern heathens.

On the domestic side, Thor is married to Sif, the beautiful goddess with Rapunzel-like blonde hair. When Loki succeeds in cutting off her hair while she sleeps, Thor becomes enraged and forces Loki to go and obtain replacement hair for her. And yet, their marriage is certainly not perfect. Thor has a mistress, the jötunn Járnsaxa, with whom he has a son, Magni, and possibly a second son, Móði, both of whom will outlive him. Sif has her own son, Ullr—a god of winter, archery, and skiing—from another relationship. Together, Thor and Sif have a daughter named Thrud, who is the subject of unwanted attention from a dwarf that Thor manages to defeat not by might, but by distraction.

Some mythologists see the marriage of Thor and Sif as in part a representation of the union of earth and sky. The myth of the sky god who "fertilizes" the earth goddess is ancient, and these two gods might be a remnant of a very old Germanic belief that derives from Indo-European sources. Sif's golden hair could represent crops ready for harvest, while Thor, who commands thunder, lightning, and rain, brings those crops to life.

Thor rides in a chariot pulled, a bit comically, by two large goats, Tanngnjóstr ("Teeth Grinder") and Tanngrisnir ("Teeth Gnasher"). But he doesn't always use it. When the gods meet each day at the World Tree, he forgoes his goat-drawn vehicle and instead wades through the two rivers of Kerlaugar ("Kettle Bath") to get there, but we're not sure why. Perhaps the goats object to having to wait around at boring meetings. These animals provide more than just transportation and dental destruction; Thor can kill them and eat them, and the next day, they will be alive and fully replenished again, a strange occurrence that might be related to older animal myths from various northern regions. This odd story might also be related to the account of the beast Sæhrímnir, whom Odin's warriors eat each night in Valhalla, and who is alive and well the next day. Unfortunately, the animals don't seem to get a say in it.

# FRIGG

Frigg is a key goddess in the Germanic and Norse traditions, present in the myths of both for centuries before the Viking Age, and she is among the most important of the goddesses. She is associated with hearth and home, as well as motherhood, marriage, and even prophetic abilities. With her husband, Odin, she has two sons, Baldr and the blind god, Hod.

Frigg is a patron of all home-related things, which were by no means trivial in the Nordic world. Women who stayed at home kept close watch over everything, and their word was essentially law, especially when their husbands were absent. The lady of the house was not to be trifled with, and neither would Frigg be. Spinning and weaving were essential for everything from clothing to making sails for the famed Viking longships. This work was mostly done by women (some of whom were certainly slaves). They would have likely looked to Frigg for inspiration and guidance. Indeed, in Swedish tradition, the stars of the constellation of Orion's Belt were called, Friggerock, or "Frigga's spindle," showing that an association between her and that all-important work continued well after Christianization.

The goddess Freya says that Frigg knows the fate of all, even if she does not speak about it. Pregnant women would honor Frigg (and sometimes Freya), and anyone with children might call on her for their protection and well-being. Frigg gives her name to the modern English word Friday: Frīgedæg, or "the day of Frigga" in Old English, completing the four-day run of days named for Anglo-Saxon gods, and showing how important they were in pre-Christian Anglo-Saxon England. Versions of these day names can be found in various other Germanic languages, meaning that it was her day across the pagan Germanic world.

She dwells at a place called Fensalir ("Fen Halls"), which is separate from Valhalla, proving that she is not just an appendage of her husband. While she represents the home, Frigg is no 1950s housewife, and she has a hall and a life of her own, sepa-

rate from Odin and his endless wanderings and adventures. The location of the hall might indicate something about how she was worshiped in the Viking Age. Gold jewelry, locks of hair, and remains of flax and spinning wheels, among other household items, have been found in Scandinavian fens and water areas, which could be offerings to Frigg. The association of Germanic goddesses with water goes back to Roman times and perhaps even earlier. Devotees of the great goddess Nerthus kept an image of her hidden on an island in a lake, which was only brought out to show the faithful at certain times. As we will see, Nerthus herself might have been the unnamed wife of the Nordic sea god Njord, or in an unusual twist, she might have actually become that god over time. We might think of Grendel's mother as another example of a magical mother living underwater, though she was demonized by the Christian overlay of the Beowulf poem. In any case, Frigg's association with fens is part of a greater tradition of water goddesses. Several other Norse goddesses have connections to Frigg, and we will cover them in a later entry.

She also seems to have magical healing powers. According to the ninth-century second Merseburg incantation (a Germanic magical charm), where she is named Frija (not to be confused with Freya), she, her sister Volla, and the god Wodan (Odin) help to heal Baldr's horse, who has injured its leg. We'll have much more to say about this incident in the Baldr entry (see page 61). But it seems significant that Frigg in Norse tradition has a handmaiden named Fulla (very similar to Volla), and that Wodan is named as a part of this charm. That their son Baldr is also there shows that the connection between the three was known in lands outside of Scandinavia and probably dates back far earlier than Viking times.

In Norse myth, Frigg appears in both the *Poetic* and *Prose Eddas*, and while she is the wife of Odin and keeper of the home, she is by no means a wallflower. She stands up to him when needed, and tries to protect her son Baldr from a dreadful death.

She comes into conflict with Loki, who deceives her in order to bring about a cruel fate for Baldr, who seems to be her favorite son. Later, Loki accuses her of having sex with Odin's brothers, Vili and Vé, perhaps at the same time, while Odin is off traveling. This might be revealing, because it's possible that Loki himself is one of those brothers under a different name (more on that shocking possibility later). She doesn't deny the accusation of infidelity, instead responding that if her son Baldr were present, he would fight Loki with fury. But by this time, Baldr is dead, due to Loki's interference.

As shown in the Merseburg incantation and the story of Baldr, Frigg possesses magical abilities to protect and heal. At the beginning of the poem *Vafþrúðnismál* from the *Poetic Edda*, Odin desires to visit with the jötunn Vafthrudnir and seeks Frigg's advice. She cautions him not to, saying that she knows of no other jötunn as powerful as he. But Odin is determined to find out just what kind of being Vafthrundir is, and to see if he can engage him in a contest of wisdom. Frigg concedes that Odin will do what he wants, so she offers him wishes of good luck and safety, but these seem to be more than just casual well-wishes. Given her ties to healing and warding, it's possible that this short little scene represents her offering up magical protection for her husband. By the way, he does come back safely.

The connection (if any) between Frigg and Freya has been discussed quite a lot. Given their similar names and occasional similar roles in various myths, some have suggested that they are actually the same goddess, but referred to with two different names. And yet, there is enough about each of them that is unique to make the case that they are two separate goddesses. Freya was unknown outside of Scandinavia (suggesting that she might be indigenous, or at least an older goddess in the region than Frigg), while Frigg can be found in older Germanic myths from outside the Nordic world. The etymologies of their names are different, even though they sound similar. One of Frigg's Germanic names is Frija, which derives from Indo-European roots. It sounds very much like "Freya," but as we'll see, Freya is a title rather than a proper name, and has a different origin.

It's entirely possible that in some places, people combined Frigg and Freya into one goddess, while people in other areas might have always seen them as separate. Both theories can co-exist. So the answer is yes, they might be the same, but also no, they're likely very different! And that's not very helpful, but it is the way of things with Norse myth.

## FREYA

Freya, or Freyja, is the goddess associated with love and sexuality, beauty and wealth, but also magic and battle. One of the Vanir goddesses, she is sister to Freyr (possibly his twin) and the daughter of the sea god Njord. All three of them came to dwell with the Aesir after the ending of the Aesir-Vanir war. She is the most beautiful of all the goddesses and one of the most powerful, and perhaps most feared. Still, Freya had countless worshippers, both women and men, and her cult was strong throughout Scandinavia. She was seen as kind and loving, responding well to her people's needs.

Her hair is blonde, strawberry blonde, or red (perhaps she can change it any time she wishes?), and she possesses a cloak made of falcon feathers, which allows her to shape-shift into a falcon and fly to any of the realms. She has a great love for gold and beautiful things. She coveted an exquisite and priceless necklace called the Brísingamen so much that she agreed to a "special arrangement" with the four dwarves who crafted the piece in exchange for it. Stories of Freya's generous sexuality exist in more than one account, and it was said that she gave herself willingly to both immortals and mortals alike if she favored them. Many jötnar lusted after her and wanted to possess her, but she always resisted and maintained her own autonomy and agency. Loki accuses her of promiscuity with all of the assem-

bled gods (and possibly goddesses?), and even of having sex with her own brother, Freyr.

In any case, Freya is married to a mysterious being named Óðr (Od). They had daughters named Hnoss and Gersemi, but Óðr then disappeared. Despite Freya's attempts to find him (she has searched throughout all the worlds), she never has. She cries tears of gold for his absence. Amber—that beautiful, fossilized pine resin found all over the Baltic Sea region—was often known as "Freya's tears."

She is a master of magic and of the ancient magical workings of Seidr (seiðr), used for seeing the future and learning hidden secrets in other realms. So valuable was this skill that Odin asks her to teach him the practice of this ancient magic, quite an odd request for a male god. In Viking times, certain magical arts like Seidr were considered to be the domain of women. Human men who practiced them were viewed with suspicion and hostility, if not outright contempt, for being overly "feminine," but this doesn't seem to have affected the people's or the gods' perception of Odin. And the women who did practice it probably were devotees of Freya.

Indeed, she must be a powerful goddess, because she rides in a chariot pulled by two cats (Norwegian forest cats? Lynxes? Tabbies? No one knows!). Anyone who has cats knows how difficult it is to get them to do anything they don't want to do themselves. Their names, unfortunately, don't appear in any surviving text. She also rides a boar named Hildisvíni, who seems to be an animal form of a human lover, named Óttar.

Freya dwells in a hall called Sessrúmnir ("Seat Room"), set in a field known as Fólkvangr ("Army Field"), and it is said that, like Odin, she chooses some of those slain in battle to join her in her hall. In fact, she seems to have first choice over Odin! This links her to the Valkyries, and to the disir, the female ancestors with great power (see the entry on them on page 99). And yet, Freya herself does not ride into battle, at least not in any of the stories about her that survive. Her role in the final battle of Ragnarök, if any, is unclear, as is her fate.

As noted in the previous entry, some scholars have suggested that Freya and Frigg are the same goddess, and that her husband Óðr is none other than Odin. It is possible that in Germanic times, Freya/Frigg were one entity, and split into two different goddesses by the time of the Viking Age. But no one is certain.

Another plausible theory suggests the opposite, and supposes that as a member of the Vanir, Freya was an older goddess in the north. In this view, worship of Frigg was brought in later with the arrival of the Germanic peoples, which, as we've seen, might also reveal something of the historical source behind the Aesir/Vanir war. The two goddesses might have been combined into one deity in some places, but they were almost certainly separate entities in others. The fact that Freya was essentially unknown outside of Scandinavia (and Iceland) suggests that she might have been local to that area, or at least older. Certainly, by the Viking era, the two goddesses governed different aspects of life and belief.

Though her name is similar to Frigg's, her name simply means "Lady," and is a title. She is also known by many other names, including Vanadís (the Dís, or "Lady," of the Vanir), Mardöll ("Sea Brightener"), and Blotgydja ("Priestess of the Sacrifice"). Strangely enough, none of these are her actual name, which remains unknown. Even so, she had many designations and was honored throughout pagan Scandinavia.

Despite Christian attempts to stamp out worship and devotion to her—or even the acknowledgment of her existence—she remained a popular figure in northern folk belief for centuries after the Viking Age. A sexually liberated goddess was the last thing the new Christian church wanted, especially when it held up the Virgin Mary as a new ideal! Indeed, one angry Icelandic Christian (before the general conversion to Christianity in the year 1000) flat-out called Freya a b*tch, no doubt to inflame and anger those who worshiped her. But she seems to have had the last laugh, at least for a while. Snorri, writing in thirteenth-century Iceland, referred to her as the sole goddess that remained, probably meaning that she was still worshiped in his time. It's said that well into the nineteenth century, Swedish country folks would offer up toasts to her or speak simple charms for her favor. She was a beloved goddess who made a powerful impression on the people, and her presence wouldn't so easily disappear.

## FREYR

Freyr or Frey, another of the Vanir, was one of the most important gods of Viking Age Scandinavia, showing that if the Vanir were the older gods in the region, they were not about to be supplanted by the new gods so easily! He was worshiped alongside Odin and Thor, and was especially revered as a god of prosperity, bounty, and fertility (both male and earthly). While he was sometimes revered as a god of battle, many non-warriors, such as farmers and those who lived off the land, were devoted to him.

He is the son of Njord and the brother of Freya. These three Vanir came to live with the Aesir after their divine war as part of the peace agreement. While these gods represent the more sensual aspects of life and peace, Freyr, like his sister Freya, is capable in battle. While Odin was more often invoked by warriors and berserkers, Freyr seems to have had his own warrior devotees.

His warrior nature is evident in the animals and objects in his possession. He rides a magical and potent boar named Gullinbursti, a gift from the dwarves; in fact, he's often associated with boars. Other accounts say that he rides a horse named Blodughofi ("Blood Hoof"), a swift steed that can race through fire, though Freyr eventually gives up this animal in an attempt to woo a jötunn maiden, Gerd. Freyr also possesses a magical sword that can strike on its own and never misses its target. But in one tale, he foolishly gives it away and must ever after use a large antler as a weapon instead, a strategy that will come back to haunt him in the final battle at Ragnarök. Why he simply doesn't have a new sword forged is unknown. Freyr is the only Vanir god who is mentioned in the Ragnarök story.

He also possesses a swift, magical ship (another dwarven gift), Skidbladnir, that never loses its way. It can expand to full size or shrink down small enough to be carried in a pocket or pouch. And yet, for all these magical items, very little source material survives to tell us how or when he uses them.

A strange and potentially disturbing story tells of Freyr's infatuation with a giantess named Gerd. His servant goes to terrible lengths, including blackmail and threats, to win her love for Freyr, or at least to have him possess her. This tale can be upsetting for the modern reader, though the uncomfortable details only appear in one of the two versions of the story, so how widespread it was is unknown. It's possible that Christian writers rewrote or even invented the story to discredit Freyr; after all, he was a fertility god associated with phallic imagery. Or it might be something else entirely, a dramatization of an older ritual representing summer's victory over winter. We'll explore these possibilities in the entry for the myth itself.

One work, the *Ynglinga Saga*, presents Freyr and Odin as real men who actually existed, kings who did great deeds and for this, they were eventually deified. According to this version, Freyr was so beloved that his closest followers kept his death a secret for three years! This deification—known as euhemerization—appears in several Nordic and Germanic accounts written by monks and other scribes. It is possible that some gods were actually based on real people, but in this case, it's equally possible that Snorri and other Christian writers sought to downgrade the gods by showing that they had always been human and were wrongly worshiped by their followers and subjects. This tactic was used to point out the supposed errors of the old faith and encourage people to adopt the new one. Or it was simply to avoid the anger of Christian authorities (bishops and such) who would have preferred that these stories never be written down at all.

Though Freyr is a Scandinavian Vanic god, he was apparently quite important in England, as well. The pagan Anglo-Saxons and Germans worshiped him as Ing, or Yngvi, and he served the same function in pre-Christian England as he did for the Scandinavians during the Viking Age. Here, he shares a name with the Anglo-Saxon rune Ing. Since like Freya, Freyr is a title meaning "Lord," it might be that Ing or Yngvi is his true name. While he was honored by the pagan English, strangely, there isn't evidence for the worship of his sister Freya in Anglo-Saxon England, but that doesn't mean that it didn't happen, of course. Evidence for her worship might simply not have survived. Or, if Freya and Frigg were ever considered to be the same goddess, then Freya might have been known in England in a different form or a different name. But Freyr was most definitely a force to be reckoned with, whether in central Sweden, Iceland, or Anglo-Saxon England.

## NJORD (NJÖRÐR)

Njord is the father of Freya and Freyr, and like them is a Vanir god, perhaps the chief of the Vanir. In the aftermath of the war between the two groups of gods, Njord, along with his children, was sent to live in Asgard, and the three became fully accepted among the Aesir. Njord is a god of the sea, the sea winds, fishing, and all things oceanic. Given how important the sea was to the Norse peoples (at least to those that lived along its coasts), it's reasonable to assume that Njord was highly regarded and commonly worshiped. He dwells near the ocean in his home of Nóatún ("The Place of Ships"), something that will prove to be a bit of a domestic problem for him later, after he inadvertently ends up marrying Skadi.

While Njord is father to Freya and Freyr, there is no mention of their mother. Some speculate that she might have been the ancient Germanic goddess Nerthus, whose worship was described by the Roman writer Tacitus in his work, *Germania*. If Njord and Nerthus are connected, it's possible that her cult didn't migrate to Scandinavia, leaving Njord as the sole god representing that branch of their divine family. Another intriguing suggestion is that they were one, a hermaphrodite god/dess. It's also possible that Njord *is* Nerthus, who underwent a change of sex sometime during the migration period, an Earth goddess transforming into a sea god, even as he/she kept many of the same divine qualities. How was this possible? There might have been a realignment from a goddess-centered cult to a god-centered one at some point. Certainly not all scholars accept these explanations, but the names Njord and Nerthus do seem to be related and indicate a connection that has become muddled and confused over time.

But if Freya, Freyr, and possibly the rest of the Vanir, are older to the northern regions than the Aesir, why would their parent(s) be from the Germanic gods that were presumably brought in with the migrations? And even within the stories themselves, there are contradictions. In one version, Njord, Freya, and Freyr were sent to the Aesir at the close of the ancient Aesir/Vanir war to help settle the peace. But in another account, Njord only fathered these two after his failed marriage to Skadi, long after he had settled among the Aesir. Another account hints that Skadi is at least Freyr's mother! Again, we see evidence for differing beliefs and traditions in different times and locations, with the surviving written accounts trying to bring them all together in ways that sometimes work and sometimes don't. There are so many more questions than answers to many of these fascinating characters and their conflicting stories.

Njord was undoubtedly held in high esteem by seagoing adventurers and travelers, as well as by the fishermen and migrants of the Viking age, and it's possible that folk devotion to him continued long after the region was Christianized. As with Thor and Freya, everyday people might well have gone to church on Sundays, but continued to make quiet, private offerings and prayers to the gods of their ancestors, even if these later became more superstitions than genuine beliefs. In Njord's case, saying a quiet prayer when stepping onto any boat or sending a loved one off to sea seems entirely reasonable, as would thanks after a safe journey.

It seems that Njord will survive the doom of Ragnarök and will either return to his own realm or perhaps join with the younger gods to help create a new assembly of gods. While his son Freyr is destined to die, Freya's fate is not revealed; it could be that many people at the time believed she would survive the destruction of the worlds along with her father. However, the idea of some gods returning after Ragnarök, as well as even some of the details of the tale of Ragnarök itself, might be later Christian inserts, and/or might be specific to Iceland. It's even possible that the Ragnarök story was not widely known in Scandinavia proper during the Viking Age and that Njord continues his long reign over the sea.

## LOKI

The infamous Loki is the quintessential trickster, a type of figure well known in myths around the world as being an agent of chaos and upheaval, but also one that brings positive change and even benefits to humans and the other gods. Today, Loki is one of the most well-known and popular of the Norse gods, perhaps because of his many appearances in the Marvel movies and television shows, where he is portrayed splendidly by Tom Hiddleston.

Loki is a complex and intriguing figure that offers up more questions than answers. His name is probably related to the Proto-Germanic *lugô, meaning "liar" or "deceiver," and not, as some suppose, to the Old Norse logi, "fire." His name might also be connected to the Proto-Germanic *luką, or "lock," suggesting entanglements or traps. Is he even a god at all, or one of the jötnar? Might he be Odin's brother? He is said to be the son of a jötunn named Fárbauti and a goddess named Laufey, though little is known about them. Whatever his origins, he is clearly involved with the gods of Asgard from a very early point in the mythology, and belief in him probably dates back many centuries before the Viking Age. Artwork from some Germanic sources might show Loki and Odin together, indicating that the trickster has been making trouble for a very long time.

Many mythological tricksters can shapeshift, and Loki is no different. He can change into pretty much anything he wishes: a horse, a fly, a fish, and many other forms. He can also swap sex, taking on a female form more than once, and even giving birth to other creatures in a few instances. Indeed, this change happens often enough that in one story (the *Lokasenna*, or "Loki's Quarrel"), the other gods insult him for it and show their disgust. They see his sex changes as odd, even repulsive.

So, can Loki even be said to be a "he" at all? Well, primarily, Loki takes a male form, but modern discussions of Loki sometimes describe him/them as nonbinary and gender-fluid, which work in a contemporary understanding. However, the peoples of the Viking Age would not have understood or even known these concepts. Still, Loki doesn't seem constrained by the usual boundaries of gender identity or biological sex, which makes him an outsider to the gods. He is often tolerated and even useful when the gods need something, but he is rarely fully welcomed.

What of his allegiances? At an earlier point in the tales, he seems more like a self-absorbed adolescent, doing things that amuse him, usually causing trouble all out of proportion to his actions, and then having to make things right on pain of death, or at least of being beaten up! There is often an element of comedy in his antics, and he is a reminder of the chaotic element that makes things go awry so that the real adventure can begin. But there is a darker element to his character that comes more and more to the front as the greater story of the gods progresses,

a malice that shows itself as his relationship with the gods of Asgard deteriorates.

He becomes increasingly hostile and antagonistic, to the point of causing genuine, irreparable harm to the gods and starting them down the path that leads to their destruction. But is he the cause of this strife, or is he simply revealing those dark aspects in the gods that they don't want to confront? The gods severely and brutally punish him for this behavior, but he eventually breaks free. At the end, only his wife, Sigyn, shows him any mercy. By the time of Ragnarök, he is almost a satanic figure, fallen from grace and eager to destroy what he once eagerly enjoyed: the halls of Asgard and the good company and feasts of the gods. He will ultimately meet his own demise at the hands of one of these gods, Heimdall (who seems to despise him even early on), but he will kill Heimdall in turn.

So is Loki evil or misunderstood? Is he a mixture of both? Does he become more evil over time in response to the way he is treated by the gods? The simple answer of "yes" might apply to each of these questions, but of course, the truth is less definitive. Tricksters can push others in directions they need to go, but they can also cause much trouble in doing so, taking things too far. They are complex creatures, balancing light and dark, so it isn't really accurate to describe them in a good/evil binary.

That said, Loki might well have been "satanized" by Snorri and other Icelandic Christians, eager to insert a "Big Bad" into the Norse myths, comparable to the biblical devil. Based on Loki's behaviors, doing so wouldn't have been too difficult for prudish or uptight Christians. It's possible, however, that Loki might have fallen out of the gods' favor before Christian influence, with these stories perhaps illustrating the fate of one who deceives too often and breaks oaths. In any case, he is not the cause of evil in the world (that existed before him and the gods), and many of his actions are simply done out of self-interest, rather than from some diabolic plan. But it would have been easy for Christian writers to cast him in the role of the great enemy, a role they already knew very well.

Loki might have even operated in Asgard in a way that was later taken up by the medieval fool, the loyal servant to the king who was able to say and do outrageous things without fear of harm. Despite his title, the fool was actually wise and kept the king honest, even if he risked his own life with his words and antics. Think of the loyal fool in Shakespeare's *King Lear*, for example.

Was Loki a kind of "fool to the gods"? A cosmic clown who takes things too far? A teller of uncomfortable truths who pushed everyone's buttons so much that they eventually imprisoned him? In the poem *Lokasenna*, this trickster interrupts a feast and proceeds to insult various gods and goddesses by revealing what seem to be dark secrets about each of them, often of a sexual nature. Affairs, incest, threesomes, murder, gender-swapping ... all of it is laid bare. Is it true? We can't tell, but the gods are so enraged that Thor ultimately threatens Loki and makes him leave. Was this account a reflection of real life in the mead hall? Were there topics that were off-limits in conversation, even among drunken companions? Very likely. We will explore this poem in much more detail later.

It's not clear if the Norse peoples actually worshiped Loki, or if he was simply acknowledged or perhaps appeased. The Arab (possibly Sephardic Jewish) traveler Ibrahim ibn Yaqub, also known as al-Ṭarṭûshi, recorded that in the town of Hedeby (in modern Germany near the Danish border) in the 960s, some people worshiped the star Sirius. This star has been associated with Loki, especially in Iceland, where it was known as "Loki's Torch," so it's possible that there was a localized cult to Loki in that region. If so, there might have been many more elsewhere. It's also possible that some people on the margins of society—outcasts, criminals, people seen as troubled or degenerate, people who identified as "other" in some way—drew closer to Loki or found some comfort in his status as an outsider to the gods. Perhaps worship of this enigmatic figure was frowned upon by society and convention, and only the brave, the outcast, or the defiant ventured down that path.

# HEIMDALL

L ike so many of the Norse gods, Heimdall is enigmatic. He keeps watch over the Bifrost Bridge, the great rainbow that connects Asgard to Midgard ("Middle Earth," our world). He is always on the lookout for jötnar and other potential invaders. He lives in Himinbjörg ("Sky Cliffs") with a good stock of fine mead, and from there he can see out over all the realms. When Ragnarök arrives, he will sound the great horn, Gjallarhorn. It is the only time he will ever blow it, which might resemble a great drinking horn or perhaps a large lur, such as those used in the Bronze Age. It might be significant that he has both a large drinking horn and a stash of mead. The Norse peoples very likely used ceremonial horns in their rituals, so one being held by a god to signal the great change in the cosmos seems natural enough.

To help him keep his watch, he needs less sleep than a bird and has remarkable hearing and eyesight, being able to see over great distances during both day and night. His hearing is so keen that he can hear wool growing on a sheep or grass growing from the ground. This is all the more remarkable because it's possible that he has only one ear.

As a god, he has several unusual attributes. He is said to have nine mothers who are sisters. While this seems like an anatomical impossibility, these mothers might represent ocean waves, indicating that he has a connection with the sea. The sea gods Aegir and Rán (who are different deities than Njord) have nine daughters who are equated to the waves, so there might be a connection between Heimdall and them, though in one source, the names of his mothers are different from those of Aegir's daughters. If there is a connection, that would make Heimdall Aegir and Rán's grandson, though there is nothing in the sources that confirms this. One of Heimdall's other names, Vindlér, means something like "wind-sea," so it's possible that he does have a connection to the gods and spirits of the ocean.

In the form of a being or man called Rig, he has sex with

three married women, one of each social class of Norse society—slaves, farmers, and nobility. These liaisons produce the children whose own children populate the world. The husbands seem to be present at these unions, raising some interesting questions. The poem *Völuspá* (the Seeress' Prophecy) begins by speaking of all the races or tribes as the offspring of Heimdall, so it seems that there was an existing myth of his establishing the social order. At the very least, as we shall see in the tale of Rig, Norse chieftains and kings would have been only too happy to have their place in society preordained by a god.

Heimdall is also called "the whitest of gods," though this doesn't seem to have anything to do with skin color. Its meaning is unclear, but it might refer to him being very handsome. And yet, this designation would seem to contradict descriptions of Odin's son Baldr as "the shining one," who is said to be the fairest of the gods. Once again, we see confusions that might indicate different traditions and sets of beliefs. Heimdall is said to be "golden toothed" (the meaning of another of his names, Gullintanni) and to have a fine horse named Gulltoppr ("Golden Mane").

One source speaks of how Heimdall's hljóð is hidden under Yggdrasil, the World Tree. Hljóð can mean "horn," so it might be that the Gjallarhorn is stored by the World Tree for safe keeping, so that no one else will blow it before Ragnarök. But *hljóð* can also refer to his hearing, or even an actual ear. Might there be some connection between hearing loss and ear horns or trumpets? Some scholars say that this word indicates that Heimdall sacrificed one of his ears, perhaps to enhance his hearing in the remaining one and perhaps even his eyesight. If true, he would be joining several other gods with disabilities and missing body parts like Odin (who sacrificed his eye for wisdom) and Tyr (who gave up a hand in the jaws of the wolf Fenrir). As noted, several Norse gods have disabilities, which makes sense in a culture that praised its warriors, some of whom probably did lose body parts but survived.

"Heimdall" might mean "one who illuminates the world," and

could be connected to the name Mardöll, or "Sea Brightener," which, as we've seen, is another name for Freya. In one source, Heimdall is listed as being of the Vanir, but this isn't mentioned anywhere else, so we can only speculate on what his relationship, if any, to Freya might be.

In a fragment of one tale, Heimdall does battle with Loki (both of them in the shape of seals) in order to win back Freya's famed necklace, the Brísingamen, which Loki stole (the entirety of the Freya and Brísingamen myth is told later in this section). In addition to the seal battle, he does seem to have an antagonistic relationship with Loki. Indeed, Heimdall and Loki are predicted to kill one another at Ragnarök, though there is little in the lore that suggests a build-up of such anger and tension between them. The battle over Freya's necklace might have been only one of several stories about their quarrel that sadly do not survive.

Speaking of animals, he seems to be associated with the ram. It's possible that this animal was sacred to him, and that his worshippers sacrificed them at rituals in his honor. Perhaps he was once viewed as having ram's horns, though most scholars don't make that leap.

More importantly, he is associated with the idea of borders and boundaries, both of space and of time. He guards the Bifrost, the border to Asgard, against jötnar attack. If he is a son of the daughters of the sea gods, then he might represent the shore and the border between land and ocean. He came from the sea, but lives on land. The myth of Rig even speaks of him walking along the seashore. And when he does eventually have to blow Gjallarhorn, he signals the end of an old world and the chaotic start of a new one, since nothing can go back to what it was.

# TYR (TÝR)

Tyr might have been a much more important god at one point in Germanic belief, possibly even more so than Odin. But his power and prominence eroded over the centuries as he was displaced by that "other" war and death god, until he was almost a minor player in Norse myth, except in the Fenrir story, as we'll see. It might or might not be significant that a one-eyed god replaced a one-handed god at some point.

One source says that Tyr was the son of Odin, but another states that he was the son of the jötunn Hymir. Again, there was probably more than one set of tales and beliefs about him, especially if Tyr had a bigger role in the earlier myths. He was certainly a war god in older Germanic belief, and Roman writers assigned him the identity of Mars, which they saw as the logical correspondence with their own god. Tyr was a popular god in Germanic lands (as Tiwaz) and in Anglo-Saxon England (as Tiw), where he gave his name to Tuesday (Tīwesdæg, or "Tiw's Day"). A third-century inscription on an altar at the Housesteads Roman Fort at Hadrian's Wall in northern England seems to refer to him, indicating that Germanic soldiers (as legionaries or mercenaries) were stationed there and had brought his worship to Roman Britain. In the *Getica*, Jordanes' sixth-century history of the Goths, he records that the Goths worshiped Mars (i.e., Tyr) and dedicated a share of the spoils of war to him, hanging enemy swords and other treasures from trees as offerings. While the *Getica* isn't always historically accurate, this particular ritual doesn't seem far-fetched at all, and shows that Tyr was probably more important outside of Scandinavia.

Tyr lost his right hand to the jaws of the wolf Fenrir, whom he essentially betrayed when the wolf was bound and couldn't escape. Since he is a war god, it might seem odd at first for him to be missing his most important limb. And yet, there must have been some Vikings and warriors who lost a hand (or worse) in combat and lived to tell the tale, against the odds of infection and very limited medical treatment.

Tyr seems to have more importance than the number of surviving myths about him would indicate. In many, he's nothing more than a bit player, and yet at the end of the world, he rushes out to do combat with a different mighty wolf, Garmr, the Hound of Hel. The two slay each other. But wouldn't it be more likely that Fenrir would want that revenge? Well yes, and that's one of the problems. Fenrir attacks Odin, while Tyr faces another canine entirely.

Tyr is associated with victory in battle, as well as justice, or at least resolution of conflicts and the handing out of punishments, if needed. Snorri even claims in the *Prose Edda* that he is the one who chooses who will win or lose in battle, which seems to undermine Odin and his Valkyries, and is yet more evidence that Tyr might once have been at the top of the god heap. It's possible that in Roman times, he and Wotan (Odin) were seen as equal.

For whatever reasons, Odin and Thor partially replaced him in the hearts and minds of Scandinavian worshippers. But traces of his prominence remained. Tyr's name can also be a generic term for "god," again hinting at his importance. Odin is sometimes called a týr in poetry, as is Thor.

Even if Odin did replace him, Tyr is not merely, or even primarily, a "war god." Snorri further relates that he is the bravest of the gods, and that men of action should invoke him. Those who advance with that same bravery in their hearts and do not retreat are said to be "Tyr Courageous." Tyr is also clever and wise, and those who are the same might be called "Tyr Wise." The Germanic rune Tiwaz shares his name, and it might have been engraved on certain items (such as on wood or stone) for protection (though evidence for the use of runes for magic is sparse, even if it probably did happen). But the fact that he shares his name with a rune seems to show that he was much more important at one point. Odin doesn't have his own rune-name, after all.

Sif is Thor's wife, and while she obviously holds a place of importance among the Aesir, information about her is lacking. She is famed for her lustrous, long, golden hair, which is a treasure and a delight. And of course, Loki finds a way to cause trouble, resulting in her losing her locks and needing to have new hair made (more about that on page 165). She is also the mother of Ullr, though Thor is not named as the father. It's likely that she bore Ullr before marrying Thor, as Thor is portrayed as being his stepfather.

Her name means "relation," but that doesn't tell us too much about her. Odin and Loki both suggest at different times that she might not have been faithful to Thor, but that hardly seems to matter much in a mythology where the gods routinely have affairs outside of their marriages. Thor himself is hardly innocent in this respect. The fact that Loki is able to be close enough to Sif while she slept to remove her hair might imply that the two are also lovers, or it might not.

The lack of stories about Sif has led some scholars to infer that she perhaps had more devotees amongst the Germanic peoples, but her popularity might have waned during the Viking Age. The emphasis on her golden hair might not represent an ideal of beauty, it might refer to the importance of gold in Germanic and Norse cultures. As we've seen, it might also refer to crops such as wheat, in which case, Sif could be a fertility goddess, worshiped for good harvests and crops. Thor and Sif might have represented a sky god and an Earth goddess, long before the Viking era. Since her husband, Thor, was associated with thunder and rain, the "marriage" of a weather god and a crop goddess seems like an obvious pairing, one that shows up in myths around the world.

Was the story of the cutting of her hair a tangled weave of much older tales representing the harvest of wheat? Her replacement hair (made by dwarves) was seen as one of the greatest of their gifts. Could her original hair have been the bounty of that harvest before winter? This is all speculative, of course. Centuries of changes and folk tradition, oral culture, and the addition of newer tales while others are lost will always obscure our hopes of knowing the answers for certain, but it is fascinating to peel back some of the layers and look at what these ancient stories might be trying to say, underneath their sometimes gaudier or even surreal trappings.

## BALDR

Baldr is the "Shining God," the son of Odin and Frigg, whom all the worlds love dearly. He is praised as the best and most beautiful of the gods, so much so that light shines from him. He is also the wisest, the most merciful, and the best spoken of the gods, though he's not good at making decisions. He lives in Breidablik ("Gleaming far and wide"), a place said to be perfect and free of all impurities. So wondrous is he that many others desire him. The story of Skadi mistaking Njord's beautiful feet for Baldr's when choosing a husband (it's a strange tale!) is a good example of how he was sought after by many.

Though Skadi might have wanted to marry him, Baldr is married to the lovely goddess Nanna ("Courageous," just like her husband). Their son, Forseti, is a god of legal procedures who helps those who quarrel to reconcile. So devoted is Nanna to Baldr that after his death she willingly dies to be with him in the afterlife in Hel. They will both wait there until after Ragnarök, when they will return, and Baldr will rule over the surviving and new gods in his father's place.

There are two written versions of who Baldr was, Snorri's and Saxo's, and they differ quite a bit, though both end with Baldr dying at the hands of Hod, his blind brother in Snorri's version, his mortal enemy in Saxo's. So it seems that this aspect of his fate was long-known; we will examine this myth in more detail in the entry on Baldr's death. Some scholars have proposed that Baldr might have been a Nordic stand-in for Christ, someone who was used by missionaries for conversion purposes, since his story includes aspects of dying by sacrifice, descending into Hel (Hell), and then being reborn. Snorri likely added in some Christian elements in his description of the young god's nature.

But those looking for an exclusively Christian interpretation for Baldr might be a bit disappointed, since it seems that at least the stories of his impending death are very old, even being found in Germanic and Anglo-Saxon beliefs. Again, we'll dive into this more in the entry about his untimely death (see page 223).

Like Freya and Freyr, his name is a title, meaning "Ruler," while the Old Norse word baldr means "courageous." This seems a far cry from Snorri's depiction of Baldr as a Christ-like figure—meek, radiant, and gentle—who is unfairly taken from the world. Older accounts seem to suggest that Baldr was indeed a warrior of some ability, such as in Saxo's description of a humanized version of Baldr. In Saxo's account, Baldr is a lustful warrior who competes against Hod for a woman's affection. A group of other mysterious women (probably Valkyries) inform Hod that Baldr is all but invincible, and that only one sword can kill him. Baldr being immune from harm has echoes of Achilles' invincibility, which also shows up in Snorri's account of his accidental death. In Saxo's story, there is a magical food that, if Hod eats it, will give him the strength to kill Baldr, which he eventually does. So clearly, there are different versions of this dying god and what he represents.

It's possible that the story and figure of Baldr had some influence on the Finnish hero Lemminkäinen (more on him in the Finnish section), who also dies at the hands of a blind man. Or perhaps there was a cross-cultural exchange of myths and ideas, or both gods came from a common source.

# HOD (HÖÐR)

Hod is unusual in the collective of the Norse gods in that he is blind.

As we've seen, it may be significant that there is a fair number of gods with disabilities in the Norse myths: Odin with one eye, Tyr with one hand, Hod with blindness, Heimdall with one ear, and Hel with only half a living body. The idea of divine perfection was not as important to the Norse as it was in some other mythologies, and perhaps this reflected the harsh realities of the land and climate of Scandinavia. In a world where accidents and violence were undoubtedly common, resulting in maiming or worse, it's fitting that these realities are reflected in the gods, as well. On the other hand, in Hod's case, there might be more to it than first meets the eye, so to speak.

As son of Odin and Frigg, he is also Baldr's brother. But unlike his brother, Hod is a bit of an outcast and seems to have had a lack of worshippers. How could one compete against the beautiful god Baldr, anyway? Everyone loves Baldr, so Hod must be a shameful disappointment. This attitude might hint at a reality about disabilities in the Norse world. Even if the disabled were generally accepted, such disabilities could also make people dependent on others, which might not have always been welcome. The ideals of the *Hávamál* and its tolerance for disability were not always possible in real life.

It's possible that Hod represented something more than literal blindness to the Norse. His actual lack of sight is mentioned in Snorri's *Prose Edda*, but not in the *Poetic Edda*. Hod's name means "warrior," which seems at odds with his nature, unless he was blinded in combat in a story that doesn't survive. Perhaps it means that he is blind to what is happening around him and allows himself to be tricked by Loki with tragic consequences. The story of Hod, Loki, and Baldr appears later in this section, in all its tragic glory (see page 223). The alternate story of Hod and Baldr given by Saxo Grammaticus (who was famous for mangling the myths and reinterpreting them in his own way) might contain some hints about Hod's nature.

As we will see, Hod is famous (infamous) for one terrible mistake (with Loki's help and prodding, of course!), which brings him not only guilt and shame, but sets in motion a sequence of events that will lead to the ending of all things. No pressure though! At least Hod is prophesied to return after Ragnarök, along with Baldr.

As is so often the case with these splendid tales, there is much speculation about their deeper nature, and not enough answers.

## SKADI (SKAÐI)

Skadi is neither of the Aesir or Vanir. She is a jötunn, the daughter of the mighty Thiazi, though she is eventually welcomed into the company of the gods and honored as a goddess in her own right. She is associated with winter, mountains, ice and snow, wolves, the hunt, skiing and other winter activities, and is known for her courage and self-reliance. She is also called Öndurguð ("ski god") and Öndurdís ("ski lady"). Her name might be linked to the word "Scandinavia," which some have interpreted to mean "Skadi's Island." Given the numerous mountains and snow-covered landscapes found across these northern regions, this meaning might just be true. However, the Old Norse word skaði means "harm," which could refer to her hunting or her fierceness. This word is related to our English word "scathing."

To make things even more confusing, it's also possible that Skadi began as a male god and for reasons unknown, transformed into a female goddess over centuries of belief and practice. Another puzzle is that "Skadi" itself is a male name, and yet in the stories, she is undeniably a goddess. A human man named Skadi who is also connected with snow and hunting appears in one of the sagas. Did an earlier version of a winter god

(possibly Sámi) morph into the goddess of the Norse peoples over time? Or perhaps two different deities were combined into the final female form that was honored during the Viking Age? Maybe there's even a long-vanished myth about how the god became a goddess. Again, so much has been lost to time that we'll probably never know.

The death of her father at the gods' hands spurs her to take vengeance, but after a tense stand-off, a peace is brokered, and all are able to avoid further bloodshed. Skadi also seems to have some sort of relationship with Loki. He hints that they were once lovers (though this might well be a lie), though she also happily presides over his most severe punishment later, after he torments her about her father's death and his role in it.

For a time, she was the wife of Njord, the sea god, as part of a peace brokered between her and the gods. But this arrangement didn't suit her, and she soon left him to return to her father's mountain home at Thrymheim. Interestingly, the *Prose Edda* says that Njord became father to Freya and Freyr after this separation, which is at odds with all three of them coming to Asgard as part of the post-war exchange. Is Skadi their mother? There is no mention of this in any other source, though her mother-like concern for Freyr is noted in another tale. These kinds of inconsistencies are common and frustrating when trying to map out a definitive chronology of events and stories.

Some scholars propose that the tension between Skadi and Njord might also represent the cultural differences between the seafaring Norse peoples and the Sámi, who were more often nomadic hunters and herders. While each brought advantages to the table that the other wanted, they could never fully integrate and be at ease with each other, even though there are stories of Norse and Sámi marriages and interactions. Was Skadi originally a Sámi goddess, who was given a Norse reinterpretation?

The sources tell us that at some point, she married Odin himself, or at least had children with him. He seemed to spread his amorous attentions around to a good number of goddesses and mortals! Only one of these offspring with Odin is named, a son called Sæmingr, who later became king of Norway. As we've seen, there was often an attempt to link the gods with actual historical beings, as a way—in Christian minds—of saying that they were really just humans all along. They'd been deified by the superstitious pagan northerners, of course, but Snorri and his fellow scribes intended to set the record straight. Freyr is also recorded as Sæmingr's father, so the whole thing is a confusing jumble; so much for setting the record straight! These contradictions are to be expected, given the multitude of traditions and lost myths.

## ULLR

Ullr is the son of the goddess Sif and an unnamed god (not Sif's husband, Thor). While Loki also claimed to be Sif's lover, there are no surviving texts suggesting that he is Ullr's father, either. Given the commonplace practice of gods and goddesses carrying on with whomever they wish, it's possible that Ullr's true father is a god or another power whose name has been lost.

Like Skadi, Ullr is associated with winter, skiing, archery, and the outdoors. In fact, he is described as very good-looking and that no one else can match him on skis (presumably not even Skadi). Like Skadi, he might have been a patron for hunters and those that needed to travel in winter. It's possible that these two were at one time connected. Some have suggested that Ullr and Skadi might have been brother and sister, like Freyr and Freya, or that Ullr and Njord were originally connected in some way now lost. Perhaps Njord and Ullr once represented land and sea in a way that Skadi and Njord later came to do in their own story of a troubled marriage. And if Sif was an ancient harvest goddess, it might be fitting that her son came to represent winter, since winter proceeds from fall.

Ullr is said to live in a place called Ydalir, but frustratingly, no other information survives about this hall or where it might be located. The word means "yew glen," and since branches from yew trees were often used in making bows, the name would seem to tie into his reputation as a skilled archer.

His name provides us with some clues about his identity. The Old Norse ullr is related to the Anglo-Saxon word, *wuldor*, which means "glory." This word was used in Christian times to proclaim the divine majesty of God, but since a version of it was known in Scandinavia, it might imply that Ullr was an important god in his own right. The *Poetic Edda* describes how the other gods take oaths on his ring, implying that he is someone of great standing, but again, it's unclear what this might mean. It could refer to him being a god on which mortals would swear oaths, especially in legal disputes.

One clue might come from the writings of Saxo Grammaticus, who referred to Ullr by his Latinized name, Ollerus, and said that for a while, Ullr ruled the Aesir, a pretty astonishing claim to make! It seems that Odin began to neglect his duties out of grief and anger after Baldr's death, so the other gods decided to exile him for ten years, letting Ullr rule over them instead. Ullr took the name of "Odin" and ruled wisely. Again, this leadership role might provide a connection between the god and the law.

Saxo also claimed that Ullr possessed a magic bone inscribed with runes that allowed him to travel over the sea with ease. It's possible that this bone refers to a pair of skis or skates, rather than a boat or an oar, which would make sense given Ullr's connection to winter and skiing. Viking Age peoples made ice skates out of bone, which they strapped to their boots; they propelled themselves along the ice with a long pole. And it was indeed easy for them to get from one place to another quickly, gliding across a frozen lake or river. So Ullr's rune-infused bone might have been representative of either a pair of skates or of the pole.

# IDUNN (IÐUNN)

The goddess Idunn, or Idunna, is associated with youth. Her name means something like "Forever young" or "The Rejuvenating One." In the surviving stories, she is the keeper of sacred fruit imbued with life-giving powers. The gods presumably eat this sacred fruit regularly to keep themselves young forever. This is a striking image, considering that gods are assumed to be immortal by default. It might point to the broader idea that the gods will not exist forever and that at least some will perish during Ragnarök, or it might not.

Interestingly, the assumption is that Idunn's sacred fruit is the apple, but the Old Norse word epli can actually mean any fruit, even though it sounds like "apple," and *eple* means apple in modern Norwegian. It's possible that Snorri played up the idea of apples to make a connection with the Garden of Eden and its forbidden fruit, though again, the fruit in Genesis is not named as being an apple; that idea came along later. It's also possible that the original motif came from the ancient Greek myth of the Garden of the Hesperides, where Hebe, a goddess of youth, tended to trees of golden apples, a gift to Hebe's mother Hera, from the goddess Gaia. Idunn's apples are also sometimes portrayed as golden. The blending and interweaving of ancient myths and stories are fascinating, but alas, all too often impossible to untangle at such a distance in time.

And yet, the fruit itself might not play a part in the gods' immortality at all. In one source, Idunn seems to keep the gods young simply by her presence among them. So when she is abducted by a greedy jötunn (see "The Theft of Idunn's Golden Apples" on page 174), it could be the lack of either the fruit she tends or her very physical presence that causes the gods to begin to grow old and to panic. Don't worry, it all works out for them in the end! Sort of.

All that said, the concept of magical apples is quite old and abounds in Norse and other traditions. Apples were a symbol of

fertility and life. They have been found in graves in England and at the famed Oseberg ship burial in Norway from the early ninth century. There are also connections with the fruit to the Vanir gods themselves, and while some scholars have suggested a connection between Idunn and Freya, this seems unlikely. Idunn might correspond to the Anglo-Saxon goddess of springtime, Eostre, but there isn't enough surviving information to conclude anything about what those connections might be, if any.

Idunn is married to Bragi, the god associated with poetry, inspiration, and skalds. These two can be seen as a young couple, whose lives are far from the violence and darkness that sometimes cloud the stories of Odin, Thor, and Loki. But the idea that all the gods' very existence could depend on the careful work of a gentle and youthful goddess is itself quite striking. This concept might be related to Norse views on rebirth and new cycles beginning as old ones closed. New children carried on the existing traditions and began the cycles anew. After death, there was birth and youth again.

## BRAGI

Bragi is the god of poetry, music, and the poetic skalds. As husband to Idunn, he is talented, handsome, and represents the gentler side of the Norse gods. His name might derive from the Old Norse word bragr, meaning poem or poetry. The name itself seems to have been a popular male name during the Viking era, which makes his possible origin all the more interesting.

Some have theorized that Bragi the god might never have been worshiped as a god at all, but was based on a human skald, Bragi Boddason, who was later deified. On the opposite end, some people have doubted that the human Bragi existed at all, because of the various mythic stories associated with him. And so it goes. But Boddason does seem to have been an actual person, who was active sometime during the ninth century in Norway. His attributed works are the earliest skaldic poetry to survive, especially in the *Ragnarsdrápa*, a work written in honor of Ragnar Lodbrok, himself a semi-legendary historical figure (and a key character on the TV show *Vikings*).

In any case, Snorri describes Bragi the god as having great wisdom, being a master of words and speech, of being Idunn's husband, and having a long beard, which of course, is the most important characteristic of all. Oh, and the Eddic poem, *Sigrdrífumál*, says that he has runes carved on his tongue, which must have been very unpleasant to receive! He appears in several stories, often telling tales of his own, or recounting facts about the nature of poetry. Like many gods, he has a bit of a beef with Loki, who makes sure to insult him on one important occasion (see "Loki's Quarrel" on page 231), which almost leads to blows.

More than once, Odin sends Bragi to greet fallen warriors, but is this Bragi the god or Bragi the mortal skald, whose talents were so amazing in life that he now enjoys an afterlife in Odin's hall? The texts are unclear about this, another frustrating example of missing puzzle pieces that leave us guessing about the full picture.

There doesn't seem to be any evidence that Bragi was worshiped as a god during the Viking Age, which does lend some weight to the idea that he was a mortal poet who legends say Odin took into his court. While Snorri does separate out Bragi the skald and Bragi the god, it's possible that Bragi's divinity was invented by later writers to provide the Norse collective with a god of music and poetry that it didn't have, basically creating a Nordic Apollo. They also might have paired him up with Idunn to showcase a couple who, together, represented youth, beauty, poetry, and song. Only Bragi Boddason knows for sure, and he's not "skalding" at the moment, as far as we know.

# EIR

Depending on who you ask, Eir is either in service to Frigg and Odin, a handmaid in service to the maiden Menglöð, a Valkyrie, a goddess in her own right, some combination of all of these options, or another version of Frigg herself. Or she might serve Freya, unless Freya and Frigg are the same goddess, as some traditions say.

Also, depending on who you ask, her name is pronounced EYE-er, AY-er, or EE-er. The correct answer is probably all three, given that there were likely different Old Norse dialects in different areas and times. Her name means something like "mercy" or "protection," or even "help," which is a clue to her identity and role.

Snorri refers to her as "a very good physician," and it seems that whatever her true identity, she was associated with healing. The Eddic poem *Fjölsvinnsmál* lists Eir and eight other women—Hlíf, Hlífþrasa, Þjóðvarta, Björt, Blíð, Blíðr, Fríð, Eir, and Aurboða—who serve as handmaids to Menglöð. They live on a hill called Lyfjaberg, which means "the hill of healing." The handmaidens grant favors, protection, and good health if sacrifices and rituals are held in their honor:

"Every summer in which men offer to them, at the holy place,

No pestilence so great shall come to the sons of men,

But they will free each from peril."

Who is Menglöð? Well Menglöð means "the one who takes pleasure in jewels," which sounds a lot like Freya. In fact, none other than Jacob Grimm (of fairy tale fame) identified Menglöð as another name for Freya, and some later scholars think he was on to something.

Snorri lists Eir among the names of the Valkyries, but also among the goddesses in a separate listing, so it's possible that she was considered a goddess in her own right. On the other hand, some scholars think that she wasn't a goddess at all, and was never worshiped, though it does seem that making offerings to her and her sisters was done in expectation of healing. Did later writers simply want to include a "goddess of healing" among the Norse gods to help fill out roles they saw as missing?

Some have suggested that if Eir was a Valkyrie, she might have helped choose who would die on the battlefield and who would recover and live on. And if Menglöð was Freya and had her first pick of the slain on those battlefields, Eir's role would make even more sense. Did she work in the service of Freya, choosing some warriors to die while others would live and recover? Or is this confusion once again caused by a tangle of stories from several regions that show how these gods and mythic tales meant different things to different people at various times and places? We can answer those questions with a definite maybe!

## HEL

Hel is the daughter of Loki and the jötunn sorceress Angrboda, who are also the parents of her brothers: Fenrir the wolf and Jormungandr the serpent, both of whom will rise at Ragnarök to kill Odin and Thor respectively. Loki and Angrboda try to keep the existence of all three children a secret from the gods, fearing a potentially hostile reaction to these strange creatures. Indeed, when the gods do discover their offspring, they remove the wolf and the serpent from Angrboda's care and put them in places where they think that they will do no harm (little did the gods know!). As for Hel, she is given control over the realm of the dead.

Hel rules over the domain of Hel or Helheim ("Hel's Home"), the land of the dead. Rather like Hades from Greek myth, the names of the god and the realm were interchangeable. She is often depicted as half alive and half dead, with one side of her body beautiful and vibrant, and the other corpse-like and skeletal. Earlier descriptions of her seem to indicate only that she had a blue or grayish tint and a grim expression, so it's possible that her classic depiction was fleshed out (pun intended) later on, or was even a Christian embellishment sometime after the Viking Age. Despite her frightening appearance, she was not viewed as evil, but is the caretaker of the lands of the dead. But unlike the other gods, she is not able to travel freely, and seems to be bound to the realm that bears her name. Still, she has total control over this world and those in it. When Baldr enters Hel, for example, she has the power to compel him to remain, despite the pleas of his parents, Frigg and Odin.

Indeed, the connection between the words "Hel" and "Hell" might seem obvious, but it's actually unclear. The "Hel" where many of the Norse dead would go after death was not a place of eternal punishment and fire. If anything, it was cold, bleak, dark, and gloomy, though some accounts suggest that Hel's hall is welcoming to the souls of the dead, and they do not suffer discomfort. While heroic warriors who died in battle might go to Valhalla or Sessrúmnir to join Odin or Freya, the vast majority of folks would probably end up in Hel. It was neither a punishment nor a reward; it was just the next phase of their existence. Even gods, such as Baldr, would enter Hel upon their deaths, and it is his death that is the prelude to Ragnarök.

It's uncertain whether the Norse peoples viewed Hel as a goddess in her own right, or whether she was simply a guardian of the realm of the dead. There's no surviving evidence of a cult dedicated to her worship, but that might not mean much, as we've already seen; so much has been lost or reinterpreted. She might have entered relatively late into Norse belief, as evidence for her only goes back to about the tenth century, though death gods and goddesses certainly existed in many other lands well before then. The concept of a gloomy afterlife was well known to the Near Eastern and Greco-Roman civilizations, which might have influenced later Norse beliefs.

Hel is trapped in her realm, at least until the end of the worlds, when she and her brothers will break free, and she will unleash the dead over the worlds. She will travel with Loki in a ship made of the clipped nails of the dead (weird and a bit gross!) and populated with souls who will lay waste to the lands and bring destruction, yet she seems to take no part in the battle itself. Is the Ragnarök tale a Christianization of the myths, invoking similar imagery to Satan and his demons being unleashed on the world at the end of time? Possibly. Or was this a heathen vision? Was it a prediction of the future or a cultural memory of a time of famine and war? We know that a series of mid-sixth-century volcanic eruptions did cause mass death around the world in appalling ways. We will discuss this theory later.

The journey to Hel (the place) is fraught with peril, and unlike the other realms, it is not easily visited. It takes considerable time, even for a god like Odin, to make the journey there, and it is guarded by a fearsome wolf named Garmr (who some suspect might also be Fenrir), and by Modgud (Móðguðr), who stands watch at a bridge Gjallarbrú, which spans the river Gjöll ("Noisy"). There, Modgud keeps track of who comes and (rarely) goes. Another frightening resident of Hel is the volva whom Odin raises from the dead to tell him about the impending death of his son Baldr. It's curious that he goes to the land of the dead to raise someone from the dead; why was she not "alive" there already? It suggests that there were overlapping myths that might tell differing versions of the same story.

In summary, Hel seems to be the Norse goddess of their underworld, a place of cold and gloom, but also one of potential welcoming and reuniting with departed loved ones. It's not a paradise, but it certainly isn't "Hell," and Hel herself is by no means a satanic figure, even if later writers might have tried to make her into one.

# SOL (SÓL) AND MANI (MÁNI)

Sol, or Sunna, is the Norse and Germanic sun goddess. Sun *goddess*? Yes, in northern beliefs, the sun was often seen as feminine. In Norse myth, the roles of the gods of sun and moon are reversed from those found in many other ancient religions; while there is a sun goddess, there is a moon god, Mani. This view persisted in Anglo-Saxon beliefs, as well, and it might be why we now speak of the "Man in the Moon" in English folk belief.

Sol and Mani are sister and brother, and as usual, there are some conflicting stories about their nature and how they became who they are. The sources agree that they ride through the heavens on chariots pulled by horses, which seems to be a very old belief, dating back to pre-migration Germanic times and even to Bronze Age Scandinavia. Sol's horses are Árvakr ("Early Riser") and Alsviðr ("Swift"), while Mani's steeds don't have names. Or rather, those names haven't survived. Ominously, both chariots are pursued by wolves. A wolf named Sköll ("Mockery") chases the sun, while Hati ("Hate") runs after the moon. Each day and night, these ravenous animals try to capture and devour Midgard's sources of light, and each day, they fail. But eventually, they will catch up to them both and devour them, a clear sign that Ragnarök has begun.

Snorri writes in the *Prose Edda* that Sol and Mani's father was named Mundilfari, a character that might be Snorri's own invention. He says that Mundilfari had two children that he thought were beautiful beyond measure, so much so that he named them Sol, "sun," and Mani, "moon," after the celestial bodies. The gods were angered by his arrogance and forced the two children to leave him and drive chariots across the sky from then on, which doesn't seem fair. The sun already existed, being a spark of flame from Muspelheim, but the chariot had no driver, and so Sol was made to take the reins. In time, she became a goddess, while her brother followed behind. Sol has a passenger in her chariot, Svalinn, who holds out a shield to protect the lands and seas below from Sol's flames as they fly out in all directions.

Mani is charged with guiding the moon and its phases. According to one source, he once kidnapped two young humans, a girl named Bil ("Waning") and a boy named Hjúki ("Waxing"), and made them travel with him, creating the phases of the moon.

Surviving works seem to hint at some lost tales and beliefs about Sol and Mani. In the Eddic poem *Alvíssmál*, Thor asks the dwarf Alvíss ("All Wise") to tell him the names of the moon and sun:

"Answer me, Alvis! You know all,

Dwarf, of the doom of men:

What do they call the moon, that men behold,

In each and every world?"

Alvis answered:

"'Moon' with men, 'Flame' among the gods,

'The Wheel' in the house of Hel

'The Goer' to the giants, 'The Gleamer' to the dwarfs,

And to the elves, 'The Teller of Time'."

Thor said:

"Answer me, Alvis! You know all,

Dwarf, of the doom of men:

What do call they the sun, that all men see,

In each and every world?"

Alvis answered:

"Men call it 'Sun,' the gods say 'Orb of the Sun,'

'The Deceiver of Dvalin' to the dwarfs;

The giants say 'The Ever-Bright,' the elves say 'Fair Wheel,'

And 'All-Glowing' say the sons of the gods."

The poem *Völuspá* speaks of how humanity uses the moon and the arrival of morning to number the years, which some scholars suggest refers to the importance of the lunar calendar to the Norse people.

There is also a record of a female jötunn that Mani desired, but no text identifying who she was survives. We do know that both the sun and moon were priceless, so much so that a jötunn demanded them (along with the goddess Freya) as the price for building a new wall for Asgard. Fortunately, he wasn't successful in his request!

## AEGIR AND RÁN

Aegir and his wife Rán are technically jötnar, but the lines between the gods and the jötnar are often blurry at best. It's generally acknowledged that these two are a god and goddess of the sea. But hold on, isn't Njord the god of the sea? Well, yes. Sometimes more than one god was associated with a certain phenomenon or role: Skadi and Ullr as goddess and god of winter and skiing, Freya, Sjofn, and Lofn as goddesses associated with love, for example (more on these latter two on page 91). Aegir and Rán might be thought of as personifications of the ocean itself, in both its giving and taking qualities.

They are said to have nine daughters, which might symbolize the ocean's waves, and a son, Snaer, who represents snow (and is a separate being from Ullr or Skadi). These nine daughters might be the nine mothers of Heimdall, though that's by no means certain. It's possible that Aegir is the father of the beautiful maiden Gerd, who enchants Freyr and captures his heart, though it might be another jötunn of the same name.

And unlike some other jötnar, Aegir has a good relationship with the gods of Asgard, and on more than one occasion, he hosts them for feasts in his watery domain. He is also known for brewing fine ale. In one story, he asks Thor to retrieve a cauldron big enough to brew sufficient ale for all the gods. In another famous tale, the gods are in attendance at one of Aegir's feasts, when Loki barges in, having been chased away once already for murdering one of Aegir's servants.

Aegir's name appears in several poems, where it means "sea." Kennings for his name include such creations as "Aegir's horse" for a boat and "Aegir's daughters" for waves. In one case, a large wave is called "Aegir's terrible daughter."

Whereas Aegir is known to be more jovial and welcoming, Rán seems more temperamental, perhaps representing the unpredictable nature of the sea, which can both give of its bounty and mercilessly take lives just as easily. Indeed, she is often associated with images of a net, which she uses to ensnare unwary sea travelers, dragging them down to a watery doom. Loki borrows this net from her when he needs to collect gold to pay compensation for accidentally killing someone (see The Ransom of Otter on page 206).

The Old Norse word rán actually means something like "robbery" or "plundering," which gives some insight into how Rán might have been viewed, i.e., as one who steals away the lives of many who dare to venture out into the waters. Given how much the Norse people relied on the sea, it is understandable that they would have envisioned some power behind it to which they paid considerable respect.

Her name is used in kennings such as rán-beðr, or "the bed of Rán," meaning the bottom of the ocean. If someone were to go to sleep in Rán's bed, for example, it would be a poetic way of saying that they had drowned at sea.

Aegir and Rán were probably not the subjects of a formal cult of worship, but instead might have been powers to which fishermen and sailors privately made offerings or prayers before and after setting out. According to one tradition, sailors would carry a small piece of gold with them, offering it to Rán to prevent themselves from drowning. It seems that the souls of the

drowned dead would travel to and be welcomed into the hall of Aegir and Rán, instead of going on to other afterlife destinations, such as Hel or Valhalla. If they had ale and feasts awaiting them, it wouldn't have been such a terrible fate.

## JORD (JÖRÐ)

Jord is the mother of Thor by Odin. She is one of the Allfather's many lovers. She is also said to be a jötunn, which makes her son's dedication to slaying them all the more interesting, and even disturbing. Her identity is a bit of a puzzle, as she appears in no stories and has no dialogue of her own, and yet she gave birth to one of the most important and famous gods in all of Germanic and Scandinavian belief. Thor acknowledges her as his mother, and she is definitely a rival to Frigg. Did Odin just indulge in a random fling with Jord as he did with several other women, having a one-night stand for his pleasure, or was Jord originally something more, perhaps much more?

The *Prose Edda* gives her a definite lineage, which is something that many more prominent deities never receive (or at least their lineages haven't survived). This suggests that she might have once been very important. Jord means "Earth" or "Soil," and the *Prose Edda* says that her mother was named "Night." The idea of the Earth being born of Night is intriguing, and may link Jord back to some form of Germanic creation story that no longer survives. Some scholars have speculated that she might also have been the first or the most important wife of Odin, especially given how popular Thor was in common belief. Indeed, thunder and weather gods as offspring of the Earth and a sky god appear in several sets of Indo-European myths.

Does Jord represent a much deeper thread of belief and tradition, perhaps dating back thousands of years, across at least two continents? Did an original Germanic story become muddled or changed over time, such that a Nordic account of Thor's mother survived but its older meaning was lost to time? Why would it have changed? How did Frigg figure into this and how did she supplant Jord, if that's what happened? These are all very good questions that cannot be answered right now, but they show the endless fascination that these stories can offer when we dig deeper into them.

## OTHER GODDESSES

In addition to the goddesses already mentioned, Snorri offers up a somewhat confusing list of additional goddesses in his *Prose Edda*, who he says are very important. Yet very little is known about them, or more accurately, very little information survives. His list includes the well-known goddesses Frigg and Freya, but other named goddesses such as Sif, Skadi, and Idunn are not found in this company; we don't know why he didn't include them. It's curious that this list of goddesses survives, and yet there is so little information about them, but there is additional information about some of them in the *Poetic Edda* and other sources, as well, included below. Here is a description of these enigmatic beings, and what we do know about them. Those goddesses already detailed in this section (Frigg, Freya, and Eir) are included, just to make the list complete.

SAGA, who lives in a large home called Sökkvabekkr ("sunken bank"). Snorri says nothing else about her. She might be associated with the sea, but some scholars contend that "Saga" is merely another name for Frigg, since the poem *Grímnismál* states that every day, she and Odin drink from golden cups at Sökkvabekkr. Others have seen a possible connection with the older Germanic goddess Nerthus, and even with Freya.

EIR, Snorri tells us, is the greatest of doctors. Here, she is more than a Valkyrie.

GEFJUN receives women who have died as virgins to serve her. She plays an important role in the *Lokasenna* ("Loki's Quarrel"), where she tries to make peace between Loki and the gathered gods. When Loki insults her, Odin warns him that it is not wise to anger her, as she knows the fate of all just as well as he does, a trait she shares with Frigg. This suggests that she is very powerful, and yet, we are given no further details. She is also credited with taking her four sons (from an unnamed jötunn) who have been transformed into oxen and, with their immense plowing strength, carving out enough new land to create the region in Denmark now known as Zealand. There are other northern plowing myths and legends dating back several centuries, and folk customs in the north of women plowing a certain amount of a field on specific days. These practices might relate to earlier fertility rites and blessings for the land, now long forgotten. Gefjun might be a different version of Freya (a similar name is listed as one of Freya's alternate names, see below), or she might be an entirely different goddess, or even another version of Frigg.

FULLA is a virgin goddess who wears her hair loose, while a golden band circles her head. She is a primary servant of Frigg and carries Frigg's ash wood box; unfortunately, we're not told what is inside of it. She not only shares secrets with Frigg (sadly, we don't know what these are, because they're secret!), but also looks after her lady's shoes. When Baldr and Nanna are in Hel, they give Fulla a ring as a gift, making her the only goddess besides Odin and Frigg who is mentioned as receiving tokens from the dead gods. In the second of the Germanic Merseburg charms (ninth-century magical spells in the Old High German language), a goddess named Volla is named, possibly as the sister of Frigg, who helps to heal a wounded horse by singing. This goddess might have been associated with healing and fertility in Germanic religion, and something of her carried over into Norse beliefs as Fulla. If so, she might be a very ancient goddess, whose worship simply declined over the centuries, or was taken over by others.

**SJOFN** is a goddess associated with making people fall in love. The word sjafni ("lover") comes from her name.

**LOFN** ("Loving"), another love goddess, is so kind and gentle that Odin and Frigg give her permission to arrange marriages, even if those marriages have been forbidden in the past. This seems like a tremendous power to have, because a forbidden marriage could have considerable consequences. The Norse word *lof*, meaning "permission," comes from her name.

**VAR** ("Beloved") hears the oaths that men and women make to each other. She also takes revenge on those who break their oaths, though we are not told what this vengeance is. The jötunn Thrym invokes her when he calls for Thor's hammer to be brought to consecrate and validate his supposed marriage to Freya (who is really Thor in disguise!). This suggests that Var might well have been important in marriage ceremonies. That she punished oath-breakers only strengthens this argument. Yet some scholars propose that "Var" might originally have been another of Freya's names, and perhaps she became a separate oath goddess at some point.

**VOR** ("Careful") knows all. She (perhaps like Odin) seeks knowledge so thoroughly that nothing can be kept from her. She might have some connection to a Valkyrie named Geiravör, or she might not. And that is essentially all we know. Unlike Vor herself.

**SYN** ("Refusal") is a guardian of the doors of the hall (we don't know which one) and locks out those who are not permitted to enter. She also defends those whose cases need to be overturned in courts. She might have been invoked by those facing legal disputes or seeking to protect their homes.

Frigg charges **HLIN** ("Protector") to guard those that she wishes to be protected from danger. Her name comes from the peace or refuge (hleinir) that one attains when one escapes from that danger. The poem *Völuspá* speaks of her "second sorrow," when Odin rushes to meet Fenrir at Ragnarök and is killed. Her "first sorrow" was presumably the death of Baldr. For this reason, many scholars conclude that Hlin is yet another name for

Frigg, but others are fairly certain that she was a goddess in her own right. Her name was a kenning for women in general in several skaldic poems, which might suggest that she was quite well known and widely honored.

The unfortunately named SNOTRA is next, and all we learn is that she is courtly and wise. Her name comes from the Old Norse word snotr, meaning "wise" or "clever." Beyond one additional reference from Snorri, no other source mentions her. Some scholars have even suggested that Snorri simply invented her, though there's no real reason why he would need to do that, given how many other goddesses he chose to leave off the list. It's possible that she was a personal protector goddess of some kind, perhaps worshiped more privately than formally.

GNA travels through different worlds, performing errands and tasks for Frigg. She rides a horse named Hofvarpnir ("Hoof Kicker") who can ride through the air and over the sea. Some of the Vanir once caught sight of her passage and inquired about who or what she was that she could fly. She replied that she was not the one who flew, rather it was her steed. Of course, there might be a relationship between Hofvarpnir and Odin's horse, Sleipnir, since both can traverse different worlds.

SOL the sun and BIL who follows the moon are also listed as goddesses, as are JORD, the mother of Thor, and RIND, the mother of Vali—the slayer of Hod, in revenge for killing Baldr.

We know so little about most of the goddesses on this fascinating and tantalizing list. Some of them, such as Gna and Syn, seem to have roles of great importance, but these roles are only hinted at. Then there are three love goddesses, Sjofn, Lofn, and Var, all of whom govern different aspects of love and relationships, which seems very detailed and even micro-managed in an odd way. They might have been invoked in different places and times, or they might be alternate names for one goddess, namely Freya.

It's possible that by Snorri's time, most people had forgotten much of the lore about these goddesses, and he was simply listing all that he could learn about them. Some of them might have always been minor, or very localized, even to the level of being house guardians and spirits. It's possible that some were seen as disir, or female ancestor spirits, in earlier times (see their entry on page 99), and perhaps acquired goddess status relatively late in the Viking Age. And yet, Snorri declares that they are all important, and is content to list Frigg and Freya alongside these mostly unknown female beings. If some of them are merely different names for Frigg or Freya, this makes more sense, but that's not the only possibility for who they are. Their identities are a mystery, and it's frustrating that we might never know much more about them.

## JÖTNAR

The jötnar preceded the gods of Asgard and are a separate class of beings from them (both Aesir and Vanir). They live in their own realm, Jötunheim, and often have an uneasy relationship to the gods. They are mysterious, powerful, and frightening beings that are at the heart of Norse mythology. The word jötunn (jötnar is plural) is often translated as "giant," but this is misleading. Some of them are described as being large, even enormous, while others are the same size as gods and humans. Many of the gods are in fact offspring of one or more jötnar parents, showing that the line between the two groups can be very blurred. Skadi is the daughter of the jötunn Thiazi, a "frost giant," who lives in a wintery locale. But she is also presumably honored as a goddess in her own right, and for what it's worth, she's never described as being huge in size.

As we will see in the Norse creation story, the jötnar might represent something ancient, perhaps the very forces of nature in a wild and primal sense, while the gods are their descendants and take on the role of the "civilizers." The taming of the primal and the chaotic is a common feature in world myths and a necessary action for human societies to arise. The relationship between the Norse gods and the jötnar might be something like that between the Titans and the later Greek gods who overthrew them. Indeed, Zeus slaying Chronos, or the Sumerian Marduk killing the primal chaos dragon Tiamat, have some similarities to the Norse tale of Odin and his brothers killing the first being, Ymir.

Since the Norse gods themselves are descended from the jötnar, the distinction between the two groups, if any, is not always clear. Their differences might be more about their purpose and actions than their powers or importance in the cosmos. Did the Norse actually worship any of the jötnar, beyond perhaps Skadi and a few others? It's difficult to say, and if there were any spiritual practices, they probably were more in the vein of appeasement than worship. There is evidence of some kind of cultic activity in a lava tube in Iceland, suggesting worship or at least placation of a jötunn such as Surtr (see below), a logical place to make offerings to a being from the realm of fire. New evidence might well come to light showing cults around other jötnar, so we can leave that question open for now.

The jötnar are both friends and foes of the gods in different stories, depending on which gods are present and who seeks what from whom. Thor is often at odds with them, despite the fact that he is the son of the female jötunn Jord. He seems to spend a large amount of time seeking them out to fight and kill them, and he enjoys doing it! The jötnar generally fear him, and his arrival in their midst is often a cause for their worry. But many people probably believed that if Thor didn't keep the jötnar at bay, they would soon overrun both Asgard and Midgard, taking those realms for themselves. And yet, we also have stories such as those of Skadi and Gerd, who were welcomed into Asgard and given the highest honors, even revered as goddesses.

And while the myth of Freyr and Gerd might have something to do with the idea of summer "overcoming" winter (see the

Freyr and Gerd entry on page 186), it's worth remembering that even though Gerd is a jötunn, she is described as being among the most beautiful of all women in all the worlds, so much so that Freyr falls in love with her from a single glance. This fact dispels the idea that the jötnar are always either huge or hideous, even though they sometimes are. Likewise, they can be good or evil, though they are often lumped into a single group of generally evil beings. Angrboda—the mother of the wolf Fenrir, the serpent Jormungandr, and the goddess Hel—is described as being a jötunn, and she is usually thought of as malevolent, but was she really?

Jötnar are sometimes described negatively as trolls (well before online harassment), and their portrayal as evil and slow-witted becomes more common with the arrival of Christian tales about them. In later Scandinavian folk and fairy tales, trolls are frequently described as bad-tempered, evil, cannibalistic creatures that turn to stone in the sunlight. Bearing in mind that this was also the fate of dwarves exposed to the sun, and that some dwarves are also referred to as jötnar in the Norse lore, it's obvious that the very term "jötunn" was used a bit freely and loosely, describing almost any being that was other than the gods themselves, never mind the god's ancestry!

Curiously, the best way to reach the realm of Jötunheim changes from story to story, and it appears to be located in different places. These discrepancies might hint at something about the jötnar's chaotic essences: they are as unpredictable as nature itself.

But nature is mysterious, and the jötnar often possess secret knowledge or prized possessions that the gods do not have but that they want or need. Freya seeks out the jötunn Hyndla to learn the lineage of Ottar, a mortal man she favors. Odin wants a drink of the mead of poetry from the jötunn Suttung to give inspiration to those who seek it. Thor journeys to Jötunheim to reclaim his stolen hammer. The jötunn Utgard-Loki tests Thor by giving him several impossible tasks, which the thunder god nevertheless almost accomplishes, earning Utgard-Loki's respect.

The jötnar assume many guises and roles, but one of the most feared of them is the "fire giant" Surtr, who waits in his realm of Muspelheim to unleash his fire upon the gods and all the worlds at Ragnarök. His flaming sword will eventually set the cosmos on fire and destroy everything, though there is no mention of his fate. We might even guess that after this brutal action, he simply retreats to his realm to wait until he will charge forth again in the next cycle to do the same. Like a force of nature, he is not good or evil, he simply is. And the idea of destruction by fire would have been well understood by the Icelandic audiences hearing these tales. The volcanoes of their island could be destructive and merciless, random and unpredictable, so the idea of a primal being who would unleash the same kind of fiery chaos on all of creation from time to time was something they could have easily accepted and feared.

The jötnar are crucial to the existence of the gods and they play a critical role in many of the myths. They are as essential to these stories as the gods themselves, even if we might never fully understand them.

## MIMIR (MÍMIR)

Mimir plays an important role in several stories, especially in dealing with Odin, but exactly who or what he is remains something of a mystery. He is an adviser to Odin and is renowned for his vast knowledge and wisdom, so much so that Odin wants to keep him nearby even after an unfortunate run-in with a Vanir blade (more on that story on page 142). His name is probably related to "memory," which is an accurate description of his nature and position. In a mostly non-literate society, those with great memories, like skalds, would have been held in high regard.

Mimir might be the brother of Bestla—mother of Odin, Vili, and Vé—and if so, that would make him Odin's uncle and also one of the jötnar. This seems like a logical connection between these two, since uncles were often held in high regard in Germanic and Scandinavian societies, as mentors and guides. Odin certainly seems to rely on Mimir in this capacity. Odin later mentions that Bestla's brother, the son of Bolthor, has taught him "nine mighty spells." If Mimir is the teacher of this magic, it would further solidify their relationship, again putting Mimir in the role of a mentor.

One poetic kenning, "mischief Mimir," is a term for jötunn. This seems to indicate that Mimir is indeed one of the jötnar, but unlike many of them, he isn't one who wishes to cause trouble or harm.

After the war between the Aesir and Vanir, the Aesir send Mimir as one of the exchanged hostages to live with the Vanir and to advise Hoenir. But soon, the Vanir think Odin might have tricked them (not an unreasonable assumption) and so they do something rather awful to Mimir before returning him (or at least part of him!) to the Allfather. Thankfully, this doesn't reignite hostilities, and Odin comes up with a creative way to keep Mimir around and giving out advice.

Mimir dwells near a well, said to be under one of the three roots of the World Tree, Yggdrasil, in the realm of the jötnar of frost. This well contains much wisdom, and Mimir is able to drink from it and increase his own, possibly using Heimdall's Gjallarhorn. Odin seeks to drink from this well, too, since he is always on the quest for wisdom, insight, and knowledge. But Mimir warns him that such a gift must come with a steep price. It's one that Odin will ultimately be willing to pay.

# THE DISIR (DÍSIR)

**P**ut simply, the disir were the spirits of female ancestors who either continued to watch over their descendants or could cause them problems. The disir might protect or antagonize a family and/or a home. Put far less simply, the word *dís* could also refer to human women and even goddesses. According to Snorri, one of Freya's names is Vanadís, or the "Dis of the Vanir." If you remember, he also calls Skadi the Öndurdís, the "snowshoe dis," which emphasizes her connection to winter.

The word seems to have been used in so many ways that it's difficult to get a sense of which, if any, was the most common. Once again, we see evidence that different people interpreted a popular term or idea in differing ways. It's difficult to say that the disir were definitely one concept or another. The term might have been used pretty freely, but its core meaning always seems to have been "lady," while an earlier Old Norse meaning might have been "goddess." Even if the disir were originally goddesses, the term could also be a kenning for female ghosts or one's kinswomen (living or dead), Odin's Valkyries, and even Hel herself. The word was a common ending for female names: Freydís, Vigdís, Thórdís, and many others. It's still a popular part of names for girls in Iceland.

The disir are referred to as a group, like the Norns and Valkyries, and some researchers have suggested that the term disir might be a generic word for all of these female spirit beings. It's also possible that the Valkyries were originally known as disir. They are called Herjans disir, or "Odin's disir," in the poem *Guðrúnarkviða*. The disir are also equated with the larger group of spirits known as norns; there were other norns beyond the three Norns who dwell at Yggdrasil (more about them on page 117), whose name is capitalized here to distinguish them.

The disir were worshiped most often as house deities. If they were seen as ancestors, then they were particular to a given family or settlement. They were honored in a rite known as a dísablót, which was probably derived from an ancient practice of ancestor worship. This rite was commonly conducted at the onset of winter, though such rituals happened at other times, too. The *Hervarar Saga* tells of a dísablót taking place in autumn, conducted by a woman. Another saga, the tale of St. Olaf, describes a similar ritual happening in later February or early March in Uppsala. It was a dísaþing, a ritual for peace, prosperity, and victory to accompany the Thing, or gathering of the people, and a market fair. When Christianity forced out the old gods, the festival continued to be celebrated, though it was moved to coincide with the Christian feast of Candlemass at the start of February. The fair still takes place on the first Tuesday of February each year, and even keeps the old name: Disting. It's likely one of the oldest continual celebrations in Scandinavia.

It seems that worship of the disir was widespread, and they were as venerated as the greater gods, perhaps even more in some circumstances. And yet, other than the dísaþing, these devotions were probably usually private, or even when they were public, they were matters for the family and perhaps the friends related to the disir in question. They were not just open to everyone. There are references in the sagas to a dísarsálr, or hall of the dis. These buildings might have been public temples for people and families to conduct their private devotions.

The disir seem to have been viewed as deceased guardians of the dead, and spirits whom one would want on one's side. There are saga accounts of fighting men boasting that their disir have come to battle with them, ready to fight on their behalf. Did warriors really brag about this, or is it just a literary invention? We don't know, but privileged supernatural protection does seem like the kind of thing that opposing armies might taunt each other with, as well as use to rally their own forces to battle.

In one story that scholars believe to be about the disir, a young man, Þiðrandi, is attacked by nine women in black, riding nine black horses. Nine women in white on white horses attempt to defend him, but can't save his life in the end. If all the women are, indeed, disir (the usual assumption), this story implies that not all disir are created equal, and that one's protective family spirits might not be up to the task of fending off challengers. Some see this particular tale as a commentary on Christianity's triumph over heathenism, but if so, it's curious that the winners are dressed in black.

The Norse disir have a parallel in the Germanic female spirits known as the Idisi. The similarity in sound is obvious, and it seems that the Idisi were widely venerated by Germanic pagans, including the Anglo-Saxons (where they were called the Ides) in England before (and after) the coming of Christianity. Jacob Grimm suggested that the goddess Idunn might be related to them in some way, though this is probably a stretch; not everything that sounds similar is connected!

## THE VALKYRIES

The Valkyries are one of the more famous products of Norse and Germanic belief that have edged their way into contemporary culture. The very word conjures up images of Wagner's famed musical piece, and most people have some inkling of them as being female spirits that lead those who have died in battle to Odin's hall, Valhalla. Indeed, the very word *valkyrja* means something like "chooser of the slain," implying that they not only retrieve the souls of the dead, but actually mark out those warriors doomed to die in a given battle. But they have other roles, as well.

They appear in art as offering drinking horns of ale and mead to the Einherjar, the dead who feast in Odin's hall, and seem to be the ones who welcome those warriors to the hall to begin with. The Einherjar fight each day in training for Ragnarök, and if they are slain in battle, the Valkyries appear to be the ones who raise them from the dead so that they can fight again the next day. Yes, in the afterlife, these warriors die and

come back from the dead on a regular basis, which doesn't sound especially appealing!

The Valkyries feature in seven poems from the *Poetic Edda*, as well as in several places in Snorri's *Prose Edda*, and in various sagas. They also appear on rune stones and possibly as figurines found in archaeological digs. The little figures might have been placed into graves because they were believed to offer protection for the souls of the dead. One of the most famous images on a stone is of a woman holding up a horn as a figure rides by on an eight-legged horse; conventional interpretations say this scene represents a Valkyrie presenting a drink to Odin as he returns on Sleipnir's back. But she might be about to drink from the horn herself.

The goddess Freya takes on the role of offering the drinking horn in a story about the jötunn Hrungnir; the more drink she brings to him, the drunker he gets, and the worse his behavior becomes. Some believe that Freya has a relationship to the Valkyries, as well, especially since she is noted as choosing half of the slain warriors for herself. But this doesn't necessarily mean that she was seen as the "goddess of the Valkyries," as some have claimed. Remember that the healing goddess Eir is listed as both a Valkyrie and a goddess, and is said to serve the maiden Menglöð, whom some have identified with Freya. But there's just not enough information to reach any definite conclusions.

Despite ideas about the Valkyries being beautiful women, they were also seen as terrifying and even merciless creatures, who took pleasure in the deaths they chose on the battlefield. They were even seen as similar to ravens, who famously would pick over the bodies of the dead for good eats. J.R.R. Tolkien suggested that their name originally came from a term for carrion-eating birds who circled the fields after a battle. They are also said to ride wolves, which strengthens their connection to Odin, known for his wolves and ravens.

Even their names hint at their ferocity and fearsome reputation; various sources list names such as Hlökk ("Noise"), Herfjötur ("Battle-Fetter"), Skögul ("the Raging"), Geirahöð ("Spear-Fight"), Skeggjöld ("Axe-Age") and Gunnr ("War"). It's not clear how many of these names were actually known or used in pagan Scandinavia, versus how many were the inventions of later poets. But in any case, they are clearly not happy, friendly spirits!

Indeed, the saga of *Brennu-Njals* quotes a skaldic poem that tells of women presumed to be Valkyries who are weaving, a typical and important role for many women in the Viking Age. But these women weave together human intestines, using skulls and heads as their weights, while they use weapons as weaving tools. This imagery obviously connects the Valkyries to violent death, but it also seems to connect them to the Norns (similar to the Greek Fates), and the idea of the weaving of fate. Since the Valkyries choose who will die on the field of battle, they might be seen as having a Norn-like role in weaving and cutting as they choose. Are the Norns, the Valkyries, and the disir all related in various ways? Quite possibly, and it's likely that sometimes those terms were used interchangeably and have connections that have been lost over the centuries.

Even though they are supernatural beings, the Valkyries are always depicted as women. Indeed, they perform several roles that some human Norse and Germanic women also did. For example, high-born human women (and sometimes men) would traditionally offer drinks to guests in mead halls and at gatherings, acting as generous and hospitable hosts. This doesn't mean that such women were thought of as Valkyries, just that they engaged in similar rites, and not just in the mead hall.

Interestingly, scholars have noted that in certain circumstances, sometimes human women would choose who would die, not on the battlefield, but for sacrifices. These unfortunate people were usually prisoners of war, criminals, or slaves. The Arab traveler Ibn Fadlan (c. 879–960) wrote about an elaborate tenth-century funeral of a people he called the *Rūsiyyah*, most likely a Norse settlement, along the Volga River. The family of a dead chieftain asks for a slave to volunteer to die with him. After a young female slave does so, a woman whom Ibn Fadlan calls the "Angel of Death" facilitates the ritual that leads to her sacrifice. Was this "Angel" (and other women like her) seen as a human version of a Valkyrie? In some cases, the sacrificial victims might be determined by lots or by divination, in effect being "chosen" by a god or gods. A woman interpreting and obeying the gods' will to choose who would die seems very similar to the role of the spirit Valkyries.

The term Valkyrie took on new meanings after the arrival of Christianity. In England, the word *wælcyrge* could refer to furies, goddesses, witches, and even ravens. Some Christian missionaries and clergymen, especially in England, used the word to refer to any female sorcerer. Such clergy probably weren't interested in the word's original meaning, and in any case, they usually intended to insult and condemn, not to inform.

Still, the image of the Valkyrie lives on in popular culture, from Wagner's driving theme signaling their arrival in his opera *Die Walküre*, to the name of many fictional aircraft and weapons, to the superheroine character in the Marvel Cinematic Universe who might be the last of her kind.

## ELVES AND DWARVES

For most people, the words "elves" and "dwarves" conjure up images from fantasy novels, movies, or role-playing games. These elves are usually tall, fair, and beautiful, often with pointed ears and long flowing hair, while dwarves are depicted as short, stout, bearded, and preferring to live underground. We have J. R. R. Tolkien to thank for these descriptions. The elves and dwarves of his Middle Earth are basically the default and set the standard for all the fantasy novels and other media that followed. And yet, Tolkien himself drew his ideas and even the names of many of these characters from Norse originals, even if he changed their natures to have them better interact with hobbits and humans in his stories. So, what are elves and dwarves, really, and how do they relate to the Norse gods?

Elves, or alfr (singular alf), as they would have been known, show up in several Norse myths, tales, and references. The word "alf" means something like "gleaming" or "white," in reference to their shining presence, even though we know there are also dark elves. The word (and the very concept of elves) was so well known among the early English that it became a popular name prefix in Anglo-Saxon England, even after Christianization. The name "Alfred" might be familiar to you? It means "Elf Counsel." In more recent times, what about "Gandalf"? It means "Wand Elf" or "Staff Elf," a good description of the beloved wizard, even if Tolkien made him something other than a typical Nordic elf.

None of the elves are physical beings, so the name might refer to many other kinds of spirit entities; "alf" could simply be a generic term for spirit. Warning children not to go into the woods or the alfr would get them could mean watching out for anything from elves to goblins, trolls, or evil spirits. It's likely that some of the alfr were spirits of the dead, like the disir. It's also possible that an alf was a male spirit (such as an ancestor), just as a dis was a female one, though alfr don't seem to have been specifically male.

The alfr are not always favorably disposed toward humanity, especially in England. The Anglo-Saxons had a long-held belief that elves could cause mischief or outright harm to mortals, if they offended elvish sensibilities. Even in Christian times, people often believed that physical ailments were caused by "elf shot," or small darts and arrows fired at humans. Some anthropologists have suggested that in part, this belief might have come from people of the time discovering Neolithic arrowheads and assuming that they had supernatural origins. True or not, many held that maladies like aches and pains, arthritis, or even more serious diseases could come from elf-shot. So, cures were often a mixture of herbs and charms spoken to drive away the elves or remove the curse of their magical attacks. Despite Christian opposition, belief in the elves lingered for a very long time in England, probably well into the Middle Ages and even the Renaissance.

Indeed, there is a similarity between the Germanic/Nordic alfr and the Celtic Sidhe (fairies). Both were seen as spirits who inhabited mounds, and it was unwise to trespass on their lands, much less antagonize or anger them. Reverence for these spirits might have evolved from common origins, back when continental European Celtic and Germanic beliefs intermingled and exchanged, with each belief system evolving to reflect bits of unique cultures and locations over the centuries. Indeed, belief in the alfr, the Sidhe, and their kin far outlasted belief in the old gods.

There seem to be three categories of elves: "light" (Ljósálfar), "dark" (Dökkálfar), and "swart" (Svartálfar), the last of these being the dwarves. Possibly. Yes, things are about to get confusing yet again!

The light elves inhabit the celestial realm of Alfheim, ruled by the god Freyr. Alfheim was also once a region on the southwest coast of Sweden, near the border with modern Norway. Legends spoke of a King Álf the Old, who ruled that land and had elf blood. On the other hand, the name might have nothing to do with the elves at all, instead being related to words for river and gravel. But that's boring.

In any case, in the mythic realm of Alfheim, the light elves might be something like demigods (or even gods themselves), or those who operate on behalf of the gods in various ways. As such, they don't often interact with humanity, though they are said to be bright and beautiful. Some see a connection between the light elves and Christian angels (with the dark elves being demons) and suggest that Christian beliefs might have influenced ideas about the alfr, especially since these beings mostly appear in medieval Icelandic writings. But visions of various spiritual beings are common in many cultures, so there's no reason why a pagan concept of light and dark alfr might not have existed already.

Light and dark alfr do not appear as characters in the *Eddas*, but they are referenced on many occasions (including attending events, such as feasts). This suggests that they had a real importance in Old Norse beliefs. Indeed, the alfr seemed to have been worshiped and honored at regular festivals and rituals, just as the gods were. The ritual known as the álfablót was usually a winter feast that people held in honor of the elves, like the disáblót for the disir. If this feast was meant to honor the dead, then it probably would have been held for the dark elves. This practice might have evolved over time and had very ancient roots in the reverence for the dead in burial mounds, which were said to be the homes of the spirits of the ancestors. Such feasts, like those for the disir, could have been small, even house or family-oriented. Believers considered the álfablót to be sacred and only meant for those who held to the old ways. One account tells of a skald who, after he had converted to Christianity, was not welcome at the álfablót.

But what of the swart elves? Some scholars think that dark and swart elves are the same beings, as both are said to live underground. But it's also possible that the dark elves are the spirits of the dead who inhabit grave mounds, while the swart elves are something else, more akin to our classic view of dwarves, kobolds, goblins, and so on. Also, there is no reason that any elf or dwarf needs to be tall or short, just as the jötnar are called "giants" but can be of any size.

So, if light elves dwell in Alfheim and serve Freyr and other gods, and the dark elves inhabit the mounds of the dead, and the swart elves are possibly the same as dark elves, what of the dwarves? They are master smiths and forgers, and love nothing more than working with gold and gems, and producing masterpieces of art and magic, very often unique pieces that are the finest ever made. They produce many of the gods' great possessions: Thor's hammer, Odin's spear, Freya's necklace, Sif's new hair, Fenrir's fetter, and others. But despite their abilities to craft objects of exquisite beauty and function, dwarves can also be selfish or even outright evil, as in the story of Kvasir's murder by the dwarf brothers, Fjalar and Galar, or how four dwarves demand Freya's sexual favors in exchange for the Brísingamen necklace that she desires.

One of their curious features is a tendency to turn to stone if they are exposed to sunlight, a trait that would survive in folklore for centuries. One amusing poem tells of how Thor tries to fend off a dwarvish suitor for his daughter by keeping him occupied long enough with spouting out his knowledge that the sun finally rises and eliminates the problem!

These beings appear far more often than elves in the *Eddas* as actual characters, often with their own agendas, for good and bad. Dwarves are named in detail in various sources; there are several long lists of them that can get tedious for the modern reader. The collectors of the Eddic poems and stories evidently thought that the dwarves were worthy of the extra attention, or perhaps stories of the dwarves circulated in Iceland for far longer than those of some other beings.

As with elves, dwarves and their kin became a part of Germanic folklore long after the pagan age, and many people still believed in them into nearly modern times. Along with the alfr, there are other types of beings, which, as we will see in the next entry, encompass whole categories of spirits, and belief in them persists, especially in countries like Iceland.

## WIGHTS AND HULDUFÓLK

Nordic spirituality almost certainly has at least some roots in animism—the belief that various kinds of spirits inhabit the natural world—even in the Viking Age. Indeed, people would have made offerings to beings known as land wights, or landvættir, who were spirits local to one's home, sometimes honoring them more often than the gods. These entities could inhabit any natural feature, from a rock to a tree to a whole field. Like the disir, they might be spirits of the dead, but wights were also believed to have inhabited places never before settled by humans, especially in Iceland.

The landvættir were often tied to the health of the land, and seeking out their friendship and protection was crucial for a farm or a business to prosper. People would regularly leave offerings of food and drink at the specific places these spirits inhabited (such as rocks, trees, or streams), a practice that continued for centuries after the Viking Age, much to the chagrin of the Christian church. If one were to anger or drive away the wights of a given location, disaster might befall the perpetrator of the offense. The spirits were there first, after all.

So alongside the great gods and powerful forces of the Norse cosmos, these spirits dwelled in close contact with people, and it might have been much more effective to call upon them than one of the more powerful beings for daily matters. The Romans had a similar relationship with their house spirits, whom they honored daily, while the "big" gods might receive far less attention until a major holiday. As for the Norse gods, Odin probably wouldn't be interested in helping you find a lost key, after all! And Loki might have hidden it, to begin with.

In particular, many believed that Iceland was protected by powerful wights who had lived there long before the coming of the Norse settlers. The *Saga of King Olaf Tryggvason* tells of how King Harald Bluetooth (whose name would be used for wireless technology centuries later) desired to invade Iceland, and so asked a wizard (possibly a Sámi man) to journey to the island in the form of a whale. As he swam around the coast to investigate its defenses, he saw that land wights were everywhere, in all sizes.

He tried to swim into one fjord, but a wight in the shape of a dragon flew toward him, along with other wights in the shapes of insects and snakes, each defying him and spitting poison. He tried again at another location but was threatened by a wight in the shape of a gigantic bird, accompanied by smaller birds. Trying a third time, a wight in the form of an angry bull confronted him, along with others of its kind. He tried one last time to come ashore, but met a giant holding an iron staff, along with other jötnar, who made it very clear that he was not welcome. He scoured the shores for places where ships might land, but found no place safe. Thus, he had to go back to Bluetooth empty-handed and tell him that trying to invade Iceland would be a very bad idea.

These four wights were seen as the protectors of the four directions of Iceland: Dreki the dragon for the east, Griðungur the bull for the west, Gammur the eagle for the north, and Bergrisi the giant for the south. They are still displayed on Iceland's coat of arms, showing how an ancient tradition can survive many changes of belief and rulers over the centuries.

Indeed, in Iceland, belief in the "hidden people," or Huldufólk, persists to this day. They are a part of folk tradition and while people may laugh or even scoff at the idea of an ancient superstition surviving into the modern world, there are several well-attested stories of human activities going horribly wrong because they either angered or refused to recognize the spirits on the land that were already there.

Equipment malfunction is a commonly reported problem in the building of roads or structures that might pass though Huldufólk land. In most cases, once someone (such as a psychic, spiritualist, modern heathen priest, or the like) reaches out to these beings to ask for permission, the troubles stop and the work can proceed. Usually, one of the Huldufólk answers the person contacting them and explains that they will be willing to move if they are given a certain number of days to relocate. Be skeptical all you want, but there are many reports about builders doing just that, and finding that once they resume their work at the appropriate time, the equipment runs fine, and they have no further troubles. There are similar stories in Ireland about the fairies, and while many people laugh at them, quite a few are unwilling to go to a supposed fairy mound or forest on their own, especially at night.

It seems likely that there is a connection between the hidden people of Iceland and Scandinavia and the fairies of the

Celtic world. Given that Germanic and Celtic traditions sometimes intertwined in the early centuries of their existence, it's entirely possible that their beliefs about animistic nature spirits influenced one another. Both Celts and Germanic peoples maintained strong beliefs in these unseen neighbors long after their pagan religions were replaced by Christianity, developing elaborate and complex hierarchies of types, ranks, and duties, for good and ill. And there was a strong cultural interaction between the Vikings and the people of Ireland, who while Christian in name, retained their belief in fairies and other beings for a very long time.

## FENRIR AND JORMUNGANDR (JÖRMUNGANDR)

Fenrir the giant, ravenous wolf and Jormungandr the dreaded serpent who circles the world are two of the greatest and most feared of all creatures in Norse mythology. Along with Hel, they are the offspring of Loki and the jötunn Angrboda, and they are destined to bring ruin to the world and slay two of Asgard's mightiest gods at Ragnarök, Odin and Thor.

Wolves feature prominently in these stories, as we've already seen. But sometimes, it's not quite clear who is who, which shouldn't surprise you at this point. Fenrir is undoubtedly Loki's son, but we have already met the two wolves, Sköll and Hati Hróðvitnisson, who chase the sun and moon endlessly. It's likely that these two are the offspring of Fenrir. Hati's second name tells us that he is the son of Hróðvitnir ("Famous Wolf"), another name for Fenrir, so that seems pretty straightforward. Snorri tells us that Hati's mother is a jötunn who dwells in the forest of Ironwood, where she gave birth to many jötnar, all in the form of wolves, including these two. So, the two wolves who chase the sun and moon are siblings. But the poem *Vafþrúðnismál* from the *Poetic Edda* states that it is Fenrir himself who will devour the sun.

So is the devourer the father or the son? Or were they once the same? And there is another problem. Garmr, who stands guard in Hel, is predicted to break loose and attack Tyr at Ragnarök, where they will slay each other. But this seems odd, since the two have nothing to do with each other until that point. As we will see in the story of the binding of Fenrir, it is Tyr who develops something like a bond of trust with Fenrir, which breaks when the gods successfully bind him in an unbreakable fetter. In anger, Fenrir bites off Tyr's hand.

Yet at Ragnarök, Fenrir attacks and devours Odin (not Tyr), while Odin's son Víðarr will slay the great wolf in revenge. This makes little sense. Even though Odin was one of the architects of the deception that led to Fenrir's binding, it was Tyr that offered his hand to the wolf's jaws as a sign of trust. To break that oath would have left Fenrir raging at the thought of having revenge on the now one-handed god. So, either a lost version of the myth reveals that Fenrir attacked and killed (and was killed by) Tyr, or Garmr is another name for Fenrir. But then, who kills him? Is it Odin's son Víðarr, or Tyr?

We probably have conflicting traditions, two different versions of the same myth told in different places and times. Some kings probably wanted their skalds to elevate Odin to a position of greater importance in this final battle. But in doing so, the narrative becomes less satisfying, because the real feud is between Fenrir and Tyr, not Fenrir and Odin. Given that Tyr might have been the senior god at one point, it would stand to reason that there could be separate myths about them both meeting their ends by the jaws of a mighty wolf bent on vengeance. Perhaps all of these wolves were at one time one single antagonist, who over the ages was split into multiple characters to suit different versions of the stories.

The second of Loki's monstrous children is Jormungandr ("Vast Snake" or "Vast River"), also known as the Midgard

Serpent. This enormous sea serpent dwells in the ocean and encircles the whole world, biting its own tail. It grew to that size after Odin tossed it into the sea as a way of dealing with the gods' concerns about the ever-growing creature. But that was just kicking the problem down the road, for Jormungandr will return at Ragnarök to devastate the world and kill Thor, though Thor will in turn kill the serpent.

Thor encounters the beast at least three times, once while trying to lift what he thinks is a house cat and failing to do so, because the cat is really the serpent in disguise; once on a fishing trip that goes horribly wrong; and finally at the end of the world. The cat story is comical, but the encounter with the serpent on the fishing boat is terrifying. There are two versions of the tale. In the first, Thor seems to successfully kill the creature by striking its head with his hammer. In the second, he merely injures it and drives it away. The killing is odd, since it means that Jormungandr cannot return to slay Thor in the last conflict. Thus, we probably have two different traditions, suggesting that Thor's death at Ragnarök might not have been a universal belief among the Norse peoples, even if it is featured in the tale in later centuries.

Thor's dangerous fishing trip is detailed in art as well, some of which predates written poetry. One possible depiction, on the Ardre VIII stone on the island of Gotland in Sweden, might date back as early as the eighth century, even before the start of the "Viking Age" as we know it. So this battle might be a very old myth that survived mostly intact into the written era, except for its two possible endings. Perhaps Thor did kill the serpent in the original version, but the alternate ending was added later to allow for the creature to come back at Ragnarök.

The idea of a warrior god battling a serpent is definitely not unique to the Norse, and is a common theme in Proto-Indo-European mythology. An ancient Indian myth tells of the god Indra and the dragon/serpent Vritra, the Greek Zeus fights and defeats the dragon Typhon, and the Sumerian Marduk faces the dragon Tiamat. In the stories of Zeus and Marduk, both are a sky or weather god striking a serpent with a hammer or lightning to release torrents of rain. This seems an obvious connection to make: the crashing of thunder and lightning before the release of the storm. A myth telling how a god had to do battle with a serpent to release life-giving rains to humanity would be an entirely appropriate interpretation of these natural phenomena. It's likely that the tale of Thor and Jormungandr, though it differs in some ways from simply being a weather myth, has very deep roots going back to ancient, even prehistoric times.

Unlike Fenrir, who is bound by fetters put on him in a betrayal by the gods, Jormungandr bites his own tail, implying that he in some way imprisons himself, perhaps unwillingly. Maybe he cannot let go, but both brothers will free themselves from these bindings at the end, though we're not told exactly how this will happen.

Jormungandr plays a major role in the climax of Norse mythology, but he is not the only serpent lurking in the dark places of the worlds, wanting to burst free. The serpent Nidhogg (Níðhöggr) lies in wait under Yggdrasil, gnawing at its roots, slowly weakening it (see the entry on page 120). The relationship between these two monsters, if any, is unknown. Might they have been the same creature at one point, or in the beliefs in some areas? It's possible. Given how Fenrir's identity seems to be mixed with Garmr's, and that Nidhogg is also released at Ragnarök to bring destruction, there might have been two (or more) myths basically telling the same story—a serpent breaks free to go on a deadly rampage—from more than one perspective. Or they might have always been separate creatures. The difference is that Nidhogg doesn't die, and seems to survive into the next world, again bringing menace and maybe implying that evil never fully goes away. The gigantic Midgard Serpent, on the other hand, falls to Thor's hammer after poisoning him in the exchange.

# THE NORNS

The Norns are among the most curious and enigmatic of all the beings in Norse Myth, the mysterious entities who weave and control the fates of all. No one is certain what they are.

The word *norn* itself might mean "to twine," which would explain the idea of them weaving together the strands of people's fates. But another possibility is that it means something like "communicate secretly," which also seems appropriate, for they know the secrets of fate. Some skaldic poetry suggests that they have a role in pronouncing legal judgment, at least over whether someone lives or dies.

Always represented as female figures, they dwell beside the Well of Urðr (Urðarbrunnr) at one of the roots of Yggdrasil. Their names are Urðr ("Fate"), Verðandi ("Becoming"), and Skuld ("Ought to Be"). They embody cause and effect rather than past, present, and future. Among their tasks is to draw water from the well to nourish the roots of Yggdrasil, preventing it from withering and rotting. They thus help preserve the order of the universe, at least until its destined end. Their origin is not clear, but as we've seen, they might be the three female jötnar who arrived in Asgard early on, ending the Golden Age of the first gods and setting the stage for all that followed. Or not. Why they arrived when they did is not known, which is perhaps appropriate for these mysterious women.

In history, the Norns might have evolved from various Germanic and Celtic beliefs in matronly goddesses, and perhaps these concepts were combined in some form with Greco-Roman ideas about the Moirai, the goddesses of fate. Although they have some similarities to the Fates of Greek mythology and the Maiden-Mother-Crone imagery of some Celtic traditions, they have their own unique properties. In Old English, the word for destiny or fate was the better-known "wyrd," the equivalent word and meaning for Urðr.

The texts indicate that the Norns appear as young women. If they are indeed the three jötnar who end Asgard's carefree days, then they are referred to as "girls" and "maidens" in the *Poetic Edda*. But they don't seem to have been goddesses in the traditional sense, and it's not clear if they were ever worshiped or received religious devotions in Scandinavia. More likely, at least some people acknowledged their role as an essential part of human existence, which of course could have found its way into various rituals.

Neither good nor evil, they simply enact the will of fate in the universe. They choose when things come into existence, when and how they live, and when they pass away. The poem *Völuspá* tells us that they made laws, allotted life to mortals, and set their fates.

Further, the poem *Hamðismál* declares:

"We have fought well, over the Goths' bodies we stand

By our blades laid low, like eagles on branches;

Great will be our fame, though we die today or tomorrow;

No one outlives the night after the Norns have spoken."

We might see this belief as fairly fatalistic. If one's fate is determined before one is born, how can anyone struggle against it, or do anything new, much less break free from it? The answer, of course, is that while the Norns know our fates, we do not. It's a conundrum that calls to mind the Christian problem of free-will vs. predestination, or God knowing all that will happen. How can we truly be free if someone, somewhere, already knows what will happen to us? It's a very old dilemma! Some Nordic heroes even resort to blaming the Norns for their unfortunate fates, or engaging in acts of recklessness, reasoning that if it is their time to die, the Norns have already decreed it to be so. A warrior might gain quite a sense of fearlessness and bravery in battle going into a fight with that attitude!

The three "main" Norns are not the only of their kind who are mentioned. Both *Eddas* relate that there are other norns, both

good and bad, who can bring fortune and misfortune into the lives of mortals. These lesser norns might have been similar to the disir and Valkyries, if not the same. There are even dwarf and elf norns, suggesting that the word might have signified a title or a role, rather than describing a specific kind of being. Snorri declares that Skuld, the youngest of the three Norns, is also a Valkyrie who rides with her sisters, but whether this was his invention, a mix-up, or a long-standing tradition isn't certain. We can clearly see a relationship between the Valkyries who choose the slain on the battlefield and the Norns who determine each person's fate. Again, many of these roles are murky in their definitions and might indicate different beliefs in different places and times.

Snorri also uses the idea of the Norns to question the unfairness of life. If the Norns determine each person's fate, then why are some people so blessed, while others appear to be cursed? The answer comes in the presence of those other norns. The good ones bring benefits to the lives of humans, while the bad norns try to bring misery and misfortune. Indeed, blame for particular tragic incidents might be leveled against a specific "bad" norn or group of norns. We are reminded of the white and black disir fighting over Þiðrandi's life. Are they norns, too? Or is the idea of "good" and "bad" norns a Christian attempt to make them into angels and demons?

Many questions remain unanswered about these strange and unnerving beings, and their role in the Norse cosmos. They were revered and respected by mortals and gods alike, and the gods even take counsel from them in the most dangerous of times.

## YGGDRASIL

Yggdrasil is the enormous ash tree at the center of and supporting the cosmos, around which all of the worlds and realms are arrayed, though the exact arrangement and even the number of worlds themselves is frustratingly unclear (see The Nine Worlds on page 132).

The tree is mentioned in many poems and accounts, both in the *Prose Edda* and the *Poetic Edda*, which suggests that it was central to the spiritual beliefs of the Norse peoples and was probably a very old and important part of those beliefs.

Its name might mean "Odin's Horse," which doesn't refer to Sleipnir (Odin's steed), but is a kenning for the gallows. Odin hung for nine nights on a tree (presumed to be Yggdrasil) to take up the runes, so the tree is indeed a place for the hanged. Other suggestions for the meaning of the word are "terror tree" and "yew pillar," which would be strange if it is said to be an ash tree. Again, we might be looking at more than one tradition blended into a common myth.

The concept of a tree connecting worlds is found in other cultures, especially across north Asia and into Siberia. In some lore, the shamans of Siberia can mount an animal in spirit form and ride through the various worlds via the tree, which calls to mind Odin riding Sleipnir through the worlds as he sees fit. Whether or not any Norse belief is a direct borrowing of some Siberian shamanic tradition (perhaps passed on through the Sámi), or a diffusion of an idea over many centuries is hard to determine, and as you can imagine, different scholars have different opinions.

The belief in a large World Tree itself probably came from the Germanic lands, or farther east. The Saxons of Northern Germany revered a tree or column that they called Irminsul, which might be a predecessor of Yggdrasil, or at least a similar idea developed from a common origin. The Christian Emperor Charlemagne made a point of destroying a large representation of this tree in his wars against the Saxons in the year 772. Ten years later, he executed about 4,500 Saxon pagans who refused to convert to Christianity. Clearly, the Irminsul held a special place for the Saxons just as Yggrasil did the Norse, so much so that they were outraged by Charlemagne's actions and were willing to die

for their beliefs. Indeed, there was a long-standing Germanic belief that humans were descended from trees, and the importance of a world tree as an axis for all creation must surely be related to that belief.

Another idea supporting Yggdrasil's origins in Germanic and or mainland Scandinavian belief is in how the gods journey to Yggdrasil each day to meet in assembly, known as a "thing." The Norse people also met together at things, especially in Iceland, which is a bit strange, because Iceland doesn't have grand or impressive trees. The native trees in Iceland tended to be small, and settlers felled and used them up quite quickly, leaving the land mostly treeless. So, the Norse people in Iceland very likely brought the story with them from across the sea.

In myth, Yggdrasil is large beyond comprehension. Its branches extend into multiple realms, and its three roots reach into three different worlds. One root goes to Niflheim, the realm of the dead; the second goes to Asgard; and the third goes to Jötunheim. At each root's end is a well:

One is at Urðarbrunnr, where the Norns dwell and cover that root daily with water and mud to help preserve the tree. This well also shares a name with the Norn named Urd (Urðr), which suggests that she is the most important of the three Norns. Two swans also feed from this well, which is said to be exceptionally blessed and holy, and from them all other swans have come. It is at this well at the base of the tree that the gods come every day to meet.

One is at the spring Hvergelmir in Niflheim. The serpent Nidhogg and many other serpents live beneath it and gnaw on the root, trying to undermine it for their own dark purposes. And yet, all rivers also flow from here, fed by a stag that feeds on the tree's branches.

One is at the well of Mímisbrunnr ("Mimir's Well"), where the frost jötnar dwell and where Ginnungagap, the great primordial void, used to be. This well is a source of much wisdom and it is where Mimir (whose name means "The Rememberer") resides (or at least his head does!). Odin sacrificed one of his eyes to drink from this well. The well might also contain one of Heimdall's ears.

Quite a lot happens in this cosmic tree, from the daily care that the Norns give it to the daily attacks by Nidhogg, as well as animals that chew on its branches and a rather curious little messenger that scurries up and down its trunk, delivering insults to its opposing denizens.

But despite its importance, Yggdrasil seems to be somewhat fragile, prone to being weakened by the many attacks it endures daily; it could conceivably die. Even so, its other names portray it as a place of refuge and sanctuary at the end of all things. Yggdrasil might also be known as Hoddmímis holt, where the two remaining humans who will repopulate the world during the chaos of Ragnarök. It is also called Mímameiðr ("Mímir's tree") and Læraðr ("shelter," among other possible options).

Yggdrasil's fate in the aftermath of Ragnarök is not specifically revealed, but its protective role implies that even though it will be damaged, it will survive the great destruction brought by Surtr and renew itself in the world to come.

There are stories of real-life trees that might have inspired or even represented the World Tree in Midgard. The eleventh-century chronicler Adam of Bremen, who wrote about the pagan Norse (and not in a flattering way, it must be said!) records that an enormous tree stood near the famed temple in Uppsala, Sweden (north of modern Stockholm). It was an evergreen, but no one knew exactly what kind of tree it was. Adam didn't see this tree firsthand, so he might have been exaggerating, or even making it up, but the idea of a large sacred tree near a major temple doesn't seem far-fetched at all. He also says that there was a well at the base of this tree, calling to mind Yggdrasil's roots. Was the Uppsala tree meant to represent Yggdrasil? Or did it speak more to the general reverence for trees found among the Germanic and Norse peoples?

In Scandinavia and parts of Germany, there was a tradition of planting "warden trees" on farms to be guardians and to bring luck. People made offerings to them in the hopes that they would continue their protection and prosperity. They might leave food or pour out ale at the tree's base on specific holidays, calling to mind the Norns and their bathing of Yggdrasil's roots. As you can imagine, the Christian church was less than thrilled with this activity, but like many pagan traditions, it became a part of localized folk customs (practiced even by those who considered themselves to be good Christians) and survived many attempts to eradicate it. In fact, it survived long after the Viking Age, well into the nineteenth century. The tradition continues in some Scandinavian regions even today. Or perhaps it's been revived since there is no more opposition to it.

## NIDHOGG, RATATOSKR, THE EAGLE, AND OTHER ANIMALS

In and around Yggdrasil dwells a host of animals and animal-like creatures that both do good things and stir up trouble. Gnawing at the base of the tree is the fearsome and terrible Nidhogg or Níðhöggr ("Malice Striker"), a serpent or dragon who forever tries to undermine its structure. In some writings, he lives in Náströnd, a place in Hel set aside for those who have committed murder or adultery or who have broken oaths. We're told that he also gnaws upon these unfortunate dead, sucking on their corpses and (presumably) causing them endless misery. This latter concept might be a Christian invention, with its ideas of eternal punishment, though it does appear in *Völuspá*.

Nidhogg dwells with other serpents. Six are named in the poem *Grímnismál* from the *Poetic Edda*, and it is said that they too gnaw on the World Tree, causing it much agony. But the poem tells us that there are many more malevolent serpents there, far more than any fool could ever imagine. The imagery evokes the idea of the serpent undermining the axis of the universe from within. The suggestion is that someone or something will always try to tear down what has been built. So, we can understand why the Norns tend to the tree to keep it healthy, at least for as long as the universe is destined to exist. It's not clear if these serpents are related to Jormungandr in any way, whether they were once part of the same brood, or are an entirely different lineage.

But we do know that other animals make use of the tree, including an unlikely creature, the squirrel known as Ratatoskr. Ratatoskr ("Drill Tooth") scurries up and down Yggdrasil, and according to the *Poetic Edda*, he brings messages from Nidhogg to an eagle who resides at the top of the tree. Considering that the World Tree encompasses the Norse cosmos, this is a long trip to make on a regular basis!

Snorri adds some extra information in the *Prose Edda*, saying that the eagle knows many things. He also must be a very large bird, for between his eyes, there sits a hawk named Veðrfölnir. What the hawk is doing there is never made clear. Some have suggested that Veðrfölnir might play a role similar to Odin's ravens, flying off to bring back information to the eagle, though it's curious that the hawk is named and the eagle, who quarrels with Nidhogg, is not. The image of a bird atop a tree and a serpent coiled beneath it can be found in other mythologies, especially from Asia, so it's possible that this imagery was influenced by an older tradition that was imported from the east at some point in the distant past.

Apparently, Ratatoskr's main task is to deliver gossip to both eagle and serpent, making them angry, presumably at each other. One can imagine them hurling insults at one another, with the squirrel being the messenger who delivers these ripostes. Does he enjoy doing this, or is it a tedious job? Perhaps Ratatoskr distorts their communications, thus inflaming the ire of both. He might have the form of a squirrel, but he might actually be a troll (pun intended!).

So, what is this really all about? There are various theories. Ratatoskr might represent a troublemaker who brings harsh words back and forth between two parties to keep hostilities go-

ing. Such a person would have been viewed very negatively in Norse society, where blood feuds could erupt and last for years. Assigning this unsavory task to a squirrel might have been a way of commenting on the nature of those who gossiped or actively tried to bring about strife. One can only speculate if Ratatoskr has any relationship to Loki, who also likes to stir up trouble with his words and deceptions.

Animals on the top and bottom of the tree gnaw at it, gradually weakening it, and Ratatoskr might be another of these creatures. Are they evil, or do they merely represent the decaying forces of nature and time?

Another named creature is the deer Eikþyrnir ("Oakthorn"), who is said to sit atop the hall at Valhalla, grazing on the branches of Lærad, which might be another name for Yggdrasil. From his antlers flow droplets (perhaps of water) into the spring of Hvergelmir, which ultimately form a multitude of rivers that flow through the world. So, Oakthorn takes from the tree, but also gives something back.

The stag has a counterpart in the she-goat Heidrun ("Heiðrún"), who also chews at Lærad and produces mead from her teats that fills a cauldron every day, so that Odin's Einherjar warriors can drink from it and never run out. These two animals might have once been a part of Heiðþyrnir, the bright sky, which was split into two parts, creating a male deer and a female goat that produced mead and water respectively. It's possible that there is a more ancient source for this myth, lost to time.

In addition to Eikþyrnir, the poem *Grímnismál* mentions four other stags: Dáinn, Dvalinn, Duneyrr, and Duraþrór (there will be a test on this later), who are described as stretching up to gnaw at the highest branches, eating the foliage. It might or might not be significant that Dáinn and Dvalinn are also the names of dwarves. One nineteenth-century Danish scholar proposed the idea that these stags might represent four different types of winds that "gnaw" at the tree, just as the wind does when it blows away leaves and rips off small branches. This is speculation, but it presents an interesting image, since four dwarves are also said to hold up the sky in each of the four directions. But these animals might just be another version of the Eikþyrnir myth, which became split into four stags over time in a separate tradition.

Finally, we have three roosters: Gullinkambi ("Golden Comb") who dwells at Valhalla, Fjalar ("Deceiver") who dwells in a forest called Gálgviðr ("Gallows Wood") in Jötunheim, and an unnamed rooster in Hel. Gullinkambi will crow to wake Odin's warriors at the beginning of the arrival of Ragnarök, alerting them that their time has come. Perhaps there is one rooster for each world: one to alert Valhalla, one to announce to the jötunn that Ragnarök has arrived, and one to announce to Hel and the dead that their gruesome ship (with Loki aboard) must sail.

Like Eikþyrnir, the tree in which Gullinkambi roosts is assumed to be Yggdrasil, though it isn't specially named. There aren't any complex theories about the significance of a rooster announcing the great battle. Perhaps it's simply that they are loud and annoying, and when they crow everyone will hear. Everyday people living on farms and rural environments would have been more than familiar with the rooster's crow, so it should be good enough for the gods, too!

In any case, Yggdrasil seems to have a lot of animal activity, just as trees in the real world do. Seeing these various creatures interact with each other in nature: birds, squirrels, and more, might have stimulated some of the thoughts about what goes on in the mythic World Tree.

## RUNES

Most readers probably have some sense of what runes are. Strictly speaking, runes are letters. But rune collections are not properly referred to as "alphabets" since they use a different order of letters than our English alphabet, and don't begin with A and B. Modern writers and scholars use the term "Futhark" when talking about runic alphabets, which refers to the letters/sounds made by the first six letters in a rune collection: F, U, Th, A, R, and K. Generally, three runic systems from before the Middle Ages survive: the Elder Futhark, the Younger Futhark, and the Anglo-Saxon Futhorc. The Anglo-Saxon runes are called the "Futhorc," since the sounds for O and C replace those letters in the Scandinavian runes.

Given the angular shapes of the letters, runes probably have their origins in Latin, Etruscan, and possibly Greek scripts, and might have been created in imitation of these, but the exact origin is uncertain, and scholars are still debating about it. Certainly, there are several runes that closely resemble Latin letters in our modern alphabet.

The Elder Futhark was first mentioned in Roman writings from the Second Century CE, and represents the runes of the Germanic peoples living outside of the Roman Empire. This Futhark has twenty-four letters grouped in three sets of eight letters. The simpler Younger Futhark became the alphabet of choice in Scandinavia during the Viking Age. It has only sixteen letters, because a number of these runes took over several sounds, making it a kind of shorthand, which can be confusing for modern people trying to read runic inscriptions from the Viking era. Context provides the meaning of each word, since the reader would have understood which letter represented which sounds, if there was more than one choice. Modern readers are not so lucky, and it can be confusing trying to figure out what a particular word means.

In contrast, the Anglo-Saxon runes expanded to twenty-nine letters to cover a wider variety of sounds. These are detailed in the *Anglo-Saxon Rune Poem*, an eighth or ninth-century work that lists each of the runes in the Futhorc. Four more letters were added to the Futhorc sometime later to accommodate the needs of the Old English language, bringing the total number of runes to thirty-three. This obviously makes for much easier reading, but sadly, few runic inscriptions in the Futhorc survive.

Why mention the runes in this book at all? Because they are inextricably bound up with Odin, who legend says snatched them up after hanging for nine nights as a sacrifice to himself (more about that myth on page 153). This implies that the runes had special meaning or symbolism, and were seen as something out of the ordinary, a treasure that held secrets. But what does that mean?

The tendency these days to ascribe various magical or divinatory meanings to each rune might or might not have any historical precedent, and seems largely to be based on the *Anglo-Saxon Rune Poem*, which tells the reader what each rune is supposed to symbolize. But was this to convey magical and esoteric meanings, or was this merely a useful way of memorizing them? Devotees of New Age spirituality and neo-paganism tend to see the runes as a divinatory system, akin to tarot or the I Ching. But were they? In the year 98, the Roman writer Tacitus described a divining method in one Germanic tribe in which an oracle would cut sticks, mark them, cast them, and read their meaning. This might be a description of casting runes (which might have been carved on the sticks), or it might be more like casting bones and looking at the position in which they fall. Tacitus's description is, unfortunately, not all that clear. We don't know if these marks were Elder Futhark runes, an earlier version of runes, or something else entirely.

So, what might the runes have meant to people in the Viking Age? They were undoubtedly used for writing; numerous carvings have been found on stones, wood, and bone and other hard surfaces showing that at least a small portion of the population was literate and could understand them. Unfortunately, these are always short inscriptions, and often practical, even mundane, in nature. It's possible that runes were used for writing out magical spells and charms, though the evidence for this is limited. That might just mean that nothing survives, especially if runes were inscribed on materials that could rot away over the centuries, such as wood, cloth, animal skins, and so on. And if runes were used in magic and divination, it's hard to get a clear picture of what these techniques were and how they were practiced.

It's not at all unreasonable to suggest that runes had magical meanings to some people in some places, but what might they have meant in a mythic context? Why would Odin hang in misery for nine nights to have the chance to take them up? One possible answer is simply because they were a form of writing and that is magical all on its own. The ability to put words down onto something permanent that can be read and re-read is a stunning achievement that we all take for granted. Even the simple act of reading this book is quite remarkable when you really think about it.

So runes were probably mainly for writing but might have had other, hidden uses meaningful to individual users. The letters are beautiful to look at, and inscriptions often give tantalizing glimpses into life at the time. Did the Norse peoples specifically use them for magic or divination? It's certainly possible, but alas, many of those mysteries vanished forever after the Viking Age came to an end.

## THE NINE WORLDS?

Discussions of Norse mythology often mention "the Nine Worlds" to describe the celestial realms where various entities live. Yggdrasil is said to grow through all of them, connecting them like an axis. It provides a nice, easy reference for how the Norse might have viewed their place in the cosmos and the otherworldly dimensions around them.

But this model really isn't all that accurate of a description. Are there nine worlds? Technically, yes, but there are more than just nine, and when nine worlds are listed, the collections vary from source to source. These are the most common:

1. Muspelheim, the realm of fire
2. Niflheim, the land of eternal cold
3. Asgard, the home of the gods
4. Vanaheim, the original home of the Vanir
5. Jötunheim, the land of the jötnar
6. Midgard, the "Middle Earth" where humanity dwells
7. Alfheim, the land of the light elves
8. Svartálfheim, the underworld of the dark elves, or dwarves
9. Hel/Helheim, the realm of the dead

This is a nice and tidy list, but it's not the only such list of worlds out there. There's also a list in the *Prose Edda* that substitutes the realm of Nidavellir, a home of the dwarves, for Hel. But don't the dwarves already have a realm in Svartálfheim, if, indeed, the dwarves and the dark elves are the same beings? Maybe? It's possible that Nidavellir is a part of Svartálfheim and not a realm unto itself. But what of Hel? Other sources say that the souls of the dead go to Niflheim, which would imply that Hel lies inside that realm. That would mean that Hel also isn't its own separate world.

The poem *Grímnismál* gives a list of locations that the gods preside over. Among them, Thor dwells in Thrúdheim (Þrúðheimr), Valhalla is in Glaðsheimr, and Skadi dwells in her father's home of Thrymheim (Þrymheimr). None of these "heims" are considered to be separate worlds, even though the list also mentions that Freyr rules over Alfheim, the realm of the elves. So, what's happening here?

Well, the suffix -heim can mean many different things, depending on context: home, country, territory, or world. So, it *can* mean a whole separate world, but it doesn't always. It can be an entire dimension or a house on the outskirts of a village. With that in mind, trying to figure out how many realms there are becomes much more complicated. Why, for example, does Freyr get a whole realm to himself, while Thor apparently only rules over a hall, even though both have -heim as a suffix?

Perhaps the problem is in the use of the word "the." No primary source ever speaks of *the* Nine Worlds. The seer that Odin raises simply says she has seen nine worlds, but that doesn't necessarily mean all of them. And Yggdrasil has three roots, not nine, which reach into the realm of the living, the realm of the gods, and the realm of the dead. In fact, mentions of the number nine seem to refer mainly to the dead, so perhaps there were nine different realms for the dead, depending on where someone would go. And given that many believed that the human soul had multiple parts, did different aspects of one's spirit go to different places?

We also have to account for the fact that warriors who died in battle were said to go to Odin in Valhalla or to Freya in Sessrúmnir. And not only warriors went to Freya. It seems that some women who died in childbirth might have joined her. Those mortals who died of old age or outside of battle most likely journeyed to Hel, while those who died at sea were said to go to the realm of Aegir and Rán. So, the idea of nine realms for the dead might not be far-fetched after all; there might even be others, whose names have not survived.

Some have suggested that "nine worlds" is simply a poetic device, rather like calling the oceans of the world "the seven seas." "Nine" might have also sometimes been a synonym for "many." But it seems to have more importance than just a different way of saying "a lot."

The number nine is quite significant in Norse belief. It appears over and over in Norse lore when describing many different concepts, usually when there are more than a few items to list. So, it makes sense that it would show up in reference to their concepts of all creation. Consider these other collections of nine:

1. Nine realms
2. Freyr waits nine nights to meet with Gerd
3. The sea god Aegir has nine daughters

**4.** Heimdall has nine mothers

**5.** Hermod rides for nine nights on Sleipnir when going to Hel to beg for Baldr to be returned

**6.** Odin hangs for nine days and nights as a sacrifice to take up the runes

**7.** Nine disir attack and nine defend the man Þiðrandi

**8.** The large gathering at the temple at Uppsala was said to happen every nine years

**9.** Snorri writes of "nine heavens," one of which will provide shelter during Ragnarök

**10.** Odin encounters nine thralls working in the fields

And these are by no means all the references! So, it seems improbable that there must be exactly nine worlds, when the number held so much symbolic meaning. It's more likely that there were different conceptions of how many worlds existed, and the importance of each, as well as who went where when they died.

So, if you read an article or book telling you with confidence that the Norse believed in *"the* Nine Worlds," view that assertion with skepticism. Whoever wrote it probably hasn't done their homework!

Now let us turn our attention to some of the most important surviving tales from Norse mythology.

## THE CREATION

*Based on the Poetic Edda and Prose Edda (Gylfaginning)*

Before the existence of the earth or sky, of the sea and sand, of grass and wind, there was Ginnungagap, the great, endless void. But the void was not entirely alone. Somewhere out in the nothingness was also Niflheim, the Dark World, and from a spring at its center flowed rivers. These rivers, called Elivagar and

the Storm Waves, flowed far from their origin, and as they did, they cooled and solidified into ice. The waters reached so far that they became hoar-frost in the northern portion of Ginnungagap.

Far away was the realm of Muspelheim, a world of fire and heat, whose flames make it impassable to all not from that region. It is still guarded by a fire jötunn named Surtr, who waits with his flaming sword to march forth against the gods at the end of time.

Eventually, the ice of the north and the fire of the south mingled, and from them a life force began to spring. There arose a primal being called Ymir. As it slept, it would sweat; the sweat under its left arm created two jötnar, a male and a female. At the same time another male jötunn was begot between Ymir's legs. From these came the clans known as the jötnar of the frost.

As the ice continued to drip, a cow named Audhumla formed. From her udders flowed four rivers of milk that fed and nourished Ymir. The cow licked at salty blocks of ice, and from one of them, a male jötunn was formed, who took the name Buri, who was said to be handsome and strong. From him sprang a son, Bor, who with his mate Bestla produced three unique sons, the brothers Odin, Vili, and Vé.

However, Odin and his brothers were dissatisfied with the order of things and set about to remake it. They attacked and killed Ymir. So much blood flowed from his wounds that it washed over the frost jötnar, killing all of them save two, Bergelmir and his wife. They climbed into a boat-like wooden box and escaped, and from them a new generation of frost jötnar arose.

Odin and his brothers took Ymir's body to the center of Ginnungagap, and from there, they began to fashion the world from the remains. Ymir's blood became the lakes and the oceans, which would surround the world and make it all but impossible to cross them. Ymir's flesh became the ground, and its hair became the trees, while mountains came from the bones and stones arose from the broken teeth. From Ymir's skull they fashioned the sky and set a dwarf at each of its corners. These dwarves are called North, East, West, and South.

As the world came into being, sparks from Muspelheim flew about, and Odin and the others fashioned them into lights and set them in the sky to illuminate the heavens and the Earth. The sun and moon and the stars above did not yet know their places. The edges along the shores of the sea became known as Jötunheim, while from the eyelashes of Ymir these first gods fashioned Midgard, the Middle Earth, and a wall to protect it, for this is where humanity would eventually dwell. Odin and his brothers tossed Ymir's brains into the sky to form the clouds.

The three sons of Bor then walked along a sea shore and found the remnants of two trees, Ash and Elm. They took them and created the first man and the first woman, Ask and Embla. The first son gave to them life and breath, the second imparted intelligence and the ability to move, while the third son gifted them with their forms, as well as sight, hearing, and speech. And thus were the first humans made.

Then the gods set about building their own home, which they called Asgard. Odin and his wife, Frigg, had children (with each other and with others of their kind), and from them came the gods known as the Aesir. They set about building two great strongholds: Gladsheim, the Home of Joy, for the gods, and Vingolf, the Friendly Quarters, for the goddesses.

There remained much work to be done, and so the gods set up forges to work metals like iron and gold into all manner of beautiful and useful things: tools, jewelry, adornments, and more. It was truly a Golden Age. All this happened before outsiders from Jötunheim came and began to bring strife upon their homes.

Some parts of Ymir's body remained unused, and maggots came to feast upon them. The gods deigned to change their forms into the dwarves, giving them the likenesses of humans and imbuing them with great forging skill, that they might make the most exquisite items from gold. The dwarves would continue to dwell within the Earth, as it was made of Ymir's flesh.

And now the worlds were made, and the gods were pleased. The great tree, Yggdrasil, grew at the center, with its three great roots stretching into different worlds. The three Norns waited by a well at one of these roots, tending to the tree and weaving the fates of all living things. They know the events that will unfold, even if the gods must seek their own answers in their own time.

BACKGROUND: The Norse creation stories are long, complex, and more than a little bizarre. To make matters more confusing, there isn't just one, definite account. This phenomenon isn't unique to the Norse myths; even the Book of Genesis has two different accounts of how the world was made. Many scholars have spent hours poring over these texts looking for similarities with other creation myths and trying to find signs of influence. It's a worthy academic goal but doesn't need to concern us here.

The idea of an immense void waiting eternally before *something* appeared seems oddly scientific and modern in its imagery, not dissimilar to the idea of what our universe might have been before the Big Bang. This concept appears in creation myths around the world, perhaps showing how many ancient peoples intuited that before there was something, there was nothing. Visions of fire and ice colliding and producing life suggest that the *Poetic* and *Prose Edda* versions of the Norse creation story were composed in Iceland, where volcanic eruptions and lava would have come into contact with glaciers and ice flows, resulting in some spectacular steam and smoke. It's probably significant that the cosmos both begins and ends with this dance of fire and ice, something that would have resonated deeply with Icelanders.

The story tells us that as flames and frost mingled, a single, hermaphroditic being, Ymir, emerged at some point, a living thing that gave birth to all other living things, directly and indirectly. The first three gods also arise, the ones who will change the cosmic order. But why do they kill Ymir? There are no indications that Ymir is a tyrant, and yet we see them overthrow the primal being and kill the first jötnar in doing so, even if accidentally. It calls to mind the Greek gods overthrowing the Titans and might represent a similar kind of mythic conception: a primal world that needs to be tamed and "civilized." Throughout the Norse myths, the jötnar often seem to represent the forces of nature.

But whatever the reason for this cosmic murder, these three brothers bring about dramatic changes and set about creating a new order that is more to their liking. But who are these brothers? In Snorri's *Edda*, Odin is certainly one of them, but the others, Vili and Vé, are virtual non-entities in Norse mythology after the beginning of time. One would think they would have a greater role to play, but perhaps they do. In the *Poetic Edda*, Odin's brothers are named as Haenir and Lodur, and it is these three who give life to the first humans.

As we will see in later stories, Odin more than once travels with two companions, Hoenir and ... Loki. It is possible that at least in some traditions, the first three sons of Bor were Odin, Loki, and Hoenir, which would explain why they are together often, and why Loki is always hanging around with the gods. Loki even refers to himself as Odin's blood brother. Some have thought that this means simply that they have sworn a sibling-like oath to one another, but what if it's more than that? Loki, the one who will eventually march against the gods of Asgard at the end, might have been there right at the beginning. The texts aren't clear about this, but it is an intriguing possibility.

And what about the wives? You might have noticed in the tale above that the wives are just ... there. This conundrum afflicts many creation stories: a being or beings emerge, usually male, then they have children with their "wives." So, where did the female beings come from? The short answer is that we don't really know. We can only conclude that they were spontaneously generated like the other primal jötnar and not linger over details too much!

After the gods create the worlds, they build their own homes and the time is said to be a golden age. Literally. Everything, even the furniture, is made of gold. This must have been uncomfortable to sit and sleep on. But this idyllic setting doesn't last forever. Three female beings intrude on it, bringing a sense of sobriety and solemnity to the gods' never-ending party. Scholars aren't exactly sure who they are as they are never identified. We do know that they're said to be from Jötunheim, and might be a trio of antagonistic jötnar, as they are sometimes described as "ogre-like." Some scholars suspect they are the three principal Norns, who remind us that fate will unfold as it will, and that not even the gods can escape that. The party's over, and it's time to get to work!

With the worlds, the Tree, the Norns, and the first gods now all in place, the next great event, the war between the Aesir and the Vanir, will begin.

## THE WAR OF THE AESIR AND VANIR

*Based on the Poetic Edda, Prose Edda (Gylfaginning), and Ynglinga Saga*

In the far distant past, the Aesir dwelled alone. But one day, a newcomer came to Odin's hall. Her name was Gullveig, said to be of the Vanir, a different order of gods. Strife arose between them, which escalated into armed conflict. The Aesir killed her with spears, and then burned her body. But she rose from the dead. So, the Aesir tried to burn her again. Three times they burned her and three times she rose, showing that she could not be killed. With her third rebirth, she took the name Heiðr and began the practice of Seidr magic by going into trances. She bewitched the minds of gods and jötnar and spread her magic far and wide.

The conflict between the Aesir and Vanir continued, and the two groups of gods went to war, a destructive conflict that lasted for many years. But try as they might, neither side could fully gain the upper hand. Finally, the Vanir pressed the attack and won a victory. The Aesir sought peace, as well as terms for how tribute would be paid. In order to secure peace, the two groups agreed that some from the Vanir would live among the Aesir, while some among those Aesir would journey to the realm of the Vanir and live with them.

The Vanic sea god Njord and his two children Freyr and Freya were sent to live among the Aesir, while Hoenir and Mimir were sent to live among the Vanir. In time, the Vanic gods became close allies and friends of the Aesir, but there was discontent among the Vanir. This strife was because Hoenir always seemed to take council from Mimir, rather than having ideas of his own, and the Vanir suspected that they had been cheated in the exchange, giving up such an illustrious trio as Njord, Freyr, and Freya for a half-wit and a fool. To prove that Hoenir could decide nothing without Mimir's advice, they seized Mimir and beheaded him, sending the head back to Odin in Asgard.

Such a violent act could have reignited hostilities, but thankfully, it did not. Odin took the head and filled it with herbs to preserve it. He then cast magic over it to bring Mimir back to life, and thus his head became an adviser for Odin, revealing secrets that he needed to know.

**BACKGROUND:** Many scholars have noted that this story might be a retelling in myth of a conflict between two groups of Germanic/Nordic peoples at some point in the past, a conflict that raged for some time before the two sides reached an agreement and called a truce. It is also possible that they combined their gods as they settled in to live among each other. Were the Vanic gods, who governed fertility, remnants of an older cult that was absorbed by the more war-like and action-oriented Aesir? And if so, did this happen in Germanic lands, or in Scandinavia itself? Or is it simply myth, telling how the different portions of a society came to function together? Any of these options is possible.

Some speculate that this tale might be a mangled version of an older myth that told of a war between the gods and the jötnar, which again would be something like the clash between the Greek gods and the older Titans whom they replaced. Some

scholars have proposed that Gullveig is actually a jötunn who comes to initiate the downfall of the gods of Asgard. As such, she endures her tortures and eventually becomes Angrboda, who brings Hel, Fenrir, and Jormungandr into the worlds.

Indeed, the figure of Gullveig is fascinating. She is said to be of the Vanir in some way and sparks disagreement and strife. When the Aesir try to kill her, they cannot, and she transforms into a powerful worker of Seidr magic, taking the name Heiðr. It's possible that Gullveig is a representation of the Vanic goddess Freya. The name Gullveig can translate in several ways: "gold lady," "gold power," "gold drunk," or even "gold lust." Freya was well known for her love of gold. Gullveig's new name, Heiðr, means "bright" or "honor," both of which are related to one of Freya's other names, Mardoll, which means "Sea Brightener." These connections, combined with Heiðr's use of Seidr—which she practiced far and wide and was favored by women—certainly strengthen the theory that Gullveig/Heiðr is an early version of Freya. If so, the story might represent a transformation, even a rebirth, into the being that Freya is meant to be.

Remember that Gullveig is killed three times but returns after each and becomes a master of Seidr magic. Odin also undergoes a similar transformation. Odin stabs himself in a sacrifice to himself and hangs on the World Tree for nine nights (three times three) to take up the runes and the knowledge they impart, coming back to life transformed. It might also be significant that later, Odin's son, Baldr, is also stabbed (by mistletoe) and dies, goes to the realm of Hel, and then apparently is reborn as the new leader of the gods in the new world after Ragnarök. These stories do seem to represent the idea of the holy man/woman or magic-worker undergoing some kind of spiritual trial or symbolic death and being reborn into their new role, after which they will never be the same again. Are these myths memories of ancient spiritual practices that might have originated in shamanic Siberia and traveled west across the Arctic north, where they were adopted by the Norse, the Finns, and the Sámi in different ways?

In any case, the story of Freya as Gullveig—the beautiful goddess of love, sex, and magic—disrupting the ways of the Aesir plays into an old sexist trope of the temptress coming between friends and ruining those bonds and possibly the social order, thus leading to war. Or maybe she was sent to try to undermine the Aesir as the war was already raging? But then Odin, in his never-ending quest for knowledge, realizes that he has much to gain and seeks out Freya to learn her strange and compelling feminine magic, possibly in secret. Unless Gullveig becomes Angrboda, in which case, her role might have been to deliberately undermine the gods all along. Is she one of the three jötnar who come to end the gods' golden age?

And what of poor Mimir? He is revived, kept alive, and remains known for his wisdom. Since he is Odin's advisor, this imagery makes sense, but this story might contain remnants of older mythic symbolism and rituals, perhaps involving decapitation as a sacrifice, be it animal or human ...

As always, the picture is incomplete, and the details are frustratingly sparse. But whatever the missing parts, the story concludes with the Aesir and Vanir finally allied.

## KVASIR AND THE MEAD OF POETRY

*Based on the Prose Edda (Skáldskaparmál)*

As the Aesir and Vanir made peace, they met to discuss terms. When they had agreed on how to settle their hostilities, the gods sealed the pact by each spitting into a large vat. This was the sign of their truce, and not wanting it to be lost, they took the spittle and created a man from it, whom they named Kvasir. Fully formed, Kvasir was said to be the wisest man in the world, such that there was no question that he could not answer.

He traveled throughout the world, spreading his knowledge wherever he went. But once, he happened to stay as the guest of two dwarves, Fjalar and Galar. These two were not welcoming, though they feigned hospitality. When they had the chance, they asked to speak with Kvasir privately, and killed him. They desired to preserve his essence and so let his blood flow into a cauldron called Óðrerir, where they mixed it with honey to create a mead that would bestow the gifts of poetry and wisdom on all who drank it. Thereafter, they lied to the gods and told them that Kvasir had choked on his own knowledge.

After this, they invited a jötunn named Gilling and his wife to visit, but again, their intentions were not honorable. They asked Gilling to go to sea with them, and they rowed down the coast. At one point, the dwarves steered the boat over some rocks, overturning and throwing Gilling into the sea. He could not swim, and the dwarves did nothing to save him, so he drowned. Upon their return, they told his wife that he had accidentally fallen in. She was distraught and cried bitterly. Fjalar asked her if she would like to go to the point where he sank, if this would comfort her. She agreed, but as she was leaving their home, Fjalar told Galar to drop a heavy millstone on her head. He did so, and she was also killed.

But this time, there were consequences. Suttung, son of Gilling, heard what had happened and realized that the dwarves were responsible. He traveled to their home, captured them, and rowed them out to sea. He left them on rocks that would soon disappear under the incoming tide. They begged for their lives, offering the mead of Kvasir in compensation for the loss of his father. Suttung decided that this was an acceptable price and rowed them back, taking the mead with him as he left. He hid it inside a mountain known as Hnitbjorg, and tasked his daughter, Gunnlod, to watch over it.

Mead is thus known as Kvasir's blood, or sometimes the liquid of Óðrerir, Boðn, and Són, the three cauldrons where Suttung kept the precious drink. Mead was also called the ship of the dwarves, or Hnitbjorg's liquid. But there is more to the story, for the mead might have lain in secret forever, if not for Odin.

In the Allfather's travels, he came to a place where nine thralls were harvesting hay. Seeing that they struggled, he asked if they wanted him to sharpen their scythes for them. They agreed, so he took out a whetstone and set to sharpening the blades. They were very happy with his work and offered to buy this whetstone from him. Odin said that he would sell it for whatever price they deemed reasonable. Every thrall wished to purchase it, so he tossed it into the air. As each of them scrambled to catch it and lay claim to it, their newly sharpened blades got in the way, cutting their throats and killing them all.

After this, Odin needed a place to stay for the night and came to the dwelling of the jötunn Baugi, who happened to be Suttung's brother. Odin called himself Bolverk and asked for lodgings. That night, Baugi was angry. He complained that his wealth had been diminished because nine of his slaves had just died, and he would have no chance of finding others. Odin decided to compensate Baugi for the loss he had caused (though he withheld the details of his involvement). He offered to do the nine men's work, only asking for a drink of Suttung's mead in exchange. Baugi made no guarantees that he could indeed provide a drink of the mead, because Suttung guarded it so carefully, but said that he would try. And so, that summer, Odin did the work of nine men in Baugi's fields.

After harvest, as winter approached, Odin (still playing the role of Bolverk) asked Baugi for his payment. He and Baugi went to Suttung, but Suttung said the mead was his alone. He would not share a single drop with anyone. Baugi and Bolverk left, but Bolverk suggested that they should use trickery to try to gain access to the mead. Baugi agreed, and Bolverk brought forth a drill that he called Rati. He asked Baugi to drill a hole into the mountain of Hnitbjorg, so that they might reach the mead that way.

After drilling for some time, Baugi finally said that he had made it through the mountain. Bolverk blew into the hole, but chips of rock flew out, meaning that Baugi had not yet drilled through. Baugi had not been truthful. Bolverk deduced that Baugi would betray him. He asked Baugi to drill some more, and the jötunn did. As he blew again, the rocks flew in the opposite direction. At once, Bolverk changed himself into a snake and slithered into the hole, before Baugi could strike at him with the drill.

The snake moved ever inward until he came to where Gunnlod stood watch. Transforming back into his true form, Odin seduced her and lay with her for three nights, convincing her to let him have three drinks of the mead. But these were not mere sips. With the first drink, he drained Óðrerir, and with the second, he swallowed all of Boðn's contents, and with the third, he finished off Són's. He then changed into an eagle and flew away.

Suttung, enraged, also changed into an eagle and pursued him. But the gods were ready for Odin when he returned to Asgard and placed vats out for him. Still in an eagle's form, he spat out the mead into the vats. He also blew some of the mead out of his rear. This was the poor mead, destined for bad poets and singers. Suttung nearly caught up to him, but could not retrieve the rest of the mead, which became the property of the gods. It was shared among them, and with those mortals who were most deserving of it.

And so, poetry is known as Odin's drink, Odin's gift, the drink of the gods, and many other names.

**BACKGROUND:** This strange tale contains many bizarre details, even for Norse mythology! There is a lot of symbolism implied, though the myth only appears in Snorri's account, so perhaps the story was something he embellished. Or perhaps it had a deeper symbolic meaning that has been lost over time. The story gives us the source of poetic inspiration, saying that it has divine origins, first in the form of a man, and later through his blood. Poetry is then, literally, from the blood of the gods, as Kvasir was formed of their spittle. Poets ask Odin for inspiration, since he first procured this magical drink and gives it to whom he favors.

We can assume that Fjalar and Galar are eager for wisdom and knowledge, though their murders of the jötnar have no real motive; maybe they're just evil?

Odin doesn't come off looking especially good in this tale. He wanders in disguise and meets nine slaves who are struggling with their field work. At first, it seems as if his gift of newly sharpened blades will help them, but soon they all lie dead. This could imply that being a follower of Odin is tricky, at best. While he can be generous, he will not hesitate to betray some if he so chooses. Sometimes he would withdraw his support from his followers and give it to their enemies because he wished to bring those followers to Valhalla. In the story of the mead, by sacrificing the nine slaves, he can take their place and work the fields. This then leaves Baugi in debt to him, and brings him that much closer to obtaining the drink.

It seems that Odin feels some guilt about his actions and offers his work as compensation; legal disputes were often settled by making offers of payment of some kind. But really, he covets the mead of poetry and wants a drink of it. And of course, he doesn't just want a small sip. He wants all of it for himself and the other gods and is prepared to do anything to steal it.

In the *Hávámal*, or "The Sayings of the High One," he recounts his actions in seducing Gunnlod, and admits that his behavior is poor, to say the least:

> Gunnloth gave on a golden stool
> A drink of the marvelous mead;
> I let her have a harsh reward
> For her heroic heart,
> And her sorely troubled spirit.
>
> Hardly, I think, would I home have come,
> And left the giants' land,
> Had not Gunnloth helped me, the good maiden,
> Whose arms had been around me.

On his ring Odin swore the oath, I think

Who now will trust his troth?

Suttung's betrayal he sought with drink,

And he left Gunnloth to grief.

Breaking an oath was a huge transgression in the Viking world, so for the Allfather to do it (and it's not the only time he will do so) is a big deal. A ring oath was particularly sacred.

But what of the mead from Odin's rear, said to be drunk by less accomplished poets? Here, Snorri might be poking fun at those he saw as inferior poets in his own time, or perhaps it's a reference to a general perception that poets and poetry just weren't what they used to be in the good old days!

Not that mead vomited up by Odin is all that much more appealing. But this is the "good" mead that will serve as inspiration for gods and humans alike. If we look past the off-putting image, we must remember that skaldic poetry comes from the mouth, not the hand, as with the written word. It makes sense that the mead that inspires poetry must also come from the mouth. And this is not any mead from any mouth. It's from a god's mouth. Remember that Kvasir was created by divine spittle, which also comes from the gods' mouths. These images reinforce skaldic poetry as an oral art form.

And mead itself is a fermented, alcoholic drink. Alcohol can loosen the tongue, weaken inhibitions, and lead to inspiration. But too much can also lead to bad judgment and, yes, vomiting. The vomit of the gods is good, but the vomit of the poet, not so much!

In any case, with Kvasir's death, the Aesir and the Vanir lose a symbol of their peace treaty, but with the capture of his blood, they gain wisdom and insight, as well as a drink to share in good fellowship, which might be just as valuable.

# ODIN'S SACRIFICED EYE AND TAKING UP THE RUNES

*Based on the Prose Edda (Gylfaginning) and Poetic Edda*

Odin, the Allfather, was ever seeking new knowledge and wisdom. On this ongoing search, he went to the Well of Mimir, down under one of the roots of Yggdrasil, where Mimir lived. Mimir was known for being unmatched in all the worlds for his own knowledge and wisdom, which he gained from drinking from his well each day. Odin asked Mimir for a drink from this well, so that he might also grow in wisdom.

But Mimir did not give him a drink. He said that he could not offer such a prized gift unless Odin was willing to make a great sacrifice. Because the Allfather desired to see more, he must be willing to part with one of his eyes in exchange. What he would give up in normal vision would be more than compensated for in vision for far greater things. After all, it was in this same well that Heimdall left one of his ears, so that he might be made more aware of all that was around him.

Odin deliberated for a time but finally agreed. He plucked out one of his own eyes and threw it into the well, where it remains hidden still. Mimir drew a horn of the precious liquid from the well and gave it to Odin. After he had his drink, Odin grew in wisdom and insight, becoming wiser than all the other gods. And from that time forward, he would have only one eye, as he was so often depicted.

And yet, Odin desired more knowledge, more insight. In an act of supreme determination, he took his spear and impaled himself against the World Tree, a sacrifice of himself to himself. For nine long, windswept nights, he hung upside down on the tree, given to himself. He gazed ever downward, having no bread or drink for comfort, intent only on gaining that which he sought. And then, after the nine nights, he beheld the runes. His sacrifice accepted, he was at last able to attain his goal. He reached out and took up the runes. He screamed as he held them and fell, released from his ordeal at last.

Soon, he began to grow wise in the ways of runic lore and magic. He learned mighty spells and the ways of the runes, how to carve them and empower them. Some from among the elves, dwarves, and jötnar also learned this wisdom and made their own. Such was his knowledge that he would then ask of others if they knew runic lore: how to carve them, how to read and interpret them, how to mark and color them, how to question and test them, how to ask them, how to make sacrifice, how to send, and how to offer and slaughter. He then spoke of eighteen mighty spells that he had learned that would greatly benefit those who would learn them.

**BACKGROUND:** These tales of Odin's sacrifices are well known and give us insight into his character, as well as introduce two of the best known images in all of Norse mythology: his only having one eye, and the runes. But what is actually happening here?

These accounts might be mythologized writings about spiritual initiation, what some have called "shamanic," though this is something of a problematic term when divorced from its Siberian origins. Still, the wizard or wise woman/man undergoing a trial of some kind to transform into who they are meant to be occurs in myths and stories all around the world.

In the first tale, Odin wishes to increase his wisdom in the hopes of matching that of Mimir. A few questions immediately arise: Is this the same Mimir who was decapitated and whose head was sent back by the Vanir? It would seem so, since Mimir was the wise one who counseled Hoenir, and it's possible that Odin placed his head by the well for safe keeping. But then, is his head just sitting beside the well? And if so, how does it drink from the well each day? One can imagine an amusing image of one of the Norns or another being coming by with a straw to fit into his mouth. And if he was only a head, how was he able to draw from the well and offer a horn to Odin? Perhaps we're not meant to be bothered by such mundane details in a mythic setting.

Another question: Which well is this? It might be the well of Urd, but it's not completely clear. And we have the interesting snippet of information that Heimdall has left his horn/hearing/ear in the well, as well. It would make sense that he would have sacrificed an ear to become more aware of his surroundings and so guard Bifrost better; the well asks different things of those who seek it out. Heimdall gives an ear, Odin gives an eye.

In any case, Odin takes up his role as the one-eyed god of wisdom after this encounter, an image found in Germanic images well before the Viking Age, indicating that some form of this myth is very old, but the age of the myth of his sacrifice is not known now. It's not unreasonable for a battle god to be missing an eye, just as might have happened to some of his worshippers.

In the second myth, Odin offers "himself to himself," an unusual action, but if one understands that sacrifices to Odin (prisoners of war, criminals, and so on) were usually speared, hanged, or both, one can see that this makes sense. Odin undergoes the same ordeal, and he accepts his sacrifice, allowing him to gain the runes, learn their secrets, and pass them on to humanity. As we've seen, the runes have a very human origin, but this story offers a wonderful mythic explanation for where they come from, and an insight into their mysteries. Even if they were primarily used for writing (as seems to be the case), there must have been some sense of power about them, for simply being able to write out sounds is magical in and of itself.

Hanging on the tree represents another spiritual trial, of a type found in many traditional cultures around the world. The would-be shaman or wise one undergoes an ordeal, sometimes painful, sometimes life-threatening, in order to transform into a new being and take up a new life. Like Gullveig-as-Freya and (as we will see) Baldr, these ordeals speak of being stabbed or pierced and then being reborn into something new, something better. By his actions at the well and the tree, Odin is remade into the god that history and legend praise so highly.

# THE REBUILDING OF THE WALL OF ASGARD AND THE ARRIVAL OF SLEIPNIR

*Based on the Prose Edda (Gylfaginning)*

In a time after the war between the Aesir and the Vanir, the wall surrounding Asgard was still in ruins. One day, a cloaked stranger came to the gods with an unusual offer. He said he would repair the wall, making it strong, high, and mighty, such that even the jötnar could not breach it. Odin thought this was a generous offer and asked the stranger's conditions for accomplishing this considerable task. The cloaked one said that he would need three seasons to finish the work and he wanted Freya as his wife and his prize. He also demanded the sun and the moon.

Freya was none too happy about this arrangement and refused. Odin likewise said no; what the stranger asked was simply too much. But Loki, ever the schemer, was already devising a way that the gods could have their wall repaired without having to pay the ridiculously high price asked by this mysterious builder. He advised Odin to accept the offer, but to insist that the task must be finished in only one winter and with the help of no others. If it was not completed by the first day of summer, the agreement would be canceled. Loki reasoned that this was impossible, but at least the gods would have a part of their wall rebuilt at the end of the allotted time. Odin agreed (and Freya fumed). The builder also agreed, but only if he could use his own horse, Svaðilfari, to bring rocks from the quarry for the wall. Odin and the other gods agreed to this one condition, a decision they would soon regret.

And so, the cloaked man set about constructing a new wall for Asgard. The gods were confident that he would fail. Who could rebuild the wall in such a short amount of time? But the stranger worked day and night without stopping, his wall becoming impressive and strong. As the deadline drew near, he seemed poised to finish his work on time. The gods feared that he might just accomplish the task. They were in a quandary. They would be forced to honor their agreement, but no one wanted to give him the sun and the moon. And Freya had no intention of being his bride.

The gods were furious with Loki and demanded that he remedy the situation and make the stranger forfeit his claim, or else Loki would face a horrible death. They told Loki to devise a new strategy to disrupt the builder's work. While the stranger toiled away on the last portions of the wall, a beautiful mare appeared one night and lured Svaðilfari away. The builder's horse was consumed with the urge to mate, no longer caring to help his master finish the gods' wall. Svaðilfari was gone all night, which delayed the building by just enough time that the project ran too late. He could not fulfill his promise of finishing the wall in time. The agreement was forfeit.

The builder was furious. He claimed he'd been tricked and accused the gods of being nothing more than a group of thieves. And indeed, he'd been duped by the greatest trickster of all, for the mare that had tempted Svaðilfari was none other than Loki the shapeshifter. In this form, he tempted Svaðilfari to pursue and mate with him as the mare, and in doing so, became pregnant.

But Loki was not the only one with a hidden identity. The builder revealed himself to be a jötunn, and he demanded his price regardless, because he'd been tricked. Thor told him he would receive what he was due, albeit in a different way. He struck the giant, smashing his skull and killing him at once. Now rid of the jötunn, the gods had their new wall, and the crafty builder could take away neither the sun, nor the moon, nor Freya, much to the relief of all.

And as for Loki? He later returned to Asgard, once again in his original form, accompanied by a magnificent gray foal with eight legs. In the shape of the mare, he'd given birth to Svaðilfari's offspring, a very unusual horse, indeed. Naming the beast Sleipnir ("The Slipper"), he offered the animal as a gift to Odin, who gratefully accepted him. Sleipnir was the best of horses among both gods and men, and would become Odin's valued steed, bearing his master through the realms on many adventures.

**BACKGROUND:** This tale of the gods employing a builder has some parallels in Greek myth in the story of the building of walls around Troy. The gods Poseidon and Apollo go to the city in disguise, offering to build new walls for King Laomedon within a certain amount of time. The king agrees to their price, not knowing that they are gods. But when their work is complete, or nearly so, the king goes back on his word and refuses to pay them. The gods take their revenge by sending a sea monster and a plague to the city. The king later learns that the sea monster can be appeased by occasionally sacrificing a young woman to it. When that fate befalls the king's own daughter, Hesione, Herakles (Hercules) agrees to rescue her in exchange for a payment of fine horses. He kills the creature and saves her, but the greedy king again goes back on his word. Herakles leaves in anger but comes back later to kill the king in revenge.

Did the Norse learn of this Greek myth from trade routes to the south and east? Or did Snorri, who was already fascinated with Troy (and presented the gods in the *Prose Edda* as humans from the city) invent this version as his own spin on a known Greek myth? Either option is possible, but it's also just as likely that the Norse and Greek tales came from a common source.

While the stories are not exactly the same, they share similarities: a supernatural builder in disguise being cheated out of his payment, a woman offered up in payment (Freya and Hesione), and a horse as a prize. Even later folk tales, such as the Germanic Rumpelstiltskin, exhibit similar motifs. In this beloved tale, a man claims to the king that his daughter can spin straw into gold; the king locks her in a tower with straw and a spinning wheel and demands she produce gold. Of course, she can't do such a task. But Rumpelstiltskin (an imp or a dwarf, depend-

ing on the retelling) agrees with the daughter to do it for her, but she must give up her necklace, her ring, and finally her firstborn child. He agrees to give back the child if she can guess his name within three days. When the woman discovers his true name, he is forced to give back her child. As we will see, rings and necklaces are also common props in Norse myth: Freya's prized necklace, the cursed ring for the ransom of Otter, and others.

But of course, there are differences. Loki's shape-shifting and switching of sexes is the most unusual aspect of this story and of his character, and is unique to the Norse version. This strange being, who sires the monsters Fenrir and Jormungandr, as well as the goddess Hel, is also the mother to a special horse that will become Odin's favorite and most faithful steed.

What does this transformation signify? It might say something about the role of gender and identity in the Viking world. Men who used magic were sometimes viewed as suspicious, because magic was often a "feminine" practice meant for women. So, for Loki to change not only his form but also his sex might have reflected attitudes about human men who engaged in magic. Indeed, Loki's actions disgusted some of the gods. And yet, male magic users and sorcerers were known to exist at the time, even if they were sometimes social outcasts. Does Loki represent these men who lived outside of the "natural" order of things?

If this tale weren't strange enough, Sleipnir has eight legs, twice as many as a normal horse, and just as many as a spider. Loki was occasionally associated with spiders, who appear as tricksters in several other myths around the world and even in nineteenth-century poetry. While this is probably a coincidence, it's not hard to see how a creature who weaves beautiful and sometimes seemingly invisible webs could be perceived as one who plays tricks on those around it.

There might be real connections, however, between Loki's transformation and myths and stories from Siberia. Some scholars have noted that there are tales of Siberian shamans who ride animals, often horses, to other worlds. One such myth of the Buryats of Mongolia tells of an eight-legged foal. This could point to an influence on the Norse myth via the polar regions, coming from Siberia all the way to the north of Scandinavia. Many have argued that Odin himself has probable connections to these powerful shamanic world-travelers, and the presence of a magical and unusual horse might point to that influence.

In any case, this is not the only time that Loki assumes a female form and gives birth. As we will see, in his quarrel with the gods later, he will be soundly mocked and detested for doing it again.

## HEIMDALL'S THREE SETS OF OFFSPRING

*Based on the Poetic Edda (Rígsþula)*

In the early days, Heimdall went wandering in the lands of Midgard. He walked along a seashore, and came upon a rustic old house. He entered this house, choosing to call himself Rig. Inside, there was a hearth fire and a couple, hoary and old; Ai and Edda they were called. Rig spoke to them, and they offered him bread and broth. Soon he rose from his chair and went to go to sleep, taking their bed. The couple lay themselves down on either side of him. He stayed with them for three nights and then left.

Nine months later, the woman Edda gave birth to a son with black hair. They named him Thræll. His skin was already weathered, and his hands were rough. His fingers were thick, and he was ugly, but as he grew, he was found to be good for hard work. To him came a woman, Thir, and in time, they had many children, sons and daughters, who cared for their home, watched over the pigs, and tilled the soil. And so, from them came the thralls, the slaves.

Now, Rig went forth and came to a hall, where he met Afi and Amma. They were busy with their tasks—he chopping wood, and she with her spindle. Rig knew what words to speak, and soon, they had offered him food, better than that of his previous hosts. Soon he rose and went to go to sleep, taking their bed. The couple lay themselves down on either side of him. He stayed with them for three nights and then left.

Nine months later, the woman Amma gave birth to a son with a ruddy face. They named him Karl. As he grew, he worked the oxen and plough with great skill, and he learned to build houses, barns, and carts. They brought him a bride, Snör, who wore goatskins and held a collection of keys. They exchanged rings and made a home ready for themselves. They had many children, sons and daughters, and from them came all the yeoman and farmers.

Now Rig journeyed onward, and he came to a hall facing south. He went in and met the couple that resided within, Fadir and Modir. Fadir made strings for a bow, and Modir smoothed cloth. They were dressed in fine clothing, and they were bright and beautiful. Rig spoke to them, and they offered him the finest of thin white bread, well-cooked meats, and a pitcher of wine. They sat together and talked for a long time. Then Rig rose and went to go to sleep, taking their bed. The couple lay themselves down on either side of him. He stayed with them for three nights and then left.

Nine months later, the woman Modir gave birth to a son with blond hair and bright cheeks. They named him Jarl, and as he grew, he learned to brandish a shield, to use the bow and lance, to ride a horse, to unleash hounds, and swim in the waters. Rig returned to him, striding from a grove of trees. He taught Jarl to use the runes, and claimed him as a son, telling him to be proud of his heritage.

Jarl went forth through dark forests and freezing crags, until he found a hall. Taking up his weapons, he fought enemies and won land for himself, eighteen halls in all. He became wealthy and shared it, offering gold and rings, jewels and arm rings to his loyal people. He married Erna, daughter of Hersir, and they lived in joy together. And so did their many children, sons and daughters, who grew wise and powerful, these children of Rig-Jarl.

**BACKGROUND:** This strange story tells of the god Heimdall going into the mortal world in disguise, though the identification of Heimdall with Rig was only added in an annotation to the poem *Rigsthula* in about the year 1300. It seems possible (especially given the runic instruction for the noble child) that Rig was actually Odin in disguise, especially given Odin's wandering eye and equally wanton desires! The poem itself probably dates from the mid-tenth century, and is a blatant and shameless propaganda piece to show how the Norse system of slaves, free workers, and nobility came into being; it was the will of the gods, of course! The thralls are ugly and only useful for low work, the peasants are average but do necessary tasks, while the nobility are beautiful and worthy and accomplish great deeds with the gods' favor. The poem was probably created to satisfy a king, to "prove" that his lineage went back to the gods. It might have been composed in Denmark, but it also shows Celtic influences; the word rig was Old Irish for "king."

Even more striking is Rig/Heimdall/Odin simply barging his way into each couple's home and then into their bed, where they lie on either side of him. Did each husband agree to let Rig have his way with the man's wife? Why are they even there? Is their presence merely symbolic to indicate their positions as the first of their social classes? Were the men somehow magically asleep, missing the whole thing? Were they willingly cuckolded? Is there a homoerotic subtext here, and did Rig have his way with both of them? Would mortals be wise to refuse a threesome with a god?

Any of these options are possibilities, but the text doesn't tell us. *Rigsthula* is a strange poem and a bit of an outlier from the usual collection of Norse myths, because it provides some interesting insights into the social structure of the time, and views about everyone's proper roles within it. The idea of divinely appointed rulers was one that would remain popular long after pagan Europe had vanished, for Christians found the idea equally useful. Belief in the "divine right" of kings to rule would persist in Europe well past the Renaissance.

# SIF'S GOLDEN HAIR AND
# THE DWARVEN GIFTS

*Based on the Prose Edda (Skáldskaparmál)*

The goddess Sif, renowned for her long, exquisite golden hair, awoke one morning to a shocking realization: her luxurious locks were gone, hacked off while she'd slept. She cried out in shock, and Thor responded at once. He was furious and knew who was most likely responsible: Loki, playing another of his tricks. Finding Loki, Thor threatened him into a confession. Loki had indeed done it, as a joke that none but him found funny. Under threat of Thor breaking every bone in his body, Loki yet again promised to make amends.

The trickster set off at once for Svartálfheim. There, he sought the three sons of Ivaldi, who were reputed to be the most gifted smiths in the whole of their realm. Greeting them, Loki explained that Sif's hair had been lost in a prank (but he didn't tell them how), and he wanted them to fashion new hair for her out of gold, in threads so fine that they would be indistinguishable from her real hair, yet would glimmer even more gloriously.

The three were certainly capable of this feat, but they wanted much in return. Loki offered them the friendship of the gods and promised that he would be indebted to them. He would help them in a time of need and repay them for crafting Sif her new hair. They were suspicious, but agreed, knowing that the friendship of the gods was no small thing, even if the word of a trickster was not to be fully trusted.

And so they set about crafting the hair. Soon, they returned to Loki with not one but three gifts. The first was the golden hair itself. The second was a spear they named Gungnir, which would never miss its mark. The third was a fine ship, Skidbladnir, which could grow to carry a full crew, or shrink down to fit in a pouch. Loki was delighted with their generosity. Taking these three beautiful things, he set off for Asgard at once.

On the way, he decided to visit two other dwarves, Eitri and Brokk. He showed them the work of the sons of Ivaldi and asked if they had ever seen such fine craftsmanship. Eitri proclaimed that his own work surpassed theirs. Loki was skeptical of the dwarf's boast. He countered that he would bet his own head that they could not create treasures as beautiful as these. They accepted his wager and set to work.

Not long after, they returned to Loki. They would have finished sooner, Eitri said, but Brokk had nearly failed in assisting his brother. Brokk protested that a fly had stung his eyelids, and in wiping blood from them, he had trouble seeing the bellows well enough to operate them properly. Loki smiled, for he was a shapeshifter ...

In any case, they offered him their own creations.

Brokk traveled with Loki back to Asgard, where he believed that the gods would judge Eitri's work superior, and Brokk would then collect Loki's head as payment. Loki insisted they would not be having his head on this day, or any other.

In Asgard, the gods were impatient and skeptical as they waited for him to bring back Sif's new hair. But their moods changed quickly when Loki showed them his new gifts. Loki offered the spear to Odin, who was greatly impressed with its beauty and magic. Loki next offered the ship to Freyr, who was likewise taken by its craftsmanship and its magical properties. And to Sif, he offered his apologies and gave her the luscious new golden hair, which wove its way seamlessly into what little remained of her own, such that it appeared just as hers had, only more beautiful than ever.

But Brokk stepped forward and announced that he and Eitri had made their own gifts, and that the gods should judge which were finer. He presented Odin with the arm ring, a bracelet called Draupnir, an enchanted ornament from which eight more just like it would drop every nine nights, like ripe fruit from a tree. To Freyr, he offered Gullinbursti, a shining, illuminated boar who could travel through air and over land and sea, and no horse could outrace him. Freyr was delighted with his new companion. And to Thor, Brokk offered Mjolnir, an unbreakable war hammer crafted just for him, which would always return to him. This mighty weapon would guarantee that the gods would always be protected from jötnar and other threats, though it had one flaw: the handle was shorter than intended, because at the moment of crafting it, a fly had stung Brokk's eyelids. But to Thor this was no matter, and he and the others accepted these gifts with much gratitude.

So impressed were the gods that they concluded that the gifts of Brokk and Eitri were indeed superior, glorious though Sif's new hair was. They told Brokk to name his price, and the dwarf proclaimed that he would have Loki's head, even though Loki offered Brokk his own weight in gold instead. But Brokk would not be moved and instead demanded his payment.

Loki fled, but Thor pursued and caught him. Brought back before Brokk, Loki had one last trick: Brokk could have his head as promised, but Loki had never offered his neck. Realizing that he could not take Loki's head without at least part of his neck, the frustrated Brokk came up with one last trick of his own. Since he could not have Loki's head, he could at least silence him. Taking up needle and thread, he seized Loki and sewed the trickster's mouth shut, sending him away in humiliation.

Brokk was satisfied that the debt had been paid, and the gods were satisfied with their gifts. But Loki would not soon forget Brokk's painful insult.

**BACKGROUND:** In this story, the gods receive some of their most famous possessions, all due to Loki, but once again, his trickery gets him into trouble. Why did he cut off Sif's hair? Was it simply a prank that he found amusing? It's possible that this was just more mischief, though some have attempted to make a connection between the cutting of her hair and the harvest of wheat or other grains, especially if Sif had any links to a fertility cult. As we've seen, her ancient worshippers might have thought of her as the bountiful Earth who was married to the sky (Thor). But then, what role does a trickster have in harvesting the crops?

Indeed, this supposed representation of her hair equaling crops might be a stretch. Some scholars have even suggested that the story of Loki cutting her hair was invented by Snorri himself as a way of explaining how the gods obtained some of their most prized possessions. The fact that Sif receives new hair of actual gold that is as good if not better than her original hair might support this theory; she loses her hair, but gains it back, so everything is all good again. Her loss is temporary and concludes so that she regains her hair. And we must ask how Loki could have gotten close enough to her to remove her hair while she slept. Of course, he is a shapeshifter, but what would have been the real motive, if he indeed did it? In the poem *Lokasenna*, where Loki insults the gods assembled for a feast, he flat out states that he has been her lover, after she insists that she has never been unfaithful to Thor. Did Sif have an affair with Loki? If so, did she know it was him, or did he take another shape, perhaps even that of Thor himself? Alas, we're never told, but if it's true, this would have given him the opportunity to cut her hair while she slept.

This myth could be a convenient way of showing how each god received their treasures, and might have been Snorri's creation, or he might have collected different accounts of these gifts and placed them into one story for convenience. But by the end of the tale, the gods have possessions that will ever after be associated with each of them: Odin's great spear, Thor's mighty hammer, and Freyr's ship and boar (itself a symbol of battle might).

Still, Loki doesn't get off the hook that easily. Despite his efforts at making amends (sincerely or not), he has one more challenge that goes very wrong for him. His brutal silencing might be seen as the beginning of the mistrust and animosity that slowly builds between him and the gods of Asgard. He takes things too far, and even though he makes up for it, he suffers a painful punishment, presumably leaving him scarred.

# THE BINDING OF FENRIR

*Based on the Prose Edda (Gylfaginning)*

Loki the trickster fathered three monstrous creatures with Angrboda: Fenrir the wolf, Jormungandr the serpent, and Hel, lady of the underworld. Prophecies said that Fenrir would bring great strife to the gods, and so he was deemed too dangerous to be let free. The gods took the wolf into their own care, so they could watch him. All feared him as he grew to a monstrous size, and only Tyr was brave enough to approach and feed him. The gods knew that the wolf must be prevented from roaming freely. He needed to be bound, but how?

They created a fetter, called Leyding, and took it to Fenrir. They flattered the wolf by noting his strength and offered him the challenge of trying to break out of Leyding. Fenrir judged that he could do so and allowed himself to be bound. Sure enough, he broke the bonds with little effort, proving that he would be very difficult to contain indeed. So the gods set about creating a second fetter that was at least twice as strong, and they called it Dromi. They brought it to Fenrir and again flattered him by saying that if he could break this bond, he would attain great fame. The wolf once again boasted that it could not hold him and allowed Dromi to be placed upon him. And sure enough, he broke this fetter, snapping it and sending the pieces flying far and wide.

Now the gods feared that they might never be able to contain the fearsome wolf, but they tried again, this time seeking help from the dwarves. Odin sent Freyr's messenger Skírnir to Svartálfheim to have them make a new bond from six items:

1. The sound of a cat's footsteps

2. A woman's beard

3. A mountain's roots

**4.** A bear's long sinews

**5.** The breath of a fish

**6.** The spit of a bird

These things are no longer in this world because they were taken away to make this magical fetter. From them, the master craftsmen created a bond that was as thin and soft as a ribbon, but completely unbreakable. They called it Gleipnir ("open one"), and gave it to Skírnir, who presented it to the gods as the solution to their problem.

The gods then went to the lake Ámsvartnir, where they met Fenrir and asked him to join them on the island of Lyngvi ("a place overgrown with heather"). Fenrir was suspicious but went with them. There, they showed the wolf the magical dwarven fetter and passed it around, with each god attempting to tear it, but unable to do so. But they told the wolf that it would be no problem for him to break, and if he could do so, his renown would be even greater. But the wolf was no fool, and he suspected a trick. Since the bond was so thin, he would gain no fame from breaking it, but if it was magical, then he would not permit it to be put over him.

The gods answered that he had broken through two mighty chains before, so how could this thin ribbon present any obstacle for him? Further, if he could not break the bond then it meant that he was no danger to the gods, and he would be set free. But still, Fenrir sensed deception. He knew that if he was unable to free himself, there was nothing obliging the gods to set him loose, even though they had pledged to do so. They might break their word. He proposed that one of them place a hand in his mouth, as a gesture of goodwill and honesty.

Knowing that they intended to trick the wolf, all the gods were naturally reluctant to do so. Only Tyr was brave enough to step forward and offer his right hand, placing it in the creature's jaws. Then Gleipnir was placed upon Fenrir and the trial of strength began.

True to the words of the dwarven craftsmen, the fetter was impossibly strong and couldn't be broken. The more Fenrir struggled, the tighter the bond became. The gods laughed at his struggle, but the beast became enraged. He bit down on Tyr's hand, severing it at the wrist.

The gods then took the portion of Gleipnir that hung free, and calling it Gelgja ("fetter"), they attached it to a slab of stone known as Gjöll ("scream"), which they drove into the ground. They secured it with another rock, Thviti ("batterer"), and left the mighty wolf imprisoned there. Fenrir struggled against the bonds and lashed out at the gods, trying to bite each of them. But when his great maw was open, the gods thrust a sword longwise into it, such that the point lodged in the roof of his mouth and the hilt upon his jaw. Thus was he bound and gagged. As Fenrir struggled, he drooled and the spittle from his mouth created the river called Ván ("hope"). Fooled and betrayed, Fenrir would be bound in that place until Ragnarök, when he would finally break free and devour Odin in the last battle.

**BACKGROUND:** This story presents several moral dilemmas, for while the gods have heard the prophecies that Fenrir will cause great harm to them, they rely on trickery to subdue the beast, including breaking their word. They promised to release Fenrir if he could not free himself from Gleipnir, yet they flat out lied. Even worse, Tyr, a god associated with justice who was invoked for oaths (among many other things), went along with this deceit, being willing to sacrifice his hand to bring the wolf under control. Since he was the only one who had been courageous enough to approach and feed Fenrir, it is also conceivable that the two had formed some kind of bond over time, even a friendship, and yet Tyr was willing to betray the wolf just as the other gods were.

Oath-breaking was taken very seriously in Norse society, so this story seems to present the gods in a bad light, even if they did it to prevent a greater evil. Some wonder why the gods simply didn't kill Fenrir when they had the chance. He was bound, gagged, and helpless and could have been struck down, preventing a major prophecy about Ragnarök from ever happening. Snorri's *Prose Edda* informs us that the place where Fenrir was bound was sacred to the gods, and they didn't wish to defile it by spilling the wolf's blood, even knowing that he would eventually break free. This seems like an unsatisfactory answer; in that case, why not just take Fenrir away and kill him somewhere else? But the question is never answered.

The actions that Odin and the gods take with Fenrir and his siblings might help to delay Ragnarök, and while they are successful for a time, ultimately each of Loki's children are placed exactly where they need to be for the events of the end to unfold as foreseen. Jormungandr grows to his enormous size because he is cast into the ocean. Fenrir is filled with fury at the gods for their betrayal and vows revenge. And Hel has the authority to deny Baldr a chance to return to the gods after his accidental death. The message seems to be that while one's fate can be delayed and avoided for a time, it is inevitable (even for gods) and eventually, it will catch up.

Tyr must understand that the gods are breaking their word, and so he might be offering up his hand as a sacrifice, some compensation to Fenrir for that dishonorable action. Once he loses his hand, the balance is restored, and justice is maintained. It's also possible that Tyr saw a greater plan in the cosmic cycle, and knowing that Fenrir must fulfill his destiny, he went along with the deceit in order to bring that plan to pass, even though it would ultimately mean the death of himself and many of his fellow gods. This might just be a modern reading of the myth, though.

Perhaps this is why Tyr is associated with justice. He received his own "justice" by losing his hand, for engaging in deceit. Is he an example for humans to follow, or a warning to them not to break their own oaths?

It's also been suggested that the story reflects the real-life phenomenon of wolf cubs turning on their parents or caregivers, which must have been known to the Norse people. Was this myth originally in part an attempt to explain that unpredictable behavior? Do all wolves do this because Fenrir once did?

In any case, Snorri also tells us that the phrases "to loosen from Leyding" and to "strike out of Dromi" were common expressions in his time, meaning to overcome difficulties or to free oneself, which shows just how deeply embedded some of these stories were in the popular consciousness, even a few centuries after Christianization.

## THE THEFT OF IDUNN'S GOLDEN APPLES

*Based on the Prose Edda (Skáldskaparmál)*

One day, Odin, Loki, and Hoenir wandered in Midgard. Dusk approached and they were weary and hungry. While there might be food aplenty in the villages, they decided instead to make camp and slaughter an ox from a nearby herd to use as their meal. After the deed was done, they boiled the ox's carcass in a cauldron over an open fire. But something was wrong. No matter how long they heated the meat, it would not cook; it remained as raw as when they had first placed it over the flames.

Odin suspected that there was an enchantment upon the animal. Just then, an eagle who was perched on a nearby branch spoke up, telling them that indeed, magic had affected their would-be food. But if the gods allowed the bird to take his own share of the meat, he would break the spell, so that they could satiate their hunger. Reluctantly, Odin, Loki, and Hoenir agreed, and told the bird that he could eat his fill.

The eagle greedily tore off enormous chunks of meat (a leg and two shoulders) for himself, and made to fly away, the spell still not broken. Realizing they'd been tricked, Loki ran after him. He struck the eagle with his staff, but the bird grasped it with its talons and rose into the air, taking Loki with him! Try as he might, Loki couldn't let go. He knew then that this was no mere eagle, but an enchanted creature in its own right, a jötunn. And he was no mere jötunn, but Thiazi himself, a great and powerful frost giant.

As they soared higher and higher, Loki begged to be set free. Thiazi, a very crafty one, offered to let him go on one condition: Loki was to bring him Idunn, keeper of the apples that brought youth to the gods. Loki agreed, and Thiazi set him free. Ever the trickster, Loki returned to Odin and Hoenir, but said nothing to them about his pact with the eagle. Was their ox cooked by then? Probably not.

After the three returned to Asgard, Loki went to Idunn and proudly proclaimed to her that there was another tree that grew its own magical apples, equal in every way to her own, and that she might find them quite valuable. Naturally, Idunn did not believe him.

But he asked her to come with him, and to bring her own apples to compare. Curious, Idunn agreed to go and see this wondrous sight. But as they made their way to a place that did not exist, the wily Thiazi, again in an eagle's form, swept down from the sky and grabbed Idunn and her apples, speeding them away, back to his own mountain stronghold of Thrymheim.

After only one day, the gods began to notice the effects of the missing apples. Odin called an assembly of the gods, and saw that each one of them was beginning to show signs of aging. They all knew that Idunn and her apples must be found at once. Odin learned that the previous morning, Idunn had gone away with Loki. Odin was outraged, knowing of Loki's propensity for mischief. He ordered the trickster to be brought before him.

Loki confessed to the crime, but defended himself by saying that Thiazi had given him no choice but to swear to deliver her and the treasured fruit. Odin said that he should have come to the gods and told them at once, but because Loki had caused this mess, he would have to remedy his mistake on his own. Freya offered the use of her falcon cloak, so that Loki might change into a bird himself and fly to Thrymheim, where he was to rescue Idunn and her apples and return them safely to Asgard. And if

he failed to do so, Odin warned, he would face death at the gods' hands. Loki agreed, and with Freya's cloak in hand, he was soon flying on his way to the jötunn's stronghold.

When he arrived, Thiazi was out at sea fishing. Loki found Idunn held prisoner within the stronghold. Removing his cloak, he told her that he was there to rescue her. She was, of course, furious with him, but he spoke a magic charm, and transformed her into a hazelnut (some say he turned her into a sparrow, but that is neither here nor there). Putting on the cloak and again assuming a falcon's elegant form, he retrieved the nut and the basket of apples, and flew away back to the safety of Asgard.

After Thiazi returned from sea, he knew at once that something was wrong. When he went to check on Idunn, he found that she and the apples were gone. He became enraged. Seeing a falcon feather left behind, he suspected Loki had betrayed him. He again transformed into an eagle and flew off in pursuit.

Meanwhile at Asgard, the gods, knowing that the furious jötunn would seek revenge and come after Loki, prepared a large pyre and set it alight. Loki returned, basket and nut in hand. With both safely deposited, he changed again into his true form and speaking the same spell, he transformed the nut back into Idunn, who was astonished to see that the gods were rapidly sinking into old age in her absence. She knew that she must tend to them at once.

Thiazi flew down toward the gods, determined to have vengeance on Loki. But he was careless and flew too close to the flames, which burned his wings. With wings gone, Thiazi could not escape. Even in his elderly weakness, Thor set upon the jötunn and eagerly killed him for his treachery and for almost murdering them all (another source gives credit for the kill to Loki). Idunn was able to heal the gods and restore their youth and vitality. The mighty Thiazi had sought the demise of the gods, but had instead brought it upon himself.

**BACKGROUND:** Idunn, as keeper of the apples, becomes almost an afterthought in one of the few myths in which she appears. But if her task really was to provide the gods with fruit that kept them eternally young, then her role was among the greatest of all, for without her, they would soon wither and die. There is a long tradition of venerating apples in Germanic myth, so it's not at all unusual that there would be a story about their importance in the Norse tales. Archaeologists have found the remains of various fruits and nuts in Anglo-Saxon, Scandinavian, and Germanic grave sites. Remember that Idunn keeps the apples, but Loki transforms her into a nut to rescue her. Apples were also found in the famous Oseberg ship burial from ninth-century Norway, a splendid grave site for a Viking Age woman of considerable social standing. Clearly, apples meant something to people of very high rank, so it's only natural that they would have been important to the gods as well.

While Snorri's version is the best known, a skaldic poem from the early tenth century by Þjóðólfr of Hvinir in Norway tells a similar story. It refers to Idunn as the one who knows the cure or the medicine for the gods' aging. Interestingly, the work doesn't mention apples specifically, which might or might not mean something. Is there another cure? Or is Idunn's very presence the cure for old age? Her name means "Ever Young," after all.

There seems to be some discrepancy over whether Idunn is a goddess in her own right or if she is actually Freya, or some aspect of Freya. Idunn is named as the "Lady of the Gods," a title conveying a position of prime importance. And remember that "Freya" isn't a name but rather a title, meaning "Lady."

In Þjóðólfr's poem about the story, he specifically calls Loki "Thief of the Brisingr." What does the Brisingr have to do with a story about Idunn and her apples? The Brísingamen was Freya's prized necklace, which she obtained from four dwarf smiths (see page 184), and which Loki managed to steal from her and give to Odin. Is Þjóðólfr implying that Idunn *is* Freya, or an aspect of her? Some scholars see it as possible. Like Idunn, Freya is associated with beauty and youth. But this connection was not universal. There might have been a tradition somewhere in the north that commingled these two goddesses, just as some places might have seen Freya and Frigg as the same. But of course, in Snorri's version, Loki goes to Freya to obtain her falcon cloak in order to fly out and rescue Idunn. Freya is clearly a completely separate goddess in his account.

As always, we have many questions, with only tantalizing hints of answers. Who is Idunn, really? Do the gods need the magic fruit to rejuvenate, or can Idunn keep them young by herself? Why do the gods need to restore themselves at all? Is this story teaching us that everyone must face death in their own time, even so-called immortals? Does the gods' collective mortality tie into ideas about Ragnarök, when several of them will die?

## THE MARRIAGE OF SKADI … AND THE MATTER WITH LOKI'S PRIVATE PARTS

*Based on the Prose Edda (Skáldskaparmál)*

Skadi learned of Thiazi's passing some days later and was beset with great sorrow and rage. Though he had certainly been in the wrong in his greed to try to take away Idunn and her apples from the gods, Skadi could not let her father's death remain unavenged. Gathering her courage, she armed herself and set out for Asgard to confront the gods and have either her revenge or some other satisfaction, come what may.

Odin greeted her and assured her that he had no desire to continue a conflict with her. He offered gold as a payment in exchange for the loss of her father. Skadi scoffed at this offer, telling him that she had more than enough wealth already, inherited from her dead father, whom, she bitterly reminded them, the gods had killed. She would be satisfied in only one of two ways: either by blood or by claiming a husband from among the gods.

But she also wanted something else: the gift of laughter. She had not so much as smiled since her father's death.

Both demands were unusual, but the gods agreed. Odin told her that she could choose one from among them as her husband, but on one condition: she could only see their bare feet. The gods would line up, side by side behind a curtain, with just their feet showing. This was a strange requirement, but she agreed to his terms. She had to consider cleanliness as well as attractiveness, and even the shape and size of each pair of feet when making her choice.

She saw one pair that she liked more than the others, a set of beautiful feet that she was certain must belong to Baldr, the shining one, the most beautiful of all the gods. Eager to take him for her husband, she chose that pair of feet. But when the curtain was drawn back, she was shocked to see that these feet in fact belonged to Njord, god of the sea, father to Freyr and Freya. She was upset and complained that he smelled of salt (given that he was from the sea, this was to be expected), but she agreed to abide by the terms of the bargain and marry him, even though she was not happy with the arrangement.

But she still had her second demand. She wanted to laugh again and demanded satisfaction on that front. So none other than Loki proclaimed that he would bring mirth back to her life. He took a spare piece of cord at his belt and tied it around a goat's beard as a leash. Dropping his trousers, he then took the other end and tied it to his testicles. Of course, the goat jerked forward as he did this, causing him much discomfort. Both Loki and the goat began to squeal, but for different reasons. At one point, Loki stumbled and fell into her lap.

Skadi was shocked by this vulgar display, but also delighted. She let out a great laugh, unlike any she'd bellowed in quite some time. Her second demand had been fulfilled.

She thanked the gods for their gifts, and as a further offering of reconciliation, Odin offered her one more thing: he took Thiazi's eyes and cast them up into the sky, where they became stars

(in another source, Thor boasted of doing this). This way, Odin said, they would always be able to look down upon her. She was moved by this gesture and thanked him again. She had made peace with the gods, and she took her place among them, as one worthy of the same honors accorded to them.

But she now had a husband-to-be, and there was much discussion about who would live where. Njord, of course, preferred the ocean, with its salt and brine, its gulls and waves. Skadi wanted to live in her mountain stronghold, amid the snow, forests, winds, and howling wolves. Clearly, they would have to compromise, so he suggested that they take turns living at each other's homes. He agreed to spend nine nights in the mountains, at Thrymheim, if she would spend three nights in his home, Nóatún, by the sea. But how would they tolerate one another's lands, which were so foreign to each of them?

Indeed, Njord quickly grew weary of her mountain stronghold, complaining of howling wolves. Skadi, for her part, complained of the sound of the sea birds, which woke her early each morning. So they separated and went their own ways. She left and returned to Thrymheim, where she remained, content to hunt and wander on skates and skis through the ice and snow.

BACKGROUND: This tale is a direct sequel to the abduction of Idunn and details the consequences of Thiazi's actions. While he was wrong to do what he did, his daughter Skadi is honor-bound to seek vengeance. She arms herself and goes without fear to demand justice from the gods. They could have attacked her, but instead, they offer her payment for the death of her father, a system of justice found throughout the northern lands. What follows is a comical scene where she must choose a husband by his feet, and Loki then entertains her by playing tug-of-war with his balls and a goat! Even though Loki got to keep his jewels, does this myth point to some long-forgotten practice of ritual castration in order to please the goddess? Or is it simply a momentary interlude of slightly vulgar humor that would have amused listeners to the tale? Or is it both?

Some scholars propose that the union of the jötunn Skadi and the Vanir god Njord might represent the interactions of the Norse peoples, devoted as they were to the sea, with the Sámi, who were dwellers of the inland and Arctic. This myth could contain some recognition of the difficulties and incompatibilities of the two cultures. While there is no direct correlation between Skadi and a Sámi goddess, the fact that she prefers the mountains and the cold might indicate that in some ways she represents those outside of the Norse circle of people. And while she is welcomed by the gods (as the Sámi sometimes were), she is still an outsider, which she would always be mindful of. Eventually, she goes back to her father's hall, which is now hers. We will discuss this myth a bit further in the Sámi section of the book.

Some scholars have proposed that Skadi might have begun as a god and morphed into a goddess over time, just as Njord, the sea god, might have originally been the Germanic goddess, Nerthus. Skadi is a male name, and a man named Skadi appears in the *Völsunga Saga*, in a tale about hunting in which a thrall is being murdered in the snowy forest. It's unlikely that these similarities are a coincidence, but is the man named for the goddess or the other way around? Or is he a reminder of an older tradition of a male god? Skadi's behavior in this tale is more "masculine" in some ways, but there is no evidence of an earlier tale about a male winter god doing something similar to restore honor. As always, we have more questions than answers.

There are also no tales or myths detailing the transformations of Skadi and Njord from one sex to another, if such tales ever existed. If these changes did happen, they would likely have been cultural adaptations that occurred over a long period of time. Still, such sex-swapping is striking, and might have echoes in the story of the male Loki shapeshifting into a mare and other female forms, and in Norse attitudes that men practicing certain forms of magic acted more feminine than masculine.

# FREYA AND THE BRÍSINGAMEN

*Based on Sörla þáttr*

Freya loved all things of beauty, especially gold, and once she coveted a priceless necklace, the Brísingamen. It was crafted by four dwarves—Álfrigg, Berling, Dvalin, and Grérr—collectively known as the Brisings. They called themselves the descendants of the Shining Ones, and they were master smiths. Their work was unmatched and exquisite.

Freya was determined to have the finest piece of jewelry in all the realms, so she set out to try to coax it away from them. Arriving at their abode in Svartálfheim, she met with them and told them of her desire for this unique thing of beauty. She offered to pay for it, but they refused, telling her that they had all the gold and precious metals they could ever want. It was not for sale.

But Freya pressed on. She told them to name their price, and it would be theirs. They told her that the four of them owned the necklace as equals, and that therefore, they would all have to share in the payment. There was only one thing they wanted that would coax them to part from their wondrous creation, and that was the Lady Freya herself!

She was taken aback and shocked, but her desire for this object of such beauty overcame her hesitancy. She agreed to spend one night with each in turn. And so she did, and departed with her prize on the morning after the fourth night, putting it all in the past as a dim memory. What mattered is that the most beautiful necklace that had ever been made was now hers!

But Loki (of course!) had seen and heard all and knew that it was time to stir up trouble. He told Odin everything he knew, and Odin determined that the necklace should come to him. He charged Loki with stealing it and bringing it back. Loki, ever eager to make mischief, was glad to do so. He entered Freya's hall of Sessrúmnir in secret, and stole the necklace as she slept. When she woke, she was horrified to see that her treasure was gone.

Suspecting the culprit, she went to Odin and demanded that he return the Brísingamen at once.

She accused him of a shameful act in stealing it, while he countered that her carnal acts in obtaining it were far more shameful. She continued to demand its return, but Odin would not yield. Only one thing would make him return it, he said. She must stir up discord between two mortal kings and twenty lesser kings. They must go to war with each other and meet with their armies on the battlefield. As each warrior died, she would have to resurrect him so that they could continue to fight.

Freya was appalled at this request for senseless violence, but agreed to his terms and set about putting all these kings into conflict. Only then did Odin make good on his promise and return the Brísingamen to Freya. The fighting would continue until a Christian lord stepped in to put a stop to it.

**BACKGROUND:** Many think that this myth portrays Freya as being greedy and shallow. Why would anyone trade sexual favors with four repulsive creatures just for a piece of jewelry, even if it was the most beautiful necklace in existence?

Well, this story only appears in a late fourteenth-century account, the *Sörla þáttr*, in the manuscript known as *Flateyjarbók*. And it comes with some huge caveats. Most importantly, the narrative (as was typical of several Icelandic writings of the time) refers to all these characters as mortals who actually lived, which, as we've seen, was a way of robbing them of their divine and magical powers and of showing Christian superiority. Anyone who worshiped them was thus deluded. Indeed, this story specifically tells us that the war between the kings will only end when a Christian lord finally intervenes.

Another thing to note is that two priests transcribed and possibly wrote this late story, and it might well show Christian disgust with the idea of a pagan goddess devoted to sex and pleasure. The Virgin Mary was the Christian ideal, so portraying the very popular Freya as little more than a prostitute and thus shaming her behavior and liberated attitude would make her look very poor in contrast to Mary's piety and obedience. At least in the eyes of the church.

But the story might be older. The Brísingamen necklace is mentioned several centuries before in *Beowulf*, for example, meaning that it was a known item in the northern world. The myth might point to Freya as a goddess in charge of her own sexuality, who will do as she pleases without regret or shame. And recalling that dwarves are not necessarily squat and ugly, and that Freya was discriminating in who her partners would be (she constantly refused the lustful attentions of repulsive jötnar, after all), it's not impossible that the four smiths were strapping, handsome dark elves of full size! Some have even suggested that what they really wanted was her magical knowledge, and so each spent a night learning Seidr and other magical arts from her. This does seem like a bit of stretch, however!

If the story is a later invention (or a spin on an earlier tale), then we can see it as a Christian "hit piece." But despite these efforts at darkening her name, Freya retained her popularity in Scandinavian folk beliefs and practices for many centuries. As we've seen, Snorri refers to her as the goddess who "still survives" in his own time, probably meaning that people continued to worship her in semi-secret in thirteenth-century Iceland. If so, her persistence in the popular imagination would explain the need to discredit and slander her, and to reduce her to a petty and shallow human woman who would whore herself for gold.

## FREYR AND GERD

*Based on the Prose Edda (Gylfaginning) and Poetic Edda*

The gods saw that Freyr was miserable, but they did not know why. Freyr's father, Njord, sent Skirnir, Freyr's vassal, to check on him when Freyr had spoken to no one for days. But Freyr immediately told his old friend to leave, for nothing could ease his heart's pain. Still, Skirnir persisted, until Freyr was willing to share his secret. He confessed that while no one was present, he had gone to Odin's hall and sat upon Hlidskjalf, Odin's high seat, and there he had looked out across the many worlds. Turning his attention to the hall of the frost jötunn, Gymir, Freyr had become mesmerized when he beheld the most beautiful woman he had ever seen: Gerd, frost maiden and daughter of Gymir. Brightness emanated from her and shone over the sea and the sky.

Freyr was transfixed and in that moment lost his heart to Gerd, but custom forbade him from going to woo her. And so, he now sat in misery, alone with his thoughts, certain that he could never be with the one who had stolen his heart.

Skirnir was moved by his friend's woe and offered to woo her on his behalf. Freyr was much comforted by the offer, asking him to bring Gerd to him. Skirnir asked for Freyr's horse so that he might travel quickly, and his sword to protect himself from the dangers of the jötnar. Freyr was more than happy to part with both, wanting only Gerd and having no care for these things.

And so Skirnir set off. After some time, he arrived at Gymir's great hall. When asked about his business, he spoke of how he represented Freyr and wished to speak to Gerd. The frost maiden came to him and heard his plea. Skirnir spoke of Freyr's love for her, of how he desired her and would do anything so that they might be together. But Gerd was unmoved. She had no love for the gods. She only loved ice and snow. Her heart, it seemed, was as cold as the wintry land of her home.

But Skirnir was not ready to give up. In exchange for Freyr's courtship, he said, he would offer Gerd eleven of Idunn's apples of youth, but she again scorned him, saying that her love could not be bought with the promise of eternal youth. Skirnir pressed on, presenting to her Draupnir, the golden arm ring forged by dwarven smiths and a prized possession of Odin. Every nine nights, eight new rings would drop from it. It was hers, if she would say yes. But again, Gerd rejected his plea, saying that her father was among the richest of all the jötnar, and so she had no need for more gold.

Frustrated, Skirnir drew the sword that Freyr had given him, telling her that it was a weapon that could easily slay jötnar. Gerd angrily retorted that she did not fear him, that his threats were empty, and if he harmed her in any way, her father would make him regret it.

Furious, Skirnir drew his gambanteinn, a magic wand made from a powerful tree branch. He set a curse on Gerd, the most terrible that one could imagine. He declared that Odin and Thor would both be angry with her, and that Freyr would hate her. His curse would deny her any pleasure or love. She would become a spectacle; all would glare at her. She would be afflicted with madness and loneliness, and her tears would be unending.

But that's not all. She would be tormented by spirits and crawl from place to place in misery with no hope or escape. The only one who would choose her would be a three-headed monster, and if she accepted him not, there would be no one for her. She would waste away, and her mind would become as a thistle at harvest's end, finished, used up, and crushed.

She would be banished to the roots of the world, owned by the foul Hrímgrímnir, and there she would drink only goat's urine from a mead horn, while the spirits of the dead would gnaw at her flesh. Using magic, he carved runes upon her to mark her with this fate.

Skirnir thus cursed her but offered her a final chance. If she would yet consent to meet with Freyr and give him her love, the curse and all its dreadful consequences would be undone. She had only to speak the word.

Gerd was distraught and knew that she must relent. She offered Skirnir a drink of mead from a precious crystal cup. She agreed to meet with Freyr and marry him nine nights hence in the forest grove of Barri, never having thought that she would join with one of the gods. As promised, Skirnir undid his curse. He returned to Freyr with the news that Freyr wanted most to hear, though he told him nothing of his methods in obtaining Gerd's agreement.

Freyr was overjoyed, but even that joy was tempered by the agony of waiting nine nights to see his beloved and be with her at last. Skirnir must have thought him mad, he said, to love a frost maiden so much. But Freyr found his patience over those nine nights and met with her as planned. He was sure that his love for her would melt the iciness in her heart. But in giving up his sword to his vassal, a greater consequence would come than Freyr could imagine, and he would deeply regret that action at the end of all things.

BACKGROUND: This tale seems very problematic by modern standards. Skirnir effectively threatens and blackmails Gerd into a relationship with Freyr that she doesn't want in order to avoid the terrible and degrading fate that he places on her. This version of the story appears in one source, the *Skírnismál* from the *Poetic Edda*. Curiously, the other source for the myth, Snorri's *Prose Edda*, makes no mention of Gerd's unwillingness to meet Freyr, nor any curse laid on her for refusing. It's possible that this negative version was a later addition, once again intended to make the pagan gods look bad. Freyr, a god of fertility and sexuality, is revealed to be little more than a rapist, a terrible and offensive portrayal that could only help Christian missionaries in their work of expunging the old gods.

Another less unsettling, but far more intriguing, possibility is that this story is the survival in mythic form of an otherwise lost ritual and speaks of the need for summer to supplant winter, which must be done by force. Farmers and fieldworkers must break the frozen ground to prepare the land for planting. Fishermen and sailors must crack through the ice on lakes and other bodies of water to make them ready for sailing and fishing. Freyr, a symbol of summer, subdues and "conquers" Gerd, the winter frost maiden, just as summer supplants winter, if only for a while. Was the ritualistic act of a summer god "defeating" a winter goddess transferred into this more literal version of myth at some point? Did the people perform this story each year in early spring as a kind of drama to ensure that the land would be ready to plow? It's a fascinating thought and might explain its presence in the *Poetic Edda*, but not in Snorri's version, since he might have wanted to tell a more straightforward account of the union of Gerd and Freyr.

## THE LAY OF THRYM

*Based on the Poetic Edda*

One morning, Thor awoke to discover that his mighty hammer, Mjolnir, had gone missing. Distressed and angry, he went to Loki, who, naturally, denied having anything to do with it. For once, Thor believed him, but that was not the reason he'd come to Loki. Instead, he knew that Loki's cunning was needed to locate the hammer and to help him retrieve it. Loki was happy to help, though whether it was because he genuinely wanted to assist Thor, or saw a way to make yet more mischief, who can say? The only question was: who might have stolen it?

Loki already had a plan. The two of them asked Freya if they could borrow her falcon cloak, so that Loki might fly to Jötunheim and search for the hammer; perhaps he already had a sense of who the culprit might be. Freya lent him her cloak, and he flew away to the land of the jötnar.

There, he met the frost jötunn Thrym sitting on a burial mound, making golden collars for his dogs and trimming his horses' manes. Loki greeted him and explained how Thor's hammer had gone missing. He asked if Thrym knew anything about the theft. Thrym smiled. Of course he knew all about it, for he was the one who'd taken it! He had hidden it under a mountain and would never let it again see the light of day, unless the gods agreed to send Freya to him to be his bride.

Loki flew back to the gods with this news, and asked Freya to take up a wedding dress. Freya was furious, and all the gods

trembled at her anger! Her Brísingamen necklace even snapped and fell from her neck, so enraged was she. She would not be bought by the likes of Thrym to become his plaything. She demanded that Loki solve this problem on his own; she would have no part in it.

The gods met to discuss the problem, and the watchman Heimdall proposed a most unusual solution. They would indeed give Freya to Thrym, but not the Freya he was expecting. They would dress Thor himself in a wedding dress and veil, put Freya's necklace about his neck, and offer him up as a "bride" to the frost giant! Thor was none too pleased with this plan, but Loki convinced him that it was the best way to sneak into Thrym's lair undetected. Loki even volunteered to dress as a bridesmaid and go with him.

In disguise, the two made for Thrym's abode, and there he welcomed them with a great feast. When Thrym saw how much Thor (hidden beneath a veil) ate, Loki explained that Freya had fasted for eight days because of her desire to see Thrym. When Thrym asked why "her" eyes glowed under the veil, Loki soothed him by explaining that it was because Freya had not slept for eight nights and burned hot with desire for their wedding night!

This was all Thrym needed to hear. Then, his horrid sister appeared and asked for a bridal gift of gold from Freya. Thrym bade his servants to bring out Thor's hammer to "sanctify the bride" by laying it on her lap. He declared that he was more than ready to be married and to consummate the marriage. The jötnar brought Mjolnir into Thrym's hall. At that moment, Thor whipped off the veil and told them he would relieve them of their treasure as he took up the hammer in his hands. The deceit was over. Thor had regained his weapon, and now Thrym and his cronies would deeply regret their theft.

He slew Thrym first, and then all the other jötnar assembled, including the sister, who had greedily demanded gold, but instead received only a strike of Thor's hammer and death.

**BACKGROUND:** Cross-dressing gods and an unexpected dash of humor make this a highly unusual story for a Norse myth! But what, if anything, does it all mean? The simplest answer is that it might have merely been meant to be enjoyed. Scholars are still debating about it, trying to find the deeper meanings of men in drag and phallic hammers. It's possible that this poem, Þrymskviða, is a fairly old tale, dating from the tenth century, if not earlier, and it might have been well known in various locations. Alternately, some have thought that it might be a later Christian parody, though this seems strange given the gender-bending and cross-dressing, not exactly topics for which Christians of the time would have been fond of discussing! The language seems to support the theory that Þrymskviða is older than the Christian era, since it uses word forms that were long outdated by the thirteenth century. But not everyone is convinced.

If it is an older poem, there might well be several deeper meanings. Thor is a super-masculine god who keeps the forces of chaos at bay by battling and killing them with his war hammer, Mjolnir. But with his hammer stolen, he cannot play this role, and must resort to secretly dressing as a woman, Freya, in order to get it back. He must have Mjolnir in order to stop hostile jötnar from overrunning the worlds, which is the only reason he agrees to do so. On the other hand, Freya is so angered at the thought of being wed to a jötunn against her will that her necklace breaks and falls to the ground. Perhaps the objects symbolize body parts. The masculine hammer (the penis) is stolen and the feminine necklace (the vagina) is broken.

Indeed, it's reasonable to assume that Mjolnir is phallic and represents Thor's masculinity. And so, robbed of this masculinity, he is forced to don the clothing of a woman until he can retrieve the hammer and regain his manly status. The story could suggest a Norse belief about the contrast between the traditional role of a man, as active, and that of a woman, who operates passively and in secret, hammer vs. necklace. It was a world where men were openly honored for their deeds as warriors and leaders, but where at least some women who practiced the "secret arts," such as Seidr (Freya's magic), might have been viewed with suspicion, if not outright fear. Hiding behind a veil, Thor pretends to be a part of that secret world, so that he can reclaim his weapon and thus his manhood, once again become active, and smash more jötnar skulls. When the hammer is laid out for him, he seizes it and regains his masculine role as a warrior. It's worth noting that in some later Swedish folk traditions, a hammer was laid on the marriage bed to consecrate the marriage, very likely a holdover from pagan practice.

We're told that Freya's necklace breaks, but Thor wears it as part of his disguise, which means that it must have been repaired sometime before he sets off. Still, he has donned a symbol of femininity, which leaves him open to mockery and disdain. And yet, he makes some odd choices that should have seemed suspicious to Thrym. Thor travels with Loki to Thrym in his own chariot, pulled by goats, rather than in Freya's chariot pulled by her cats. Further, Thor/Freya is only accompanied by Loki in female form, whereas according to tradition, Freya should have been accompanied by a male companion of some sort. These glaring errors don't seem to alert Thrym. We can conclude that Thrym and his kin are not very bright, and that Freya is a goddess who needs no one to speak for her!

In what might seem like a modern practice, the original Old Norse poetry of this work refers to Loki in disguise as a woman. When Loki cross-dresses voluntarily, he takes on feminine designations and pronouns. This technique was used in other stories, sometimes even for humans in sagas. The implication might be that Loki really does transition into a woman, which is a notable detail, pointing to an understanding that Loki was a true shapeshifter, not just a male being in a woman's costume, and one who could easily move from one form to the next. It's no wonder that he was viewed with suspicion.

Or, the whole tale might all just be a comical cross-dressing romp!

# THOR IN UTGARD

*Based on the Prose Edda (Gylfaginning)*

Summer had come, and Thor was eager to go and challenge jötnar in the city of Utgard in Jötunheim. As he prepared to set off, Loki came to him and advised him that this was a dangerous undertaking. The trickster warned that he would need a sharp wit to survive such a journey, and Thor's own wits were as blunt as his hammer! Loki offered to go along and be the wit to Thor's strength. Thor agreed and the two set off at dawn in a cart drawn by Thor's two great goats.

They traveled the whole day and at sunset were weary and wished to rest for the night. They passed by a farm house and knocked on the door. The family who lived there was poor, but offered their home as a place to sleep. They confessed that they had little food. Thor countered that they could eat his goats because they were magical creatures. After eating them, they could simply throw the bones on the animals' hides, and they would be reborn the following morning. Loki, Thor, and the family enjoyed a great feast. But the following morning something was wrong. The goats were indeed reborn, but the son, Thjalfi, had unknowingly broken one of the goat's leg bones to suck marrow from it, and when it had been returned to the hide, the animal was remade with a broken leg.

Thor was furious. But he agreed that it was done in ignorance and took Thjalfi and the daughter, Riskva, as his servants in payment. The farmer and his wife would have to look after the goats until the goat's broken leg was mended. And so the four companions set off. As the sun set at the end of the day, Thjalfi, who'd been wandering ahead, found something and excitedly came back to tell the others. It was a strangely shaped hall in a clearing, almost like a cave. It would be the perfect place for them to sleep. Thor and the others agreed it would make a good resting place and settled in. At some point during the night, the ground

rumbled beneath them, and they feared an earthquake, but it soon stopped and they returned to their sleep.

In the morning, Thor was up and about, but he was in for a great shock, for a huge jötunn sat nearby. He called himself Skrymyr, and he told Thor that he and his traveling companions had actually slept inside of Skrymyr's glove; it was so large that they had mistaken it for a cave! Skrymyr offered to travel with them and carry their provisions for them.

At the day's end, they agreed to stop for the night. But Thor found he could not open his own bag. Fearing that Skrymyr had enchanted it, he went to the jötunn, who rested nearby. In anger, Thor struck the giant on the head with his hammer, but Skrymyr merely asked if a leaf had fallen on his head. Undaunted, Thor resolved to try again. Later that night, he took a full swing with Mjolnir on the jötunn's head while he slept. And again, Skrymyr brushed it off, asking if an acorn had fallen on his head. Thor tried one more time at dawn, and Skrymyr then asked dismissively if bird droppings had fallen on his head. Thor was furious but could do nothing more.

Now Skrymyr took his leave, but he warned the company that he was not the largest of the jötnar and that they should take great care in Utgard. Thor especially should not brag, he cautioned, which no doubt only incensed the red-haired god even more.

By afternoon, Thor, Loki, and Thjalfi reached the great city, and they must have been quite the sight as they entered and wandered through its streets. They made their way to the hall of a jötunn known as Utgard-Loki ("Loki of the Outyards" or "Outlands," not to be confused with our own trickster!), who taunted Thor. Telling him that he knew of Thor's wish for battle, he also exclaimed that the little god before him couldn't possibly be the same mighty warrior. He further stated that they could not stay in his hall as guests, unless one of them could prove to be a master at something. Thor feared that his lack of wit in these matters might be their ruin, but Loki spoke up, saying that he could indeed impress them. He bragged that he could eat food faster than anyone in the hall and was ready to prove it. Utgard-Loki summoned a giant, Logi, to challenge the trickster. Though Logi was small, his appetite was unmatched. The two dove into an eating competition, but Logi was faster and out-ate Loki.

Utgard-Loki was intrigued by the human Thjalfi and asked him what he was capable of. The young man boasted that he could run very quickly. Utgard-Loki summoned another jötunn, Hugi, to put this boast to the test. While Thjalfi could indeed run with great swiftness, perhaps faster than anyone in Midgard, he was no match for Hugi, who finished the race long before his mortal opponent.

And so, Thor stepped up. Taking a cue from Loki, he bragged about something he knew he could do very well: drink. He would outdrink anyone in the hall, he proudly proclaimed. The jötnar brought an enormous drinking horn to him, telling him that the strongest could finish its contents in one gulp, while the average person could do it in two. No one, not god nor jötnar, ever needed a third drink. Thor eagerly took up the challenge ... but could not finish the horn's drink in one gulp. He took a second mighty gulp, and yet liquid still remained. Who knew that Thor was so weak, Utgard-Loki jested.

But Thor was not done and would yet prove himself. Utgard-Loki offered him a contest of strength. Thor had only to lift the jötunn's cat off the ground, a task that should be easy enough. Thor was amused and eagerly accepted the challenge. But no matter how hard he tried, he could not lift the little animal fully off the floor. The jötnar roared with laughter as the mighty Thor was again defeated.

Thor proposed one final challenge. He would prove his strength in a wrestling match with any jötunn they would set against him. Utgard-Loki mockingly suggested Elli, his former nursemaid. She came forth, old and wizened, and the two set to wrestling at once. Thor held his own for some time, but in the end, she too defeated him.

But Utgard-Loki proclaimed that he was impressed with Thor and all his companions and announced that they would feast and stay as his honored guests for the night after all.

The next morning, Utgard-Loki walked with them outside the city. Thor confessed that he had never faced such challenges, and he was certain his host would soon tell everyone of his humiliating defeats. But Utgard-Loki had a confession of his own. Utgard-Loki was a master of magic and had been tricking Thor and his companions from the start. He had disguised himself as Skrymyr and was the one who had bound Thor's bag so it could not be opened. And when Thor had thought he was hitting Skrymyr with his hammer, he was in truth striking a mountain; his blows were so mighty that he had created three valleys.

As for the challenges, Logi was in fact wildfire, which consumes all things far faster than any mortal or god can. Hugi was a thought, which can outrun anyone. The drinking horn was connected to the sea, and so of course it could never be drained, but Thor would see just how much he had drunk when next he went to the ocean. The cat was not a cat at all, but Jormungandr, the Midgard Serpent, whom Thor had almost succeeded in lifting out of that same sea. And as for Elli, she was nothing less than old age itself, and though they might try, there was no one who she would not defeat eventually. Had Utgard-Loki known of Thor's true strength before these contests, he would not have let him enter the city.

So the challengers were far from weak, but they never stood a chance against their opponents! And with that, Utgard-Loki bid them farewell and warned them not to come back, lest he defend his stronghold again in a similar way. Thor raised his hammer to strike, but they found themselves on a wide and empty plain. Their jötunn host had left them to make their own way home.

BACKGROUND: This lengthy tale is full of curious imagery, but at the heart of it is that nothing is what it appears to be. Thor and his companions are repeatedly tricked into believing that what they see is something else. And each time it happens, they are humiliated in some way, which might be a warning to the reader or audience not to take things at face value. These illusions are a testament to the power of jötnar magic, which can beguile gods, even given that Thor is not the cleverest among them. But it seems that Loki is also deceived, a master trickster outwitted by an even more clever master! And yet, Utgard-Loki lauds Thor and the others for trying to win in the contests he sets for them, since they never had a chance.

The story of Thor's goats and how they can be slaughtered and brought back each day has commonalities with several other myths and legends, in Britain, Ireland, Sápmi (the lands of the Sámi in modern northern Scandinavia), the Caucasus, and even in Native American traditions in the Pacific Northwest. There is a Christian legend about a Saint Germanus who does something similar with a calf, and some have suggested that Snorri, being a Christian, might have borrowed this motif and added it to his story about Thor. But there are enough differences that it's probably not a direct borrowing. A good number of European folk tales also speak of killing an animal, but taking care not to damage its bones, so that it can be revived later.

The Sámi have a story about a bear (who might be a god) that allows itself to be hunted and killed under certain circumstances. So Thor's magical goats might well come from a very deep and ancient tradition of the relation of the hunter to the hunted or of the farmer to the domesticated animal. It's a story that could be old enough for migrating people to have brought with them into North America at some point in the prehistoric past. Or, it might represent a common mythical idea in our collective unconscious that has spontaneously arisen in different cultures over vast amounts of time.

But what do we know about the major antagonist of the tale, the one responsible for all the illusions and deceptions? Loki and Utgard-Loki are both tricksters who delight in confounding their companions. Some scholars have theorized that given the obvious connection in name between Loki and Utgard-Loki, they might have been the same being originally. Perhaps it was Loki tricking Thor all along. Or perhaps they were always different entities, with Loki being an ally of the gods and Utgard-Loki being their true enemy. Did Utgard-Loki originally do some of the more dastardly deeds that brought about the anger of the gods? Did Snorri and other Icelandic writers swap him out for "our" Loki, to have him be more of a fallen, satanic figure who rises against his former friends at Ragnarök? We cannot know for sure, but if so, it might explain the 180-degree shift in Loki's allegiance from the gods to their enemies by the end.

## THOR AND JORMUNGANDR, THE MIDGARD SERPENT

*Based on the Prose Edda (Gylfaginning), the Poetic Edda, and Húsdrápa*

Thor returned home from his Utgard misadventure, and after only a short time, he found himself preparing to set off again. The gods needed to replenish their own stock of ale, and they chose Aegir to brew it, who said he would only do so on the condition that he could use a cauldron enormous enough to brew ale for all of them, thinking that no such vessel existed. The god Tyr knew that his father, Hymyr, kept a massive cauldron for himself, and so the gods asked Thor to force him to relinquish it. He would visit the jötunn Hymyr and bring the giant's enormous cauldron back to Asgard. Tyr chose to accompany Thor, telling him that it would take more than brute force to steal the object away; they would need to be cunning.

And so, Thor journeyed with Tyr to Hymyr's hall, perched on a hill above the sea. Tyr would present as himself, while Thor disguised himself as a youth named Veur. But as soon as they arrived, Tyr's mother and grandmother (she of nine hundred heads) warned that both of them needed to hide in the cauldron itself, as Hymyr was not welcoming of guests in his home. Hymyr came forth and, suspecting that something was wrong, knocked down several other cauldrons, but when Tyr and Veur were revealed, the giant relented and allowed them to enter his hall.

Hymyr ordered that three of his bulls be slaughtered to make a feast for his guests. After they were prepared, he was shocked to see that Veur devoured two of them in a single sitting. Hymyr was annoyed and resolved to set out the next day to procure more food, deciding to go fishing. Still disguised as Veur, Thor asked if he might join the expedition, and Hymyr agreed, asking him to collect an animal from a nearby pasture to use as bait. Thor returned with the head of Himinhjrot (the "Heaven Bellower"), Hymyr's finest ox. Hymyr was furious.

Nevertheless, the two set out in Hymyr's boat, and Thor suggested that they go far out to sea for the best catch. But Hymyr was worried about the presence of Jormungandr, the Midgard Serpent, and so he would only go so far before he stopped the boat and set about trying to catch fish. Thor cast out his own line, with the ox's head attached to it, and let it fall into the depths of the ocean. Soon, the line tightened, and Thor knew that something had taken the bait. Thor pulled with all his considerable might, and before them, the fearsome Jormungandr rose from the depths!

Revealing himself, Thor drew forth his hammer and struck the creature on the head. It cried out with such a bellow that it was said that its howls could be heard at the top of the tallest mountains of Jötunheim. But though the blow was mighty, Thor could not kill the creature. The serpent broke free of the fishing line and sank back into the deep, dark waters of the ocean, where it will wait for Thor at Ragnarök.

Hymyr hastily rowed for home, and once they neared the shore, he asked Thor for help. Thor leaped out and dragged not only the boat but Hymyr's entire catch onto the beach, and then up the hill until it was again beside the jötunn's hall. At the hall, Hymyr, impressed with Thor's might, set him a task: Thor must try to break an unbreakable goblet made of fine glass. Thor threw

it against a stone pillar. While the pillar was damaged, the goblet remained free of all blemishes and scratches.

But now, Hymyr's wife whispered to Thor that he should throw the goblet at Hymyr's head (which was as hard as any stone), to be done with this whole affair. Thor did as she suggested, and when it struck the giant, it broke into two pieces. Hymyr was convinced of Thor's strength, and accepting defeat, he offered the cauldron to Thor, who carried it away on his shoulders. But no sooner had Thor and Tyr left the hall than they saw that Hymyr and other giants pursued them, presumably to try to take back the cauldron.

Setting down the great vessel, Thor again drew Mjolnir and with mighty blows, he knocked down each giant that opposed them. He left them defeated and dead and returned to Asgard with his prize. The gods were delighted with the cauldron, and every winter since then, they have enjoyed their own ale brewed in it.

**BACKGROUND:** The poem *Hymiskviða* combines two different tales of Thor's exploits: his retrieval of the cauldron and his encounter with Jormungandr. While there are various versions of Thor encountering the serpent at sea, this poem is the only source for the cauldron tale. The fishing story foreshadows the climactic battle between Thor and Jormungandr at Ragnarök. Thor could not destroy the monster in this instance, and he will only do so then at a terrible price. Snorri's version of the myth says that as Thor raised his hammer to strike, Jormungandr cut the line and sank back into the sea. Thor was so annoyed that he hurled Hymyr overboard.

And yet, another alternate version of the story tells us that Thor did indeed slay Jormungandr on this fishing trip (or at least implies it), which contradicts one of the main battles of Ragnarök, and so removes one of the most dramatic scenes from it. So what's going on? It's possible that there were several versions of the story, and Snorri took the one best suited to his purposes. It's also likely that the version of the myth where Thor seemingly kills the serpent is the older one, from a time before the concept of Ragnarök was fully developed. But if Thor doesn't die by Jormungandr's poison at Ragnarök, what does kill him? Does he even die? Does the other source belong to a separate tradition of myths where there is no Ragnarök at all? Unfortunately, we can't answer these questions, as all we have are the surviving glimpses.

What we can say is that the basic story itself—Thor facing a gigantic serpent at sea—is quite old and was probably well known across the north. Images of Thor in a boat confronting Jormungandr appear on four surviving picture stones in Sweden, Denmark, and northwest England. That's quite a distance for essentially the same story to travel in one form or another.

As we've seen, the account of Thor battling Jormungandr represents a confrontation that probably has deep roots in the myth of a sky or weather god fighting a serpent that represents chaos or destruction. When he is far from shore, Thor is out of his element and firmly in that of Jormungandr. He's in danger of being knocked out of the boat and swallowed up by the sea, or even the serpent itself, lost to the forces of chaos.

The second story, that of the gods desiring a proper cauldron for their ale, is unique to the *Hymiskviða* poem. Like Kvasir's death and Odin's quest for the mead of poetry, Thor's taking of the cauldron belongs to a long line of myths across several cultures about how the gods come into possession of sacred, often intoxicating drinks. Examples can be found in Norse, Greek, Indian, and Iranian tales. The drink usually must be obtained or won from somewhere else and brings great benefits with it. Just as Odin stole the mead from Suttung and Gunnlod, Thor wins the cauldron from Hymyr, who immediately tries to get it back; it doesn't end well for him. While mead brought the gift of poetry to the gods and humanity, we're not sure what the ale brewed in this cauldron does, except perhaps to increase the god's comradery and bond, which is certainly a worthwhile outcome. But like the mead, they can't seem to create ale on their own, and have to steal it from the jötnar, which implies that even with all their power, there are some things the gods cannot do.

# THE RANSOM OF OTTER

*Based on the Prose Edda (Skáldskaparmál) and Poetic Edda*

Odin, Loki, and Hoenir once wandered in Midgard, and they traveled until they came to a river. They followed this river to a waterfall. There they saw an otter that had caught a salmon and was eating the fish with its eyes closed. Loki picked up a stone and threw it at the animal, killing it. The others thought they had found good fortune and skinned the animal to use its hide as a bag. They also took up the remainder of the fish. They continued on their way until evening fell, and they came to a house owned by a man named Hreidmar.

The three travelers asked for lodgings for the night, saying that they would share their catch. They showed the fish to Hreidmar. They also showed him the otter's skin, which he beheld in shock and then called for his sons, Fafnir and Regin. Upon seeing the animal, the three men attacked and seized the three gods and bound them, taking away their possessions. It turned out that the animal was Hreidmar's other son, Ottar, or Otter, brother of Regin and Fafnir. He had been in the shape of an animal when Loki had inadvertently murdered him.

Filled with remorse, Odin and the others offered to ransom their lives by giving Hreidmar and his sons as much wealth in gold as they demanded. Taking up Otter's skin, Hreidmar made a bag out of it, and said that he would free them if they could find enough gold to not only fill the inside, but to also cover it completely on the outside. If they did this, the debt would be paid. The gods agreed to his terms, and Hreidmar set Loki free to find the gold.

Loki traveled to the sea goddess Rán and asked to borrow her net. She agreed and he took it with him, traveling to Svartálfheim. Once there, he saw a fish swimming in a nearby river. But he knew this was no ordinary fish. In truth, it was a dwarf named Andvari, who Loki knew possessed much gold. The dwarf told him that he was in this form because a norn had cursed him in his youth. Tossing the net over Andvari, Loki managed to catch hold of him, and demanded that he give up all his wealth. Andvari reluctantly agreed and led the trickster to his home. He gave Loki all the gold he had, an enormous amount, but kept for himself a small golden ring, which he tried to hide. His secret did not escape Loki's attention, and when the trickster saw the little piece of jewelry, he demanded it at once. Andvari begged Loki to let him keep this one small treasure, saying that if he retained it, he would be able to craft even more golden objects. But Loki refused, insisting that he must relinquish all of his wealth. He snatched the ring from the dwarf, and taking the rest of the treasure, he left.

But Andvari, angered by Loki's theft, called out after him, saying that the ring was cursed and would bring about the death of whoever took possession of it. Loki paid him no heed, and said that this curse didn't worry him, since he would warn any others of Andvari's words, should they desire to possess it. Loki was not keeping it for himself, after all.

He returned to Hreidmar's home, and he showed Odin the gold he had collected. Odin was pleased, and was intrigued by the little ring, which he took for himself. Hreidmar and his sons were paid the rest of the gold, and they began to stuff it into the skin of Otter. Setting the bag upright, Odin then proceeded to stack the remaining gold outside of it, so as to cover the pelt completely, as Hreidmar had demanded. But when the work was done, Hreidmar saw that one small whisker was still visible. He told Odin that unless that whisker could be covered, their agreement would not hold.

So Odin brought out the ring and placed it in the gap, covering the whisker completely, thus satisfying their ransom oath. Hreidmar was pleased and returned to Odin his spear and to Loki his shoes, freeing them. As they were leaving, Loki recounted Andvari's warning, saying that the ring was cursed and would bring about the death of whoever possessed it. And with that,

the gods departed, leaving Hreidmar and his sons to their fates. Fafnir and Regin later demanded their share of Otter's ransom, but Hreidmar refused, so Fafnir stabbed him while he slept. And thus, the cursed ring began to work its evil in the world.

**BACKGROUND:** This story will probably seem familiar to some readers, as the tale of a cursed ring is well known in Germanic mythology. This is a Norse spin on the story of *Ring of the Nibelung*, found in Germanic myth and Wagner's famous operas. The tale itself has more southern, Germanic origins, but at some point it was adapted to Scandinavian myth before finding its way into Icelandic texts. Versions of it exist in the *Poetic Edda* and the *Prose Edda*, both of which go into much detail about the adventures and tragedies that follow, as well as the deaths of Regin and Fafnir, the latter of whom is transformed into a fearsome dragon who greedily guards his treasure before he is killed. Many more characters, such as Brynhild, Sigurd, and Atli (Attila the Hun) are drawn into the story, most of whom die in terrible ways!

The dragon Fafnir had a clear influence on Tolkien's own great dragon, Smaug, and of course, he integrated the idea of a cursed magical ring into his *Lord of the Rings*. Modern audiences might also know the story of the cursed ring through Wagner's *Ring Cycle* operas, which did much to revive public interest in these old Germanic myths. These stories are vast and complex, and would require a whole section of their own to do them justice. So this entry begins and concludes with the ransom tale, and focuses instead only on the deeds and misdeeds of the gods.

Once again, Loki has set events in motion that will bring trouble and misery to many. It's not known if his contribution was a central part of the Scandinavian version of these myths, or if it was added later, possibly even in Iceland, but it is keeping in character with his behavior that he would do something for selfish reasons that would have much larger ramifications.

And it's not only Loki; the other two gods don't come off looking particularly good in this prelude to the larger story of the cursed ring. They appear selfish, cruel, and self-absorbed, and their behavior directly leads to the many tragedies that will follow. However, they don't seem especially concerned with the ramifications of their actions; they just want to be freed by any means necessary. They offer to buy their way out of their captivity, which might seem like a callous form of bribery, but it was a common enough practice. Certain crimes could be paid for if the victim (or their family, if the victim had died) was amenable. This system of justice was practiced throughout the North, and in Germany and England. The amount paid was based on the severity of the injury done.

But we have to wonder why the gods don't simply escape. How are they overpowered by mere mortals? And what exactly could those mortals do to them in any case, even after capturing them? The gods being portrayed as so weak might indicate a Christian origin to this particular tale, perhaps to show that they had no real power and had to resort to trickery and deceit to succeed, attributes already long associated with Odin and Loki. And once again, poor Hoenir has no role whatsoever. He's named as traveling with the other two, and then he just disappears from the narrative. One wonders what substantial myths, if any, existed about him, and why they might not have survived.

In any case, the gods are free once again, and a cursed ring is set loose in the world. But the gods have other problems, as conflicts with the jötnar increase and the storm clouds of Ragnarök begin to gather.

## THOR AND HRUNGNIR

*Based on the Prose Edda (Skáldskaparmál)*

Once, Thor journeyed to the east to battle the trolls. At the same time, Odin rode his horse Sleipnir to Jötunheim and there met a jötunn named Hrungnir. This jötunn asked about the one who rode so fine a steed over the sea and through the sky, and the nature of his animal. Odin responded that his horse had no equal in all the realms, and he would even bet his head that this was the case. Hrungnir admitted that Sleipnir was a fine beast, indeed, but he countered that he had a superior horse of his own, called Gullfaxi, or "Golden Mane," who could gallop farther and faster than any other. God and jötunn argued over the swiftness of their steeds, and then Odin rode away as a challenge. Hrungnir leaped onto Gullfaxi and set off in pursuit, to prove his point. And indeed, though Odin raced over hills and through worlds, Hrungnir kept pace, eventually riding all the way to Asgard.

Once there, the gods offered Hrungnir a drink, and he took it at once. He was given Thor's own drinking bowls, which he drained with ease. And as he drank, he became intoxicated, such that he began to boast of his life and deeds. He threatened that he would lift up Valhalla itself and carry it to Jötunheim, and that he would bury Asgard and destroy all the gods except for Freya and Sif, whom he desired for himself. Freya, no doubt displeased with his presumption and rudeness, nevertheless served him more ale in the spirit of being a good host. Hrungnir boasted that he would drink all that they had. But Freya and the others were no longer amused and grew tired of his boasts and taunts. And so they summoned Thor back from his battles.

Thor stomped into the hall, Mjolnir in hand. He was furious that after the gods and goddesses had been so hospitable, this jötunn fool had insulted and threatened them. Why should Freya serve him as a guest when he behaved so? Hrungnir insisted that he was there on Odin's invite and was thus protected. Thor countered that the drunken jötunn would soon regret his invitation. But Hrungnir had enough wits left to deflect. Indeed, he said, it would be better if they fought at Grjotunagardar, the Courtyard of the Rocky Fields. Hrungnir regretted leaving his weapons at home, but he insisted that Thor would be proven a coward if they did not fight a fair duel. Thor would not be so dishonorable as to kill an unarmed opponent, would he?

Thor conceded this point, but was still eager to fight the duel, so he agreed that Hrungnir should journey back to his home to prepare for battle. Word of the impending conflict spread, but the other jötnar were worried, as Hrungnir was their strongest, and if he could not defeat Thor, what hope had they? So they decided to build a giant clay man at Grjotunagardar, nine leagues tall and three leagues wide. They gave this creature the heart of a mare, but that heart trembled as Thor approached. Hrungnir's own heart was made of stone, and he stood waiting, armed with his whetstone and shield. The clay giant, named Mokkurkalfi, became so afraid that it peed itself.

Thor arrived with his human servant Thjalfi, who went to Hrungnir and announced that Thor would strike at him from below. So Hrungnir stood on top of his shield to protect himself as thunder clapped and lightning flashed all around them. Then Thor rushed at him, throwing his mighty hammer at Hrungnir. The jötunn lifted up his whetstone and hurled it at Thor at the same time. It struck Thor's hammer in mid-air and split in two, half of it falling to the ground (and from this piece come all whetstones), while the other half struck Thor in the head and lodged there. Meanwhile, Thor's hammer hit Hrungnir square in the head and shattered his skull, killing him at once. He fell forward and onto Thor, trapping the hapless thunder god beneath, Thor's head lying under the dead Hrungnir's leg.

At the same time, Thjalfi attacked Mokkurkalfi and felled it, but this tale is not even worth telling more about.

Now, Thor was trapped underneath Hrungnir, and though Thjalfi tried to lift the leg, he could not move it. The gods were summoned to assist, but likewise, they could not budge the limb. Only Magni, Thor's son by the jötunn Jarnsaxa, was able to move the leg and free his father. Incredibly, he was only three winters old at the time (some say only three days). He told Thor that it was a pity he had not been summoned sooner, for he would have killed Hrungnir with a single blow from his fist. Thor was grateful for his son's aid and offered him Gullfaxi as a reward for his deed. But Odin was displeased with this, thinking the horse should have been given to him instead, since Magni was a jötunn's son.

Afterward, Thor returned to his home, Thrudvangar, but the whetstone remained lodged in his head. Sometime later, a seeress named Groa, who was Aurvandil's wife, came to see him. She sang spells and worked magic until the stone loosened. Thor was grateful for her work and told her of how he had once carried Aurvandil across a river in Jötunheim, in a basket on his back. But one of Aurvandil's toes had been exposed outside of the basket and had frozen. So Thor broke it off and cast it into the sky, where it became the star Aurvandilstá (Aurvandil's Toe). Thor also mentioned that Aurvandil would soon return home to her. She was so happy at this news that she forgot her magic in that moment, and the whetstone stayed in place. Because of this, no one should ever throw a whetstone, for if they do, the whetstone in Thor's head moves.

**BACKGROUND:** A drunken and boasting jötunn who lusts after goddesses, an angry verbal exchange with the gods, a deadly duel, a clay statue with a horse's heart that pees itself in fear, a whetstone stuck in the head, and a frostbitten toe that becomes a star … just another day in Norse mythology!

The story seems to be quite old. It's referenced in the ninth-century poem *Ragnarsdrápa* by the skald Bragi Boddason, where he refers to Thor as "Hrungnir's skull-splitter." So, some version of the tale must have been known at the height of the pagan Viking Age. Hrungnir's bragging while drunk sets up a classic confrontation, as must have happened often in the company of drunken Norsemen! He abuses the hospitality offered to him by boasting of how he will destroy the gods and take Freya and Sif away to be his concubines. The fact that Freya offers to serve him more drink to make him even drunker is notable. She might be saying "just you try it," or she might, as the master of Seidr, see into the future, and so participate in Hrungnir bringing about his own doom.

It's noteworthy that Thjalfi, Thor's human charge, tricks Hrungnir into misusing his shield, thus setting him up to be killed. But Thjalfi's own battle with Mokkurkalfi apparently isn't worth telling. Scholars have various theories about this; the story might indicate that certain human actions are important to the gods' success, even necessary. But since this is a tale of the gods, maybe his secondary battle doesn't matter; Mokkurkalfi would have posed no threat, anyway. And Odin's irritation at Thor handing over Gullfaxi to Thjalfi for his help is also curious. Was Odin worried that this horse might actually be superior to Sleipnir?

As for the whetstone as a weapon, well, they were very hard and sometimes worn on one's person to use as needed to sharpen knives and other blades. If it was large enough, it might have made a good makeshift weapon. On a deeper level, this battle might refer to the contrast between stone and metal, chaos and civilization (jötnar and gods), and the ferocity of nature versus the taming of it by tools. Whetstones were also important to rulers as signs of authority. When Thor's hammer breaks Hrungnir's whetstone, it undermines any authority he might have had. And yet, Hrungnir has something of a last laugh, for part of it lodges in Thor's head forever, a permanent reminder of their conflict.

Thor throwing Aurvandil's toe into the heavens to create a new star has obvious parallels with Odin's throwing Thjazi's eyes into the sky to make them stars, as part of his compensation to Skadi for the gods killing her father. In fact, in another version of that story, it's Thor that throws Thjazi's eyes up, so there seem to have been different traditions about who did this. The poem *Haustlöng*, by the late-ninth-century Norwegian skald Thjódólf of Hvinir, tells the story of the abduction of Idunn and then this tale of Thor's battle with Hrungnir back-to-back, indicating that they are somewhat connected, at least as far as jötnar body parts becoming celestial objects are concerned! Thjódólf also offers more detail on Thor's journey to the duel, telling of how he flew through the sky in his chariot drawn by goats, and that his journey shakes the cosmos.

In a separate work, Bragi Boddason hints at another important incident, saying that Hrungnir abducted Thrud, Thor's daughter by Sif, and that Thor duels with Hrugnir to fight for her return. It's possible that the abduction of Idunn and the presumed abduction of Thrud were complementary myths, meant to tell similar tales about presumptuous jötnar, who abducted goddesses and then paid the price with their lives. Both stories end with body parts becoming stars, though the significance of this in relation to these tales is lost to us now.

## THOR AND GEIRROD

*Based on the Prose Edda (Skáldskaparmál)*

Loki once came to Frigg and made a simple, if presumptuous, request: he wanted to borrow her magical falcon cloak. He wanted to amuse himself and soar free for a time. She agreed to lend him the item. Draped in the precious garment, Loki soared high above Jötunheim. He came to the dwelling of the giant Geirrod. Seeing Loki in the shape of a beautiful falcon, Geirrod ordered that the bird be brought to him. Taking hold of Loki, Geirrod realized that this was more than a fine bird; its eyes gave away its true nature. He demanded to know who the bird truly was, fearing that a spy had come. But Loki would not reveal himself. Geirrod locked him in a chest for three months with no food or drink, deciding that this would loosen the little spy's tongue.

Finally, Loki, still in falcon form, blurted out his true identity. Geirrod then told Loki that if he wished to live, he would bring Thor to Jötunheim, but without his belt of might or his hammer. Loki fled and went to Thor. The trickster tempted Thor by saying that Geirrod would like to meet him, and that Thor would most certainly like to meet his beautiful daughters, which was a lie, for they were even fouler than their father. Loki convinced Thor to go with him and to leave his battle-tools behind, so as to appear peaceful. As there was no immediate jötnar threat, Thor went along unarmed, and they passed through Midgard to approach Jötunheim.

One night, Loki proposed that they stay at the home of the beautiful jötunn Grid. And she most certainly would like to meet Thor! Thus tempted, they arrived at Grid's home, and sure enough, she offered hospitality to them. But Grid warned Thor of what was to come. Geirrod hated the Aesir, she said, especially the one who had killed the giant Hrungnir, namely Thor himself.

Since Thor had killed that very jötunn, he knew at once that Geirrod's intentions were not good. Grid insisted that he take Gridarvol, her magical and unbreakable staff, as well as her own belt and gauntlets, which would protect him against attack. He agreed to arm himself with her gifts.

The next day, Thor and Loki set out to finish their journey to Geirrod's home, but they came to the river Vímur, which they needed to cross. Thor used Grid's staff to help himself wade, while Loki held onto her belt, which Thor now wore about his waist. But waiting upstream from them, one of Geirrod's daughters, Gjálp, wished to hinder them. She straddled the river and began to urinate into it. Her urine caused great waves to roll down toward Loki and Thor, nearly washing them away. Thor, realizing the cause of the rapids, threw a rock at her, which hit its mark between her legs and plugged her up, stopping her from urinating. He then grabbed onto the branch of a rowan tree to pull himself and Loki out of the river.

After their ordeal, they arrived at Geirrod's hall. One of his servants greeted them and offered them accommodation in a barn, a lowly and insulting offer. Thor was angry but weary from traveling, and desired to sleep. As he slept inside on a chair, he felt himself rising up into the air. He woke up to see Geirrod's hideous daughters, who had come to make sport with him. But using Gridarvol, he pushed back against the ceiling, forcing the chair back down with his feet, knocking both daughters into a stupor and breaking their backs. They were indeed anything but what Loki had promised they would be!

Soon, the servant returned and told Thor and Loki that Geirrod would now see them, but he wanted to challenge Thor to a special game. No doubt, he assumed Thor would be unarmed. Thor entered his hall, which was lined with fire on both sides, and the jötunn used tongs to lob a large chunk of molten hot iron at him, no doubt hoping to strike him dead. But wearing the gauntlets, Thor caught the deadly missile and threw it back at Geirrod. Geirrod ran behind a pillar for safety, but such was Thor's strength that the iron burned through the pillar and struck him, killing him at once. It didn't stop there, but burned through his body and crashed through the nearest wall, coming to rest outside. The jötunn's plan had failed, and as she'd hoped, Grid's special favors had saved Thor's life.

Thor was no doubt furious that Loki had promised that Geirrod's daughters would be beautiful, and that their father would offer him a warm welcome. Once again, Loki's trick had not unfolded as he'd planned.

**BACKGROUND:** The most obvious anomaly in this tale is that Loki goes to Frigg and asks for her falcon cloak. All the other stories tell us that Freya possesses this magnificent item. So, this discrepancy brings us back to the question of the relationship between Frigg and Freya. Are they the same goddess, at least in some traditions? There are a few possibilities:

Some people viewed Frigg and Freya as the same goddess, possibly in pagan Iceland. Or over time, Frigg and Freya became combined, especially after Christianity dominated the island. Snorri might have simply recorded this story as he heard it.

Frigg and Freya both own magical cloaks made of falcon feathers that allow them to shapeshift and traverse the realms. But this seems unlikely, since no other source gives this item to Frigg, powerful though she is.

The surviving manuscript copy of the *Prose Edda* contains a scribal error. Whoever copied and wrote down the tale (Snorri's original copy doesn't survive) confused Frigg with Freya and put her name down instead. Honestly, this seems the most likely explanation. Mistakes were just as common then as now, and no one saw fit to correct this one, since these were the tales of the heathens, after all.

In any case, once Loki has the coveted cloak, he is ready for another mischief-filled adventure.

The story is similar to some other Thor stories: for whatever reasons, Thor doesn't have his weapon and battle garments, and he must make a journey into another realm populated with jötnar. Once there, he must accomplish something, which also usually involves killing said jötnar. These are common motifs and themes in the Thor myths, and they seem to reflect his never-ending task of keeping the chaos of the evil jötnar at bay, even when facing difficult odds.

The way he kills Geirrod is unusual, though, and calls to mind other stories, such as when Odin (or Thor in one version) tosses Thiazi's eyes into the heavens and creates stars, or when Thor does the same for Aurvandil's toe. It's possible that this version of the myth is a reworked telling of something older and perhaps more cosmic and creation-oriented. Did the molten iron have more significance in an earlier version of the myth? Some scholars think the tale and the iron might have represented something more celestial. Perhaps a creator-god Thor set the iron in the sky to make the sun or another star.

There are similar versions of a missile striking a foe in Celtic myth, such as in the Welsh tale of *Culhwch and Olwen*, where the hero catches a spear and lobs it back into his opponent's eye. In an Irish account, *The Second Battle of Moytura*, the god Lug throws a sling stone into the evil Balor's eye, pushing it through his head, and preventing him from using it to burn the land. These myths are similar to the Norse tale, and might point to an older, common creation myth now obscured under the hot-headed

Thor putting down yet another troublesome jötunn.

By the end, Loki's tricks are testing the patience of the gods, as his antics get more elaborate and extreme. His behavior helps to set the stage for the final break between him and the gods of Asgard and the inevitable calamities that will follow.

## BALDR'S DREAMS

*Based on the* Poetic Edda

Baldr was the beautiful Shining God, the son of Odin, and beloved by all the other gods. His wife, Nanna, adored him, and all seemed well. And yet, he was troubled, for he was haunted by dark dreams, dreams of his own death and of loss. When he spoke to the other gods and goddesses of this, they were greatly disturbed and long debated the meaning of his nightmares.

At last, Odin stood up and resolved to find the cause of Baldr's terrible dreams. He laid a saddle on his eight-legged steed, Sleipnir, and set off for Hel, determined to find the one who could give him the answers he sought. He rode for a long time until he came to Mist-Hel, where he was met by the great hound Garmr, the dog in front of Hel's gates. It had blood on its chest, and it barked and howled at the Allfather, but Odin rode on to Hel's great hall.

From there, he rode to its east doors, where a seeress had been buried. He found her grave, and he worked a magical spell to revive her corpse. She was a volva, a wise woman. With reluctance she rose, asking what man had summoned her. For he had made her travel the difficult road back, where she had been snowed and rained upon after having long been dead.

Hiding his true identity, Odin spoke, saying that he was Vegtam ("Road Tamer"), son of Valtam ("Corpse Tamer"). He wished to know the news of the great hall of Hel. He asked her why were its benches strewn with rings of gold? The wise woman answered that the hall awaited the arrival of Baldr, and that mead had been brewed for him. Odin dreaded what was about to happen. She spoke with reluctance and then wished to be silent again.

Odin asked who would kill Baldr and rob Odin's son of his life. The wise woman spoke, saying that Odin's other son, the blind god Hod, would kill Baldr, sending that beloved son to this place. She spoke with reluctance and then wished to be silent again.

Odin pressed her, imploring her to speak until he knew all. He demanded to know who would have vengeance on Hod for this terrible crime, who would send him to his own funeral pyre? The wise woman spoke, saying that the goddess Rindr would give birth to a son named Váli, fathered by Odin. Váli would grow up at once, and at only one night old, he would kill Hod. Váli would neither wash his hands nor comb his hair until he had avenged Baldr's death and sent Hod to the pyre. She spoke with reluctance and then wished to be silent again.

Odin pressed her, imploring her to speak until he knew all. He wanted to know who were the young women who would weep over these events and throw the corners of their scarves into the air?

The seeress grew angry at these words, telling him that she now knew that he was not Vegtam as he had proclaimed, but instead was Odin, the Allfather, come to trick her. Odin countered with equal anger that she was no wise woman, but merely a mother to giants and monsters.

The wise woman commanded that he ride home to Asgard and be proud of what he had tricked her into giving away. No others would come to see her again until the time that Loki had escaped from his bonds, and Ragnarök was upon them.

BACKGROUND: This strange tale is much more about Odin's reaction to the terrible news of his son's death than about Baldr's dreams, which are never detailed. Since Odin can travel between worlds, he can ride down into Hel's domain, and up to the very hall of Hel herself, where preparations have already been made for the arrival of the beautiful god.

Odin, as he often does, uses trickery and magic to gain the knowledge he seeks, which is possibly why he resurrects a seeress, instead of visiting Hel herself. Hel would undoubtedly know him the moment he entered her hall and refuse to answer any of his questions, nor could he compel her to do so. Instead, he lies to the wise woman about his name and heritage in order to squeeze as much information from her as he can.

An obvious question about this poem is why he needs to bring her back from the dead to begin with. If she's dead, her spirit should already reside in Hel, so why is there a grave next to Hel's hall in the realm of the dead? Where was her spirit if not in Hel itself? It's possible that this tale combines elements of two or more earlier myths. Perhaps in an earlier version of the story, Odin first went to a grave mound and resurrected a seeress there, before traveling on to Hel. We can only speculate.

Odin's desperation to know more and his pressing of the seeress are not only due to his love for his son, but also a sense that Baldr's impending death is a sign that Ragnarök is approaching. But is Odin trying to do what he can to delay or prevent it, or is he resigned to his son's fate? It seems like he accepts that what will be will be, which is a curious contrast to the next tale in this section, where he attempts to bring Baldr back from Hel by having one of his loyal men appeal to the lady herself.

He presses the volva until his fourth question tips her off, and she finally realizes his ruse.

Indeed, this fourth question has confused many readers and scholars over the years. The first three questions are direct and to the point. Odin wants to know the exact details about what will happen to Baldr and how his death will be avenged. But then he throws out an obscure (to modern readers) and mysterious query. The audience for whom the poem was composed probably would have understood the reference.

He might be referring to the three Norns, or perhaps the weeping that all of the worlds will do for Baldr after his death. Or the women might be a kenning for waves, or even Baldr's funeral ship. Another theory suggests that his question is in reference to Ragnarök and speaks of the world sinking beneath the waves. The true meaning of his question is probably lost, but it is enough to alert the volva that her visitor is no ordinary man.

It might be that this question is one that only Odin would and could ask—especially if it pertains to Ragnarök—and thus he reveals himself by asking it. Does he do this deliberately, or is he caught up in the "heat of the moment," such that he accidentally gives away his identity? In any case, once he does so, his hold over the volva is broken. She unmasks him, and he responds with what we can assume is an insult before she tells him basically to get lost!

When she angrily confronts him, he insults her and her offspring. Is the volva meant to be Angrboda, or some equivalent? Some scholars even suggest that the volva might actually be Loki in disguise, yet again! Was he lying in wait, ready to intercept the Allfather? Did the hound who howled at Odin tip off Loki that he approached? Perhaps Loki has pulled off another tremendous deceit, and this conflict between blood-brothers foreshadows how Baldr's brother Hod will kill him. Loki is Odin's brother, but as a shapeshifter, he could also be the "mother" of three monsters. The volva mentions him in third person in the final verse, after all. In any case, her identity is never revealed, but whether she is Loki, Angrboda, or someone else, she must be someone with great knowledge. Her rebuke sends even the mightiest of the gods away, knowing that events are about to unfold that cannot be undone.

## BALDR'S DEATH

*Based on the* Prose Edda (Gylfaginning) *and* Poetic Edda

Baldr had suffered disturbing dreams of his impending doom, and the volva's prophecy had done nothing to ease the gods' minds. The volva explained to Odin that the halls of Hel were already decorated in anticipation and honor of the Shining God's arrival. Baldr's mother, Frigg, was so distraught that she decided to try to do whatever she could to prevent his death. She journeyed throughout the worlds and extracted an oath from all things—fire and water, metals, earth and rocks, trees, animals, diseases, and poisons—that none of them would ever harm her son. Each pledged that they would not harm Baldr.

Confident that she had protected him, Frigg returned to the gods and told them the good news. Odin and the others were greatly relieved, and in their confidence (or perhaps arrogance) they took to playing dangerous games with Baldr's safety. They attacked him with arrows, stones, swords, axes ... whatever they could throw at him. Indeed, none harmed the Shining God. The weapons simply bounced off of his body, causing him no harm. The gods marveled at this and thought that the prophecy had been averted.

But Loki was angered by the protection given to Baldr and devised a way to undermine their efforts. He transformed himself into an old woman and went to visit Frigg at Fensalir. In his disguise, he asked Frigg what was happening at the assembly of the gods. Frigg replied that the gods were enjoying attacking Baldr, confident that he could suffer no injury, for all things had promised her that they would never harm her son. Loki asked if it was really true. But Frigg admitted that one object had not sworn—the mistletoe, a small plant growing west of Valhalla. She thought it too small and young to be of her concern. Loki thanked her and left, returning to his true form. He went to where the plant grew, snapped off a small branch, and took it with him back to the assembly.

There he found Hod standing to one side, and Loki asked him why he wasn't taking part in the fun of attacking Baldr. Hod replied that because he was blind, he couldn't see where his brother was, and in any case, he had no weapon. Loki gave Hod a sharpened piece of mistletoe and offered to point him in the correct direction, so that he, too, might join in the sport to honor his brother. Allowing Loki to guide him, Hod shot the twig at Baldr. It pierced his skin and mortally wounded him, and so he fell dead to the floor. All the other gods stood speechless. None could speak, only weep. They took no action against Hod or Loki, for this gathering of the gods was sacred and could not be defiled with blood, no matter the crime.

Odin stared in disbelief. For all the efforts Frigg had made to protect their son from harm, fate had found a way, and now the end of the gods seemed inevitable. Despite her grief, Frigg came to her senses and asked who would be brave enough to ride the Road of Hel to go and beg its mistress for the return of her son. Hermod, another of Odin's sons, offered to make the journey. Sleipnir was brought to him, and he mounted and set off on the long nine-day trip through dark and dangerous terrain.

The gods prepared Baldr's body for a lavish funeral at sea. They brought it to his fine ship, Ringhorn, which they wanted to use to build a funeral pyre, but the ship could not be launched from its place on the shore. They sent for the jötunn Hyrrokkin, who came to them riding a wolf and brandishing a venomous snake. Odin asked that four berserkers stand guard as she dismounted and came to dislodge the ship. She did so, sending it into the water, but the prow caught fire. Thor became so angry and raised his hammer to strike her, but the other gods told him to stay his hand.

The ship was now free. Nanna, Baldr's wife, was so overcome with grief that she died on the spot. The gods carried her body on board to lie next to her husband's. A fire was lit, and Thor blessed it with his hammer, but a dwarf named Lit got in his way, and in anger Thor kicked him so that he fell into the fire and burned.

Many gods attended the funeral: Frigg first of all, along with Odin and his ravens, and the Valkyries. Freyr came in a chariot drawn by his boar, Gold Bristle, while his sister Freya arrived in her chariot drawn by two cats. Heimdall came on his horse, Golden Forelock. Jötnar from the mountains and the land of

frost also attended. Odin placed his magical ring, Draupnir, on the pyre, and Baldr's own horse was also sacrificed to the flames, that it might join him in the afterlife.

Meanwhile, Hermod rode for nine nights through deep ravines until he finally reached the Gjoll Bridge, spanning the River Gjoll. There he met its guardian, Modgud. She asked him who he was, since he had more color in his face than a dead man and cast more weight upon the bridge than five troops of the dead who had crossed the day before. Hermod admitted that he was not dead, and he had come to Hel to search for Baldr and asked if she had seen him. Modgud confirmed that Baldr indeed had gone through here and taken the north way to Hel. She permitted him to pass, and he rode to the very Gates of Hel. Tightening the saddle, he spurred on Sleipnir, who jumped over the gates. He then rode on to the hall.

There he was welcomed and met his brother Baldr, and was given leave to remain for the night. The next morning Hermod approached Hel and entreated her to let Baldr return to the living, since the gods were so grief-stricken by his untimely passing. But Hel was unmoved. She told him that if all things in all the worlds, living or dead, would weep for Baldr, then he could return to the gods, but if even one spoke words against him or refused to cry, then Baldr must remain in her hall. Hermod acknowledged her terms and prepared to leave. Baldr gave him the ring Draupnr to return to their father, while Nanna offered a linen robe for Frigg and a gold ring for Fulla. Hermod took these gifts and thanked them before wending his way back to Asgard, where he told Odin and the other gods of Hel's offer.

The gods sent messengers to travel throughout the worlds to ask each thing if it would weep for Baldr. All did: animals, trees, rocks, and metals, just as they do when brought out of the cold and into warmth. They came at last to a jötunn in her cave named Thokk and asked of her the same. She replied that she would only cry dry tears for Odin's son at his pyre, and that he had given her no joy. So, she was content that Hel should keep what she had. Because of this one refusal, Baldr could not return from the realm of the dead. The messengers went away dismayed. Some suspected that Thokk was really Loki in disguise, who by refusing to weep, was able to keep Baldr held in death's embrace.

**BACKGROUND:** At first glance, the tale of Baldr's death might appear to be most similar to the tale of Christ, but not only does it seem to be older than Christian presence in Scandinavia, it shares connections with other tales as well.

Indeed, it's tempting to see Baldr as some kind of "Nordic Christ," and to assume that Snorri, a Christian writing for a Christian audience, was trying to make a connection between the two: Baldr is kind and innocent, suffers a cruel death, descends into the underworld, and then returns to reign in majesty after an apocalyptic event. Snorri might well have introduced some or all of these ideas, though it could also be that Christian missionaries had already been using Baldr as an example to those pagans whom they wished to convert. The Catholic Church sometimes tried to integrate the existing beliefs of the people in pagan lands with their own to encourage conversion. They might have claimed, for example, that the pagan gods were really Christian saints, in an effort to make conversions easier. It's possible that Christians held up Baldr as just such an example with the implication that pagans who honored Baldr were actually already honoring Christ, they just didn't know it yet!

Christ-like imagery aside, much about this story appears to be from pre-Christian Germanic and Nordic pagan beliefs, including the very old idea of Baldr being a sacrificial god. For example, the second Merseburg charm indicates that Baldr's horse stumbles and is in need of healing. Odin and Frigg come to speak the necessary magical healing charm. One's horse stumbling was often seen as an ill omen. If this is the same Baldr, then there seems to be an acknowledgment that something bad will happen to him, even as the gods heal his steed.

We see similar imagery in other works written before the year 1000. *Beowulf* speaks of two human warriors, Herebeald and Haethcyn, whose names are essentially the Old English equivalents of Baldr and Hod. Haethcyn accidentally kills his brother with an arrow, devastating their father, Hrethel of the Geats who, like Odin, cannot take vengeance on the offending brother. Another Anglo-Saxon poem, *The Dream of the Rood* (probably from the eighth century) casts Christ in the role of an Anglo-Saxon warrior and notes that the cross describes itself as being shot full of arrows, and that all creation wept when Christ died. These details seem similar to the fate of Baldr, so it is possible that the story of Baldr was already known in England. The author of this poem thus incorporated motifs about his death into the Christian narrative to bridge the gap between Christianity and Anglo-Saxon heathenry with the implication that the Anglo-Saxons already worshiped Christ, they just didn't realize they were doing it.

Several archaeological finds seem to show the death of Baldr. A Danish bracteate (a gold medal worn like jewelry) depicts a figure holding a ring while a stick protrudes from his midsection. A figure with a spear stands near him along with a third figure with wings wearing women's clothes. Bracteates from other locations show similar scenes. Scholars have concluded that the wounded man is Baldr, while the figure with the spear is Odin, and the figure in women's clothing is Loki. In this scene, Odin might be giving permission for his son to be sacrificed. He did it to himself, as a sacrifice to himself, after all! Here he might be allowing Loki to commit the act, or even doing it of his own initiative.

Hod's role might be a later addition to the lore, or Hod could even be a form of Odin himself. Odin is famed for letting those warriors he wants to bring to his hall die on the battlefield, and for tricking others into killing those he wishes to die. Hod is said to be blind, though his name simply means "warrior," while interestingly, Odin is already half-blind. Are they the same figure in some traditions? And as we've seen, Saxo tells a very different story about Baldr and Hod, saying that they are bitter enemies. It's a version that might well represent a different mythic tradition, possibly an older one.

So while these images seem to tell a story that bears a remarkable similarity to the Christian tale of a god sacrificing his son for a greater good (or at least realizing that fate is unavoidable), Baldr's death seems to be wholly Germanic in its origins. Perhaps Baldr is sacrificed to keep him safe in Hel for his eventual return. Dying and resurrecting gods do bubble up independently from time to time in various myths around the world, whether from some shared deep prototype myth, from the human psyche, or for unknown reasons.

Those of you familiar with Greek mythology might have thought that Baldr's fate is strikingly similar to that of Achilles. While this is true, we see the motif of an invincible hero with one fatal weakness in other northern European lore. In the *Nibelungenlied*, for example, the hero Sigfried suffers a similar fate to Baldr's. Sigfried becomes invulnerable by bathing in dragon's blood, apart from a small spot on his back that remained covered by a linden leaf. His enemy Hagen learns of his fatal flaw. One day, while Sigfried bends down to drink from a stream, Hagen attacks him, stabbing him in the back in his vulnerable area. Interestingly, another source of this story describes Hagen as being one-eyed. Is this another telling of Odin willingly sacrificing his son?

It's possible that Baldr's death is also a mythologized retelling of an initiation ritual. Odin himself effectively "died" on a tree and after his resurrection was even mightier and wiser. Baldr dies after being stabbed by a stick and returns as a mightier version of himself. Is this myth evidence of some kind of symbolic death ritual among the Norse peoples, where the practitioner has to journey in spirit to another world and come back more whole and stronger?

Farther afield, an Irish myth tells the story of Alill, who is jealous (for various reasons) of another man, Fergus. While Fergus bathes in a lake, Alill tricks Fergus's foster brother, Lugaid, into throwing a spear at him, telling him the sound of the bathing is really a deer and her doe. Since Lugain cannot see them from his vantage point, Alill offers to direct his aim. Lugaid throws his spear and unintentionally kills Fergus. Because this story is very similar to Loki tricking Hod, it might indicate that an Irish legend influenced the myth of Baldr. Given the number of Norse and Irish immigrants who moved from Ireland to Iceland (willingly and often otherwise), this Celtic myth might well be one source of Snorri's version.

Interestingly, some anthropologists have suggested that the Mesolithic peoples of Denmark (15,000 to 5,000 BCE) might have used mistletoe as a poison on their arrows when hunting aurochs and other large wild animals. While it's very unlikely that Baldr's death by mistletoe is a memory of that ancient practice, it does suggest that knowledge of the plant's poisonous qualities is very old.

In any case, the death of Baldr sets events in motion that will bring about Ragnarök. Despite the gods' efforts, fate will not be denied.

## LOKI'S QUARREL

*Based on the* Poetic Edda *and* Prose Edda *(Skáldskaparmál)*

The sea god Aegir obtained the great cauldron after Thor took it from Hymyr, and set to brewing ale for the gods. He invited them all to his hall to share in the bounty of his drink, and they each came: Odin and Frigg, Bragi and Idunn, Freya and Freyr, Tyr the one-handed, Njord and Skadi, Sif, and Loki, along with other gods and goddesses and elves. Only Thor did not attend, as he was away in eastern lands. The gods praised Aegir's servants, Fimafeng and Eldir. But Loki resented them, and in a quarrel, he killed the servant Fimafeng. The gods were furious. They shook their shields and howled threats. They chased him away from the hall and then returned to their drinking.

Before long, Loki returned, and Eldir met him outside. The trickster asked Eldir what the gods spoke of in his absence.

Eldir said that they boasted of their weapons and being prepared for war, but that none had a good thing to say about Loki. Loki was determined to go into Aegir's hall again and trade insult for insult. He barged in and asked for a drink of mead and a place to sit. Bragi told him that he would find no welcome, but Loki reminded Odin that they were blood brothers, and that Odin swore he would not drink unless it was brought to both of them. So Odin reluctantly agreed to let Loki sit with them.

Loki hailed the gods and goddesses all. Bragi offered him gifts if he would hold his tongue and keep the peace. Loki refused and told Bragi that he was a coward and that his war skills were lacking. Bragi retorted, saying that if the two of them were outside, he would already have Loki's head in his hand.

Idunn begged her husband to calm his words and remember the ties of kinship to which they were all bound. But Loki told her to be silent, saying that she had already embraced her own brother's killer. Idunn did not let herself be drawn into the fray, answering that she only wanted to calm Bragi, who spoke too much because he'd drunk so much beer.

Gefjun spoke up, asking everyone to cease their war of words, for it was known that Loki liked a good joke. But the trickster turned his venom on her as well, saying that she had allowed herself to be seduced by a young man who gave her a jewel. Odin called Loki mad, saying that Gefjun was far wiser than that, and like Odin, she knew the fate of the world.

Loki snapped back that Odin was famed for deserting his supporters on the battlefield when it suited him, allowing the unworthy to win instead. Odin responded that Loki had spent eight winters underground, where as a milking cow and a woman, Loki had given birth to several children, a sure sign of his strange nature. Loki reminded them all that Odin practiced Seidr and acted as the seeresses did, beating a drum and cross-dressing, a sure sign of his strange nature.

Frigg spoke up, saying that neither of them should speak of such things in front of others, and that the past should be kept in the past. Loki commanded her to be silent, saying that once when Odin was gone, she took his two brothers, Vé and Vili, to bed with her. Frigg answered that if her son Baldr were there, Loki would have a true fight on his hands. Loki merely smiled and reminded her that it was because of him that Baldr would never again be seen riding to a hall.

Freya spoke up then, calling Loki mad for admitting to his hateful actions. She defended Frigg, saying that Odin's wife knew the fate of all, even if she spoke not of it. Loki sneered and replied that he knew all about Freya, for there was no one gathered in that very hall that she had not taken as a lover. Freya replied that his tongue was false, and that it would soon bring disaster to him, for the gods and goddesses raged against him and he risked their fury.

Loki shot back that Freya was a witch with ill intentions, and that once, she had lain with her own brother. He said that when the gods discovered them together, she farted.

Njord came to his daughter's defense, saying that a woman might have a husband or a lover or both, and that this was harmless. The real harm, he said, came from a trickster who changed shape and bore children. Loki reminded Njord that he was a hostage from the Vanir, and then claimed that the daughters of the jötunn Hymir had pissed in his mouth. Njord simply replied that he was happy to be among the Aesir and had fathered a son, Freyr, whom no one hated. Loki accused Njord of fathering Freyr and Freya with Njord's own sister, which was to be expected from the likes of him.

Tyr spoke up, defending Freyr, praising his boldness and honor. Loki replied that Tyr could not deal honestly with anyone, given that he had deceived Loki's son, Fenrir the Wolf, and lost a hand for it. Tyr replied that while he had lost a hand, Loki had lost Fenrir, who was now bound and must wait for the end of all things before he would be free. Loki simply taunted that Tyr's wife had given birth to another of Loki's sons, as well.

Freyr warned Loki to hold his tongue if he didn't want to be bound like his wolfish son. Loki smiled and reminded Freyr that he had bought his wife by giving up his sword, and when the time came, he would bitterly regret doing so, for he would have no defense against the fire jötunn, Surtr.

Byggvir the brewer praised Freyr's lineage and nobility, while Loki dismissed him as a nobody, a puppy wagging its tail, begging for scraps.

Heimdall spoke, accusing Loki of being drunk and talking too much. Loki mocked Heimdall's poor life, in which he was destined to do nothing but keep watch and wait in the dirt and mud.

Skadi warned Loki that he would not long get away with this insolence. He might be amused now, but soon, he would be imprisoned in a mountain cave, bound by the entrails of one of his sons. Loki reminded her that he was among the most eager when the gods killed her father, Thiazi. Skadi simply replied that he would never receive anything but coldness from her again. Loki said to her that she had been gentler and more eager than now, when she invited him into her bed, if they were to keep score on each other's misdeeds.

Sif came forward and tried to make peace, welcoming Loki with a crystal goblet filled with fine mead. She told him that he must admit that she was blameless in her actions. But the trickster would do no such thing. She might be blameless, but she had in fact had a lover of her own during one of Thor's absences. In fact, it was Loki himself!

Beyla, Byggvir's, wife spoke up, saying that the mountains were shaking, meaning that Thor would soon arrive, and that he would deal with this upstart who dared to insult all the gods. But Loki would not be intimidated. He called her worthless, nothing more than a dairy maid covered in dung.

The doors flew open and there stood Thor. He commanded that Loki hold his tongue, lest Mjolnir take it from him. He threatened to strike Loki's head from his shoulders. Loki taunted him by saying that he would not be so brave when the wolf devoured Odin. Thor again demanded Loki's silence, threatening to throw his body away to the east, where no one would ever see it again. Loki reminded him of how stupid he was to think that a jötunn's giant glove was a cave to sleep in. Thor then threatened to break every bone in Loki's body.

Loki laughed saying that he would yet live for a long time, reminding Thor again of his misadventure with Utgard-Loki and inability to even open his own food sack. Thor could only respond that his hammer would send Loki to Hel if he didn't shut his mouth.

Loki conceded that Thor would make good on these threats. He acknowledged all those gathered, telling Aegir that while he had prepared a fine feast, he would not do so again, and that everything would burn. Then he left and went into hiding, knowing that the gods, in their anger, would seek him out.

**BACKGROUND:** The source of this story, known as the *Lokasenna*, contains an abundance of details about the gods. It tells us that the trickster Loki is no longer loyal to the gods and working on their behalf, but instead, he has become their adversary. We have already seen an indication of his character arc from neutral to nefarious when he has revenge on Odin by ensuring that Baldr is sent to Hel, possibly in retribution for the fates of his own offspring at the gods' hands. In this story, Loki returns to the feast that he's already been expelled from, and to make matters worse, he proceeds to insult all of the gods assembled there. He adds insult to injury as he addresses the gods and goddesses and reveals their dirty secrets, if these taunts indeed are true. He might well just be making up scandalous accusations, but he seems to know everyone's business.

This type of poem is called a flyting, a poetic contest of verbal skill, cloaked in a barrage of insults. Skalds and audiences could well have understood the *Lokesenna* to be something of a vulgar farce, intended for entertainment, while clearly being irreverent. It might have been a kind of test of skaldic skill that became widespread because of its unusual content. In another *flyting* poem (the *Hárbarðsljóð*), Odin, disguised as a ferryman named Harbard, trades insults and threats with Thor. The Norse peoples had a different relationship to their gods than their Christian counterparts, so a tale exposing divine hypocrisy and bad behavior isn't unlikely. Consider how humans behave under the influence of alcohol and a good time. How many drunken boasts and insults would have been hurled in the feasts of Midgard over the centuries? So why should the feasts of the gods be any different?

In any case, this work is an appropriate prelude to Loki's binding and punishment (see the next entry on page 239), but both the dating and chronology of the poem are, like so many other works in the Norse collection of myths, a bit more complicated. Scholars are not certain just where to place it in the mythic timeline. These events seem to occur shortly after the retrieval of the cauldron from Hymir, but the compilers of the *Poetic Edda* use the poem to show the final break between Loki and the gods. It works quite well this way, but was that its original placement? As usual, we're not sure.

Scholars also debate who wrote the work. It might have been a long-standing poem in oral tradition, since like many of these works, it features a long list of names, but its negative tone is quite different from other works from the same time period. Would a believer in the gods go to the trouble of highlighting their supposed faults in such one-by-one detail? Even at the hands of Loki? Perhaps, but we cannot be sure.

Some experts have suggested that Christians wrote it as a kind of "hit piece" to show that the Northern gods were petty, human-like, and unworthy of worship. But would a cleric or monk have wanted to bring up all of the sordid details of these gods—accusations of adultery, incest, threesomes, and perversion, among other things—just to prove a point about the superiority of their religion? The general prudery of medieval priests and monks seems to disqualify this option. Such topics would not have gone over well at a feast for a Christian king and his court, for example, much less in a monastery or other Christian institution. For example, suggesting that Frigg had sex with both of her husband's brothers, presumably at the same time, would have been quite inappropriate.

The details about Freya are particularly confusing. Christians who wanted to present the Virgin Mary as the female ideal despised this sensual goddess, but describing Freya as farting while bedding her own brother seems a bit much, even for Christians who hated the old gods and had no problems making up lies about them! Loki also accuses Freya of literally taking everyone in the room as her whore. The word "whore" is given a masculine form in Old Norse, so it might mean that she only bedded the male gods and elves, but it could also imply that the female gods acted in a masculine (and thus inappropriate) way with her sexually. It's not explicitly stated, but a goddess of love and sex being bisexual doesn't seem to be much of a stretch, especially in the context of all the other poem's accusations and revelations.

And the detail about the jötunn's daughters pissing into Njord's mouth? Some have suggested that this is a kenning or metaphor for two rivers flowing into the sea, which seems like a good explanation. But here, it's clearly intended to be insulting. Would a Christian scribe who didn't understand the original meaning really have bothered to include what seems like a perverse behavior? Would he have just made it up for fun? It seems doubtful.

Ultimately, that anyone wrote this work down at all seems rather remarkable, given its subject matter. Perhaps the Christian scribe(s) who eventually did so meant for it to show the superiority of their own faith, using the very words of their adversaries. In any case, it's a remarkable poem that sheds light on the hidden deeds of the gods of Asgard—true or not—rather like a tabloid newspaper or a tell-all expose!

# THE CAPTURE AND BINDING OF LOKI

*Based on the* Prose Edda *(Gylfaginning)* and Poetic Edda

Loki fled from the gods and hid on a mountain. There he built a house with four doors, so that he could look out in each direction, to see if the gods were coming for him. And for a time, his plan worked. But just to be sure they would not find him, he would often change into a salmon and hide at a location known as Franang's Falls.

At both his house and the falls, he thought about how the gods might try to capture him. He wove a fishing net from linen to see if he could escape from it, fearful that the gods would try anything to take him. But as he did so, he heard several gods approaching. It so happened that Odin had discovered Loki's hiding place while sitting on Hlidskjalf. Knowing that his time was up, Loki hastily cast the net into the fire and fled, running to the river where he again assumed the salmon's form.

Back at his makeshift house, the gods entered by one of his doorways. Kvasir, the wisest, glanced into the still-burning fire and saw the remains of a net, mostly now only ashes. He told the gods what it was, and they set about constructing a new net, thinking that they might yet be able to capture Loki. Guided by a hunch, they set out to the river, taking the new net with them.

Once there, they cast it into a nearby waterfall. Thor held one side of the net by himself, whilst the other gods held onto the other side. But Loki kept ahead of them and swam deeper into the water, though the gods now knew that something was there. They cast the net again, and again, Loki managed to stay ahead of it. But he realized that he was now not far from the sea and jumped out of the water and over the net, heading back toward the falls. The gods followed him on both banks of the river, while Thor waded into the water.

Loki had two options: to try to swim to the sea, where he might face other dangers, or to once again jump over the net.

He chose to jump. As he did so, Thor reached out and caught hold of him, but Loki the salmon was too slippery and managed to twist away. Thor lunged again and got a firm grasp on Loki's tail. It is said that this is now why all salmon are narrower towards their backsides.

The gods had captured Loki at last, and he was helpless in their company. They compelled him to assume his true form and took him to a cave. The gods took up three large stones and broke holes through them. They captured Loki's sons, Vali and Nari. They changed Vali into a wolf, and in this form, Vali attacked and savaged his brother, tearing him apart and disemboweling him. Taking up Nari's guts, the gods bound Loki to the three stones, one set under his shoulders, another under his waist, and the third under his knees. Once set, his bonds became as hard as iron, and he could not free himself.

Now Skadi kept the promise she'd made to Loki at Aegir's feast. Taking hold of a venomous snake, she placed it above Loki's head so that its venom would drip down onto his face, causing him much pain and suffering. None of the gods cared about Loki's fate, save for his wife Sigyn, who found a bowl to hold over his head to collect the venom as it dripped. But she had to empty it from time to time, and then the poison would fall on his face again during the time she was away. And the pain of the venom was so great that each time it hit him, he shook and convulsed, shaking the whole of the world. And this is where earthquakes come from.

And so Loki remained there, bound in humiliation and misery until the end of the world.

**BACKGROUND:** This fascinating story seems to complete Loki's transformation to evil and follows on from the quarrel at Aegir's feast. Here, he is clearly an adversary pitted against the gods, and he will be an agent for the coming of the end of the world. It's a logical continuation of the insults, but again, the chronology is confusing, since Aegir's great feast seems to have happened shortly after Thor took the cauldron from Hymyr, much earlier on.

This account of Loki's capture comes from Snorri, and in it, some see evidence that Snorri combined several tales together, or at least different versions of tales. Some wonder if he confused different stories or simply combined them for convenience. Was the salmon tale originally part of another myth? Also interesting is that, unlike most of the Eddic poems, this story offers explanations for two natural phenomena: the shape of salmon and earthquakes. Were these two accounts simple folk tales that Snorri incorporated into his writing? It's also worth noting that the story mentions the god Kvasir, who should be long dead by now, unless he was somehow brought back to life in a myth that no longer survives, or if in this story, he's an entirely different god about whom we know nothing.

But regardless of its placement in the timeline, Snorri intends for it to be a prelude to the end. The gods are merciless in enacting justice against the trickster, but they do not kill him. Instead, he is sentenced to agony and endless pain. Skadi, who once laughed at Loki's testicle buffoonery, now gladly places the venomous serpent over his head. In this moment, she is as cold as the landscape she inhabits. Why is she the one to do it? Is there a myth about a conflict between them that we no longer have?

Loki is said to be bound until Ragnarök, but no timescale for that is given. It could be months, years, even centuries before he frees himself. And there is no surviving account of how he does slip free. The next myth we have is an account of the end, and he is already loose. Was he visited by other gods and mocked or tormented during his captivity? Does the binding of a trickster have deeper meanings and implications? Perhaps his captivity is meant to represent the taming of chaos in the world, at least for a while, though inevitably, it will return. The gods have subdued Loki for now, but the end draws near.

# RAGNARÖK

*Based on the* Prose Edda *(Gylfaginning)* and Poetic Edda

It will begin with Fimbulvetr ("Fimbulwinter"), the Great Winter, three years when winter will not release its grip on the world, and snow and ice will dominate, bringing anguish to the world. There will be no help from the sun, though she still flies through the sky. There will be no summer in between these cold seasons, and it will be a time of misery, a time of axes and swords, of splitting shields, howling winds and wolves, when the world shall fall into ruin. Brother will fight brother, and the bonds of kinship will be severed. Then the great wolf that follows the sun shall finally catch her and swallow her, and darkness will descend. The moon will be caught and destroyed by the other wolf, and then the stars themselves shall vanish from the night sky.

The world will tremble and shake, trees will rattle, and mountains will fall. Then will the fearsome wolf Fenrir at last break free of his bonds, his heart set upon revenge against those who wronged him. Flames will shoot from his eyes and nose, and his jaws shall open wide. His brother, Jormungandr, the Midgard serpent, will be freed from the depths of the ocean and surge up onto the land, spewing its venom far and wide. And at the same time, the dreaded ship Naglfar will become unmoored. It will be constructed from the nails of the dead, and for this reason, it is best to trim the nails of those who have died, lest they contribute to the building of this awful vessel. It will sail forth, commanded by a jötunn named Hrym, and he will be accompanied by Loki, free at last from his tortured fetters and the venom that has scarred his face. Hrym commands the jötnar of frost, while Loki brings legions of Hel's dead. They have one goal: to march upon Asgard.

The sky will split apart and then the jötnar of fire will appear, led by Surtr, his sword gleaming brighter than the now-vanished sun. They will advance upon the Bifrost Bridge, eager to make war with the gods and their followers at the vast field called Vigrid.

Heimdall shall see it all and know that the end is near. He will blow the Gjallarhorn for the first and last time to signal that Ragnarök has begun. The gods shall hold council, and after consulting with Mimir one final time, Odin will ride out. The Einherjar, his mighty warriors from Valhalla, will follow the gods to meet their enemies on the field. Yggdrasil will shake, and all will be consumed with fear for what must surely come.

Odin will face Fenrir. The great wolf will lash out and capture the Allfather in his jaws, swallowing and killing him. Thor will fight a mighty battle against Jormungandr the great serpent and strike a killing blow at last, but the beast's terrible venom will be Thor's undoing. As Jormungandr dies, Thor will take nine steps back and fall, perishing from the poison. Freyr must confront the great jötunn Surtr, but he will only be armed with an antler, since he gave away his fine sword to win Gerd's love. Surtr will surely destroy him for this mistake. Garmr, the hound of Hel, will leap forward to attack Tyr, and they will slay one another in the ensuing fight. Heimdall, long an enemy of Loki, will at last meet his foe in battle, and the two of them shall kill each other.

As Odin dies, his son Vidar will step forward. Wearing his iron boot, he will stomp down on Fenrir's lower jaw to hold it open. He will take hold of the wolf's upper jaw and with his might, he shall rip apart Fenrir's mouth. Then he will stab the wolf in the heart, to ensure that he is dead, and thus will Vidar avenge Odin. And so the two sons of Loki finally fall. Surtr shall set fire to everything, and the Earth will sink beneath the waters, bringing about the final destruction.

But this will not be the end of all things. A handful of the gods will survive. These new gods will take the place of the old: Vidar, avenger of Odin and Vali, will inhabit Idavoll, which will stand where Asgard once did. Thor's sons, Modi and Magni, will take up his hammer and be the new protectors of the new realms. Baldr will at last return from the underworld of Hel, freed from

his death at the hands of the mistletoe. His brother Hod will also join him, forgiven for his role in Baldr's death. Njord shall return to the Vanir. These new gods will discover remnants of the old order and remember it, even finding in the grass some golden playing pieces from a board game enjoyed in the earlier time, during the golden age.

A new home for mortals will arise, and two humans who have taken refuge in the great World Tree will emerge after the chaos and destruction. They will be called Lif ("Life") and Leifthrasir ("Life Yearner"). They will dine on the dew of the morning, and from them will come many descendants, who will repopulate the land. This new world will have its own sun, for the previous sun, Sol, bore a daughter before she was consumed by the wolf, and this daughter will take up her mother's daily course, lighting up the sky once again. And so the cycle will begin anew.

**BACKGROUND:** This dark and foreboding tale says that at some point, the universe will come to a terrible end in a climactic battle between the forces of the gods and the jötnar that oppose them. These creatures will kill several of the gods, and in turn be killed themselves, while the flames of the giant Surtr will burn everything in existence. Only after all is lost can the world, the gods, and humanity emerge again.

The doom of Ragnarök—the world burning away and a glorious new world awaiting after its destruction—might seem familiar in some ways, perhaps even suspiciously Christian. Lif and Leifthrasir repopulating the world might also seem quite a bit like Adam and Eve.

You wouldn't be entirely wrong in making these connections. Some scholars see these cataclysmic accounts as Christianized versions of older pagan myths, rewritten to fit in with the new faith of thirteenth-century Iceland. It's entirely possible that an end-of-the-world story did exist in Norse belief; there are references to some kind of Ragnarök-style event in older literature and in art on stones. But those concepts might well have changed over time to reflect (at least in part) the religion of the missionaries and conquerors. As far as we can tell, Ragnarök as a concept was not universal in heathen belief outside of Iceland. It doesn't seem to have been a part of pagan Anglo-Saxon beliefs, for example, which of course honored similar gods and presumably had similar myths.

Ragnarök as portrayed in the Eddic literature itself might be a Christian invention, with the idea being that the dreaded event had already happened, the old gods were dead, and the new one, the Christian god, had supplanted them. Here, Baldr might stand in for Christ. As we've seen, Christian writers all over Europe often noted the pagan beliefs of the people they preached to, while putting their own spins on them to try to make conversions easier. Though by Snorri's time, Iceland was technically Christian, despite the fact that many likely still adhered to at least some of the old ways in secret.

As for the final battle itself, it's curious that only certain gods are mentioned as dying: Odin, Thor, Loki, Heimdall, Freyr, and Tyr being the most important. But there is no mention of the fates of the goddesses, other than that Odin's death was Frigg's great sorrow. Are we to believe that they just sat around, waiting for the cosmos to burn, even the ones who are known for being skilled in war and combat? Freya is a love *and* war goddess, and yet she is absent. Skadi is also known for her hunting and battle prowess, but is never mentioned. So where are they? Can we presume that some of them survived? We're told that certain gods will return: Baldr and Hod, Thor's sons Vidar and Vali, and Hoenir. It seems that Njord also survives, but while his son Freyr dies, what about his daughter? It's impossible that Freya is so unimportant that her fate deserves no mention. As we've seen, Snorri alludes to how she is still present, which could either mean that she survives Ragnarök, too, or that her worship was still strong in his time, or both. There are so many inconsistencies and omissions in these depictions of the end that it's hard to make sense of them, and once again, we have to conclude that there were several versions, with only the Icelandic take on the myth surviving in written form.

Snorri also indicates that even after Ragnarök, the souls of the virtuous live on and enjoy pleasures such as good drink in numerous halls. But he also cautions that there are bad places, such as Nastrandir ("Corpse Strands/Shores"), where murderers and those who have broken their oaths will be tormented by serpents' venom. There is also Hvergelmir, where it is said the serpent Nidhogg still dwells and torments the souls of the dead (the *Poetic Edda* also mentions these latter two places). We have to ask if these ideas—golden halls of welcome and reward for the good and dark halls of suffering and punishment for the evil—are simply Christian glosses on old myths and legends. Or, do they reflect an older heathen belief that evil can never truly be banished from the world?

The idea that the world and the very universe might come to an end at some point is not new or unique to Norse spirituality, of course. But the notion of all things consumed by fire would fit in well with witnessing regular volcanic eruptions in Iceland. A fear of possible destruction by lava might have been long-standing, working its way into religious beliefs, both heathen and Christian. Likewise, the creation, with its violent mingling of primal fire and ice, could well reflect the topography of Iceland, where fresh lava flows collide with icy ground.

It's also possible that real-world events inspired the Ragnarök tale. The three winters might be a cultural memory of the events of the year 536 CE, when a massive volcanic eruption sent ash into the atmosphere, dimming the sun and drastically reducing summer temperatures. Roman writer Cassiodorus wrote that in 538, there was prolonged frost and unseasonable drought. His letters also refer to widespread famine. Several other accounts around the world from Peru to China to Ireland record poor harvests, crop failures, dim sunlight, and even snow in the summer. Additional eruptions seem to have occurred around 539–40, continuing the climate chaos and likely causing mass starvation. The exact location of these eruptions is still debated, with some scientists suggesting a southeast Pacific location such as Krakatoa and others favoring a North American site.

Did the memory of a real-life Fimbulwinter inspire a general dread of an approaching cosmic doom? Possibly. A pessimistic worldview would certainly fit with the often harsh and brief existence for the northern peoples living during those centuries. But the idea of everything dying and being reborn might not have been a significant part of it. That doesn't mean that Snorri and the collectors of the *Poetic Edda* invented Ragnarök—not at all—but they might well have embellished it to suit their own artistic, political, and religious goals.

Ragnarök brings to a close one cycle of Norse beliefs but implies that a new era is about to begin. Is Ragnarök still far in the future? Has it already occurred? And what did the Norse believe about it, if they believed in it at all? At the end (slight pun intended), we are left with more questions than answers.

# Finnish Gods, Goddesses & Myths

The vast repertoire of Finnish mythology can be found in several sources, but especially in a splendid collection of epic poems, the *Kalevala*. This nineteenth-century work collects the stories of the Finnish heroes and gods and their exploits and adventures. It's drawn from oral poems known as runes, which should not be confused with the Germanic and Norse writing systems. These tales are as unique, fascinating, strange, and wonderful as the Old Norse myths, but the way that they were preserved was very different from their Nordic counterparts. As we'll see, the most popular collection of these stories doesn't include all versions of the myths and was created for the purpose of fostering an idea of Finnish national identity.

From ancient times, the Finns were a seagoing people, like their Norse cousins, though they didn't travel as far, nor did they colonize or establish new settlements far from home. And yet, we know that there was a Viking presence in Finland, and certainly some among them joined Viking bands or war parties. Cross-cultural exchanges undoubtedly occurred, and scholars are still working out how much influence the Finns and the Norse had on one another, whether in culture or in spiritual beliefs.

But regardless of those influences or ancient common ancestries, the Finns developed many of their own unique myths, gods, and legends, some probably drawn from the Sámi, their northern neighbors, or from other peoples to the east. And like the Old Norse myths, much has been lost to time or stamped out during attempts at Christianization (as we will see, the Sámi suffered especially badly in this regard). But even if the Finnish people were made to recognize a new, single god, many of them held on to their ancient folk beliefs in secret or in stories and songs. At home, they recited or often sang their runes and brought to life the ancient heroes away from church intrusion.

Indeed, Finland has long struggled against foreign influence and control. Beginning as early as the late thirteenth century, Swedish powers ruled the Finns. In the early part of the nineteenth century, the Kingdom of Sweden and the Russian Empire struggled for control over the land we now call Finland, but the Finns had been dominated by Swedish culture for centuries. Swedish, not Finnish, was the language of choice among the elite and educated. Even so, Sweden lost Finland to the Russians, who then controlled it for over a hundred years. Like many peoples who find themselves under the thumb of an oppressor for too long, the Finns yearned for independence and the ability to express their own language and culture once more.

Beginning in the eighteenth century, partially spurred by these centuries of Swedish rule, Finnish scholars took an interest in their own myths, legends, and folklore. They knew that the Icelanders had their sagas and the *Eddas*, the Germans their *Niebelungenlied*, the Greeks their *Iliad* and *Odyssey*. Finnish folklorists and historians suspected that there was a truly rich body of Finnish folk belief that could be uncovered and brought out in a similar way. They began cataloging these stories so that they could be recorded, preserved, celebrated, and take on new meaning in their own time. Some believed that recording Finnish folklore could be a way to assert Finnish identity, heritage, and pride. But would it be possible to construct a Finnish epic out of the surviving runes that were still sung and spoken in the remote and rural areas of Finland?

Thankfully, for historians and mythologists, the answer turned out to be yes! Though several collectors made attempts, the most notable work of preserving the Finnish myths was done by Elias Lönnrot (1802–84), a doctor, language expert, and enthusiast for Finnish myth and folktales. He began his work as a physician in a poor, rural area of central and eastern

Finland; he often used natural remedies as well as emerging medical methods of the time. As he cared for his patients—often poor villagers—he developed an interest in their poetry and folklore, eventually setting out to record it.

He found that the region known as Karelia—an area that overlaps eastern Finland and western Russia between the White Sea and the Gulf of Finland—was a particularly rich source for old poems and runes, and he went to work collecting and committing to paper thousands of lines of folk poetry, both spoken and sung. He had the idea that these runes could be combined into a single, national epic, and set about creating just such a work.

His efforts didn't pass without criticism, though. Some of his contemporary scholars complained that he was by no means the first person to attempt to do this, even if he seemed to act like it at times! Perhaps some were jealous of being upstaged by a younger collector. Some critics also thought that because he had transcribed the eastern tales into a more western form of Finnish, he might have altered their content, meaning, and nuance.

But Lönnrot carried on with his exhaustive work, finally publishing his collection in book form. He called it the *Kalevala*, a word meaning something like "the land of the descendants of Kaleva," in reference to the ancient mythic Finnish land of that name (also called Väinölä). This realm contrasts with Pohjola, a mythic region found in the far north, though Lönnrot was convinced that Pohjola might represent a real place, possibly the territory of the Sámi.

He published the "old" *Kalevala*, in 1835–36, which contained thirty-two runes or cantos. In 1849, he published a revised version of the poems, the so-called new *Kalevala*, in which he expanded the total number to fifty. In both versions, he attempted to bring together the runes he'd gathered into a coherent whole, starting with the creation of the cosmos and continuing up to the prophesied arrival of Christianity and the departure of the work's main hero, Väinämöinen. Lönnrot combined many shorter runes into single longer poems. He also sometimes altered stories or combined characters for more clarity or assigned them new roles that they might not have had in the traditional works, a controversial decision that still irritates some scholars and folklore experts to this day.

Indeed, he received a lot of criticism for these changes (then and now), but Finnish scholars now estimate that he probably only wrote about 2–3 percent of the verses himself, mainly to fill in the blanks when some story or detail was unavailable to him, or perhaps lost. Finnish historian Väinö Kaukonen also believes that about 14 percent of the total *Kalevala* text was composed or revised by Lönnrot from existing variants, while 50 percent are verses that he barely touched other than some minor alterations to fit the style. Some 33 percent of the work contains original oral texts taken directly from the traditional singers in rural areas. Thus, about one-third of the *Kalevala* is completely "authentic," if that word even means anything!

Of course, just how accurately his impressive achievement reflects "true" Finnish mythology as it might have been known in pagan times is still a question that probably can't be fully answered. And we also must consider his political agenda—giving the Finns a national epic of their own—and his personal beliefs, which might or might not have influenced what he chose to include in the final work and why. Lönnrot accepted that the poems he collected were not unchanged originals from ancient history but had undoubtedly evolved over time. They were the product of more than one poet and had been combined and remade on numerous occasions over the centuries.

Researchers continue to discover more about the history of the poems. Using Lönnrot's work as a reference, scholars have tried to assess the age of the various runes and stories, and they usually conclude that the "cosmic" stories about creation, as well as the stories about the Sampo (a powerful artifact) and some of the hero stories, are probably the oldest. These likely originated around 500 BCE and continued to be remade and modified well into the Christian era, passed on through singing and oral tradition. The stories themselves are likely older than the practice of singing them, at least in the forms that Lönnrot collected. Some of the tales show signs of Central Asian influence. Indeed, there is evidence of Finnish peoples being in contact with Asian travelers on the Volga River as late as the second century CE.

Regardless of how these stories came to be, the *Kalevala* is a triumph, a treasure trove of ancient lore that is the best source for Finnish mythology that survives. Of course, other sources for Finnish myth and folklore exist today, but this book will focus mainly on the Finnish myths as they are presented in Lönnrot's *Kalevala*. As you might imagine, less scholarly work exists in English than for the Old Norse tales, so it's a bit more difficult to track down quality articles and books about the subject, at least ones that aren't in Finnish. But some fine studies can be found in the "Further Reading" section at the end of the book. The entries for gods and heroes here rely more on excerpts from the *Kalevala* poetry itself (in public domain translation, with a few alterations and modernizations) than the Old Norse portion of the book does for its sources. It is well worth seeking out one of the modern translations of the *Kalevala* and reading it in full.

Before moving on to the entries and stories, it's worth examining some of the mythology outside of the confines of the *Kalevala*. In 1551, Finnish Lutheran reformer and scholar Mikael Agricola produced a Finnish translation of the Psalms, and in the introduction, he included a list of twenty-four pagan Finnish gods and heroes (technically, one of them was the Christian devil). He named them not to glorify them, of course, but to declare that these ancient beings needed to be refuted and defeated. He also accused the pope and the Catholic Church of having tolerated these beliefs, which gave him further reason to condemn them! However, he did record some brief, useful information. Some of the beings on his list were not actual gods, but rather protective spirits and folk heroes. Agricola, who did much to establish Finnish as a literary language, was probably the first scholar to attempt any kind of catalog of supernatural beings from the regions of Tavastia and Karelia.

Beyond this short list, we must look to later scholarly writings to try to construct a picture of Finnish paganism. What did the ancient Finns believe? It seems that their practices included several components:

Animism, the belief that spirits inhabit all things: trees, animals, rocks, and the Earth itself. The Finnish people called these beings haltijat, and they might also dwell in human creations, such as homes, hearths, and other manmade objects. In addition, each place had its own magical force or embodiment of spirit, called väki, which was controlled by the spirit living there. These väki needed to be kept apart, so one would not go into a forest to hunt and invoke the forest väki, for example, and then go and try to fish in a lake on the same trip, which would require addressing a different väki. This mixing of different energies could damage the landscape.

Belief that each plant and animal was governed by its own primal spirit, the originator of its species, called *Emuu*. A person would make an offering to this mother spirit and thank her for any animals or plants that they took for human use. The ancient Finns, like the Sámi, especially honored the bear and its primal mother. In some places, such as Karelia, it was forbidden to eat bear meat. Since the bear and humanity were considered to be closely related to each other, to do so would be to commit cannibalism. In other areas, eating bear flesh was sacred, but reserved only for important rites.

Veneration for ancestors and the spirits of the dead, who could remain in contact with their descendants. They might even come back in the form of butterflies or birds to greet their still-living relatives. And yet at the same time, they also dwelled in the realm of the dead.

Belief in sacred sites, such as hilltops, springs, and certain rocks or trees. These sites were called *hiisi*, a term later changed by the church to mean a demon, in an attempt to stamp out worship and offerings at them.

Belief in an afterlife that was not a heaven or hell, but simply a place where all souls went, like the Norse Hel or the Greek Hades.

The use of poems and songs imbued with magic that could be recited and passed on.

An agricultural civilization whose spirituality was deeply tied to the seasons and other natural phenomena, especially all things related to water.

Belief that one should conduct one's activities according to the phases of the moon to ensure the best outcome.

The pagan Finns had specific ideas about the physical world itself, which was flat and covered by a large dome, sometimes called the "Lid of the Sky." This dome was held up by a great pole, which reminds one of Yggdrasil from Norse belief, though it is not referred to specifically as a tree. It's also likely that some Finns thought of this item as the Sampo itself, a magical object that is mysterious and undefined, but plays a key role in the stories of the *Kalevala*.

Outside of our Earth, the Finns believed in two additional worlds, as opposed to the multiple realms in Norse mythology. The upper world consists of the sky and the south. This realm might be ruled by the goddess Iro (also known as Ilmatar), who gave birth to gods at the beginning of time. The lower world is located in the far north of the Finnish lands and under our own. Known as Pohjola ("the Northern Place"), it also intersects with the land of the dead, called Tuonela. It was to this realm that an ancient Finnish tietäjä, a sage or healer, would journey in spirit to gain knowledge and possibly bring back help or cures. These shamanic-like journeys were later demonized by Christian missionaries who sought to re-brand the underworld as Hell. It also seems that the realm of the dead in many places might have simply meant the grave itself, which would help to explain why the dead were close by to visit the living when they chose.

These beliefs were deeply ingrained in the pagan Finnish mind. We know that, as with so many other forced conversions in Europe and beyond, many people continued to make sacrifices to their old gods and spirits in secret, sometimes even in the new churches themselves, since these buildings were often constructed over sites that had been used for pagan rites as a sign of the new religion triumphing over the old. Sometimes, churches would accept items as "donations" that had likely been offered as sacrifices previously, such as animal skins, antlers, and grain.

In more rural areas, there was a kind of syncretism between Christian and pagan Finnish beliefs that lasted well into the nineteenth century, with the two often being blended in new and creative ways. We see this in the *Kalevala* itself, with old gods and new both named in the same stories.

But even under Christian influence, many Finns held to a worldview rich with spirits, gods, animism, and enchantment. Assuming that the *Kalevala* records traditional Finnish stories reasonably accurately, and that the old runes still sung by villagers and rural folks at the time preserved much of their ancient heritage in some form, we find a wonderfully strange world, familiar but not. There are images, motifs, and characters that often seem surreal and otherworldly. Like the Old Norse myths, these tales often have a dream-like quality and a distinct lack of logic. Remember, we are in the realm of the mythic, not the rational, so it's important to be accepting of whatever a story throws at us!

But what does this work, and all of its components, actually "mean"? That's a question that has puzzled scholars and mythology enthusiasts. Some have suggested that the rivalries and hostilities between Kalevala and the northern land of Pohjola might represent friction and conflict between the Finns and the Sámi, though this is probably a bit simplistic. Further, Kalevala itself might well be a mythicized version of the lands of Karelia in eastern Finland and western Russia. As such, these stories might be imbued with ancient memories of those lands, rather than being a straight north-south divide between the Finns and the Sámi. Others have suggested that the "original" land of Kalevala might have been in what is now Estonia. Estonian mythology is related to Finnish mythology, but is also different in several ways, which presents whole new possibilities and problems about where the "historical" Kalevala might be. But that topic is far outside the scope of this book.

Was Kalevala a real place at all? Some scholars have gone so far as to suggest that Lönnrot simply invented the realms of Kalevala and Pohjola to create narrative tension that would give these stories more excitement and drama. They argue that a basic good vs. evil conflict was missing from the original Finnish myths, and that Lönnrot invented it to make the final product more suitable as a national epic. In this view, the Finnish heroes needed an evil to strive against. If this is true, it would strengthen the argument that Lönnrot assigned the role of villains to some gods or characters to give the story the opposing forces it needed, and so that good could triumph over evil.

And yet, others insist that Lönnrot was deeply affected by the runes and their history, and he wouldn't have altered the originals so much just to make a nationalistic point. He no doubt did make some key changes, but did he really alter the fundamental nature of some characters or invent whole realms for them to live in? We can't know for sure, but it seems rather unlikely.

What about Christian influence? Undoubtedly, it had crept in, both in the original runes and in Lönnrot's retellings. The Christian church exerted some control over what the people listened to and enjoyed, but in homes and remote regions, it's possible that people sang the old runes for centuries with little outside interference. And yet, these poems probably did change over time. Near the end of the epic, we learn of the virgin maiden named Marjatta, who is certainly a stand-in for the Virgin Mary. Indeed, her miraculously born son displaces Väinämöinen and will eventually establish his rule over the land, which is definitely meant to represent Christianity supplanting the old gods and ways. But did Lönnrot invent these characters? This story probably already existed and was added at some time in the past, likely by Christians who wanted to harmonize the ancient ways with the newer faith.

In any case, some Finnish mythic concepts will seem familiar; there are gods of the sea and the sky, of the hunt and the underworld, and sometimes they have personalities that remind us of the Norse gods. Indeed, there are probably some connections between the two cultures that date back far into the mists of history, while other stories might have been variations on ones taken along trade routes. That said, the Finns have their own unique gods and heroes, though undoubtedly some are the same as those of the Norse and the Sámi; they're just wearing different masks.

Let's look at a few of these epic figures. The most important character in the *Kalevala* is Väinämöinen, a wizard and seer, who is born in a most remarkable way, spending centuries in the womb of the goddess Ilmatar before seeing the light of day. Older versions of the myth cast him as the creator of the universe himself. He is a master player of the kantele, an ancient zither-like musical instrument that is still enormously popular in traditional and contemporary Finnish folk song. His adventures form a large portion of the stories, though there are other key heroes, such as the master smith Ilmarinen, who was also originally a god, and who forged the sky at the creation of the world. Also important is Lemminkäinen, an adventurer who has some similarities to the Norse god Baldr, and the tragic hero and magician Kullervo. Opposing them is the powerful Louhi, the matriarch of the realm of Pohjola. She was likely a goddess in ancient times and gradually reduced to the role of an evil witch and enemy to the heroes.

An abundance of other gods make appearances, though they are usually not as involved in the affairs of humanity as some of their Norse counterparts. The heroes often call upon them in times of need, but in general, they are not as fleshed-out as the main characters of the story. This fact might have to do with loss of knowledge, myths, and lore about them over the centuries, but it could also reflect the effects of Christianization over the same period. Or it might simply indicate what survived in the regions where Lönnrot collected his runes. But these gods have their own unique qualities, powers, and strangeness, and there is no doubt that at one time, they held sway over the hearts and minds of the Finns.

There's probably no need to locate these stories anywhere except in the world of myth and imagination. Did Väinämöinen actually exist at one time, perhaps as some kind of spiritual leader who was a prototype for the later wizard? We cannot know, and it's probably futile to try to find "historic" versions of any of these characters. It's equally possible that the *Kalevala's* characters were always mythic and perhaps represented natural phenomena so that they could be better explained and understood.

There is a good chance that some of these gods and heroes were influenced by Sámi spirituality; as we've seen with the Norse gods, when two cultures living side by side are in frequent contact, exchanges of all kinds are almost inevitable. As mentioned, both the Sámi and the Finns revere the bear in their tales and mythologies. In the *Kalevala*, the goddess Mielikki creates the bear in a colorful and imaginative way, indicating that the ancient Finns honored the creature as a special product of divine power. Väinämöinen and others give great praise and honor to the bear in a tale near the end of the epic.

But it's not the bear that towers over the *Kalevala* narrative. Rather it's an object, the Sampo, which is never fully described. One of the main stories of the epic is the quest for the Sampo, a magical artifact that the great blacksmith Ilmarinen fashions. For such an important object, it's kind of amazing that we really don't know what it is! It's like a horn of plenty (such as the Cornucopia in Greek mythology), an object that brings riches and prosperity to the people and the land that holds it. Lönnrot thought it was a mill that could make not only flour, but also gold. But the Sampo might be something more ancient, such as a World Tree that supports the cosmos, just as Yggdrasil does in Norse mythology. We'll delve more into its mystery later in this section, but the conflicts over who would possess it are a major part of the later *Kalevala* stories.

Ultimately the *Kalevala* is an amazing achievement, regardless of how well it preserves pagan Finnish myth. Its publication helped fuel already rising Finnish nationalist sentiments. It inspired a sense among the Finns that their own stories and history mattered and could take their place alongside the great works of world literature.

This section will first look at the gods and heroes of Finnish myth, and then present a (very!) abridged version of the *Kalevala* tales, focusing on the main stories and the overall narrative, from the creation to Väinämöinen's departure and the triumph of Christianity. These remarkable tales still resonate with modern readers and transport us back to a time of magic and wonder, of enchanted songs, strange creatures, totem animals, evil spirits, surreal settings, and revelations about the human condition that still matter today.

## ILMATAR

Ilmatar is a primeval goddess, the daughter of the sky from the time when there was nothing but primal waters and the endless sky itself. Ilma translates to "air," and tar is a feminine suffix. A goddess of that air and sky, she is associated with nature in general. Indeed, she is also sometimes known as Luonnotar; luonto translates as "nature," so this name would mean something like "female nature spirit," which perhaps doesn't seem very original, even if it is sufficiently descriptive.

In the *Kalevala*, she was the ancient power who gave birth to our world, though she was seen as a "virgin" goddess. Other versions of the creation myth don't give her this role, but here, she is known for forming and shaping the world, as well as giving birth to the legendary hero Väinämöinen.

The first rune of the *Kalevala* describes her existence as stretching far back into the mists of time:

In primeval times, a maiden,

Beautiful Daughter of the Ether,

Passed her existence for ages

In the great expanse of heaven

Over the prairies yet enfolded.

The maiden grew weary,

Her existence sad and hopeless,

Thus she lived alone for ages

In the infinite expanses

Of the air above the sea-foam,

In the far outstretching spaces,

In a solitude of ether.

Only the elements of air, water, and ether existed, but Ilmatar longed for more and the cosmos answered that need. From her would come all creation and the magnificent people and heroes that feature in the stories of the *Kalevala*.

Beyond this all-important act of creation, the work says little more about her. Whatever her original role, we can assume that the ancient Finns worshiped or honored her in some ways, but evidence for that worship is scant. Finns still celebrate her name day (the day associated with one's baptized name) on August 26, but scholars are not sure if this is a survival of an ancient connection between the goddess and this date, or merely a later Christian addition for the name itself.

We find various ancient primal forces giving birth to the Earth or cosmos and then retreating in many myths around the world, including Norse, Egyptian, and Greek mythology. The story of Ilmatar is likely another example of that belief with deep and ancient connections to similar myths. The prime cre-

ator does its work and then withdraws, leaving Earthly acclaim and attention to the next generation of gods, who interact far more with humanity and the world.

And yet, some believe that Lönnrot altered or embellished her story in significant ways, including claiming that she is the mother of Väinämöinen, when Väinämöinen himself is credited with being the creator in other accounts. But still other versions of the Finnish creation myth tell of Iro (who might also be Ilmatar) giving birth to Väinämöinen, as well as Ilmarinen the smith, and a presumptuous rune singer, Joukahainen. In this tale, Iro is impregnated by a lingonberry, and bears the three brother gods (made into heroes in the *Kalevala*). This method of conception reappears at the end of the *Kalevala*, when the maiden Marjatta is made pregnant in the same way and gives birth to the Christ-king that will supplant Väinämöinen and the old ways.

## VÄINÄMÖINEN

Väinämöinen is the principal hero of the *Kalevala* and of Finnish mythology in general. Whether or not he is a god depends on which text you're reading. In the *Kalevala* he's not a god, but rather an intermediary between the realms of the gods and spirits and that of humanity. In Agricola's account, however, Väinämöinen is clearly a god of songs and poetry. This discrepancy suggests that some pagan communities revered him as a god, while people in other regions of Finland lauded him as human or something like a demi-god. Clearly, he was important in the hearts and minds of the Finnish people for a very long time, whether as a god or a (semi) mortal hero.

God or not, he is a wizard, leader, adventurer, master singer and musician, and wise sage. He was born an already old man, and he lives for what seems like many centuries. He has the energy and ability of a dozen younger men and is always ready to protect the land and the people of his home. He can bend and shape reality through his magic by singing his wishes into existence, if he knows the proper spell (but sometimes he doesn't).

And yet despite all his glowing attributes, he can be foolish, selfish, uncaring, egotistical, quick to anger, and prone to making mistakes. In this regard, some scholars see a relation between Väinämöinen and Odin, who likewise was a god of poetry and magic, and who, as we've seen, could also make some rather terrible decisions! Yet the *Kalevala* constantly refers to Väinämöinen as "wise," "trusty," an "ancient hero," among other praises.

As we've seen, some scholars have speculated that Väinämöinen might have been a real figure in history, perhaps from the ninth or tenth century, a kind of holy man or magician, and someone with mysterious powers who was held in great esteem during his lifetime. Lönnrot seems to have believed this, and it might be why he recast Väinämöinen in the role of a hero to make him the chief protagonist of the epic.

To make matters even more complicated, in some versions of the Finnish myths, it is Väinämöinen who floats in the endless, primal waters and creates all things from an eagle's egg, not Ukko (see page 270) or the goddess Ilmatar. You could easily substitute Väinämöinen for Ilmatar when reading the *Kalevala* creation story and still be "correct." Here we also see the motif of the world being created from water, which calls to mind the flood myths of the Ancient Near East and other regions.

Väinämöinen's exploits feature extensively in the *Kalevala*. He spends more than seven centuries in Ilmatar's womb before being born as an old man. He takes his final leave from the land at the arrival of a baby born by Marjatta's virgin birth, an obvious reference to the coming of Christianity to Finland and its gradual supplanting of the old ways. And yet, he doesn't die at the end of the story. Indeed, he even promises to return one day, should his people need him again. In this way, he resembles King Arthur, a hero inextricably tied to his land, who will always help

his people when they have the need. A hero who is ostensibly always "available" for Finns struggling for independence and a national identity of their own certainly makes sense, but how widespread the idea was in centuries past is open to debate.

Väinämöinen himself is a mess of contradictions, perhaps due to the many different versions of his tale. On the one hand, he often tries to protect the people of his home. When a terrible plague of several diseases from the north ravages the land, he uses both his own magic and his appeals to the gods to halt these pestilences and save many lives. He duels with the young upstart and would-be rune singer Joukahainen (who has also been reduced to the status of a mortal in the *Kalevala*), who boasts that he is greater than Väinämöinen. This conflict recalls the ancient motif of warring gods (and brother gods at that). In another story of his skill, Väinämöinen constructs the first kantele (a zither-like instrument that is the national folk instrument of Finland), and his music charms and enraptures all beings: gods, spirits, humans, and animals alike. Indeed, so important is the kantele to the identity of the Finnish people and to the land itself that he leaves it behind when he departs, so that it can continue to weave its musical magic, even in the time of Christianity.

But on the other hand, Väinämöinen can be selfish, such as when his determination to have one particular young woman as his wife leads to her death. And though he feels remorse, it's still his fault that she's dead. Thus, he's not a perfect, blameless hero by any means.

Even though you might not have been familiar with this hero before now, you have very likely met characters inspired by him. Tolkien was fascinated with the Finnish language and the *Kalevala*, and Väinämöinen served in part as a model not only for the wizard Gandalf, but also probably for the enigmatic characters of Tom Bombadil and Treebeard. Each of them is very old, very wise, and like Väinämöinen, Treebeard and Bombadil are intimately tied to their respective lands and yet are mysterious and not completely understood by mere mortals.

Väinämöinen's adventures are fantastic, outrageous, funny, sad, and frequently impossible, such as when he spends time in the intestines of a dead wizard and refuses to leave until said wizard teaches him the magical runes he's looking for! He's a fascinating character, both in traditional myths and in Lönnrot's literary construction. You'll get to know him much better in the following pages.

## UKKO

Ukko, whose name means "old man," is the Finnish god of the sky and thunder. Indeed, the Finnish word *ukkonen* derives from Ukko and means "thunder." Of course, we've already met a god of thunder, Thor, and it's possible that Ukko influenced the character of Thor (or perhaps vice versa), or that they came from a common source.

Like Thor, Ukko wields a mighty weapon, a hammer known as Ukonvasara, or "Ukko's hammer," which is not an overly original name, but does the job. Sometimes his weapon is depicted as an axe or even a sword, and he uses it to create lighting. This description reveals another obvious connection to Thor's Mjolnir, and might well represent an earlier form of the myth that was grafted onto the Germanic god Thunor at some point, or perhaps Thor's own tales influenced Ukko. Throughout Finland, archeologists have found pendants and charms that resemble Thor's hammer, the Mjolnir pendants that the Norse also wore.

It's possible that Ukko, in combination with the great Finnish smith god Ilmarinen, either had an influence on the character of Thor, or that they came from a common source. Ukko seems to have supplanted Ilmarinen as a major god of the Finns at some point, and Ilmarinen became "downgraded" to a powerful, but mortal, hero.

If Thor was fully formed as the Germanic god Thunor, then any influence would have had to be much earlier in time, though it's also possible that Thor took on some of his more familiar aspects during and after the migration period, and that he was combined with Ukko Ilmari to create a new hybrid god. But again, maybe not. It's all a tantalizing mystery!

Indeed, Ukko appears to have mythological connections to deities in several traditions. Ukko could have some deep Indo-European roots or distant relations to gods like Zeus in Greece and Indra in India. However, given that the Finno-Ugric languages are not of Indo-European origin, those connections might well be minimal. He could also be related to the Estonian god Taara, whose name also bears a strong resemblance to Thor. In another link, it's possible that Ukko is related to the Sámi god Aijeke, whether by borrowing or by a connection lost over time. Aijeke was equated with another Sámi god, Horagalles, and both were gods of thunder who wielded hammers. Thor-Taara-Horagalles ... it doesn't take too much imagination to see the similarities between these various northern thunder gods, though we'll probably never know the full extent of their relationships to each other. In another etymological connection, the name Perkele, which is related to the names of Baltic thunder gods (though condemned as a devil in Christian times), might be yet another word for Ukko.

Perhaps all of this confusion stems from the fact that the Finns used the word Ukko to refer to any god, rather than one specifically.

Some scholars have speculated that Christian storytellers elevated his status so that an eternal sky god was the most important in the collection of Finnish deities. Indeed, Ukko was also sometimes known as Ylijumala, "Supreme God," which suggests Christian overlay. The Christian church certainly would have approved of elevating Ukko to the status of a "father of heaven," while at the same time trying to wipe out any genuine belief in these gods. They might have even used Ukko as a model for a supreme god that the Finns could look to when converting.

In the *Kalevala*, several powerful figures look to Ukko for assistance and guidance. In the very first rune, the primordial mother goddess Ilmatar calls upon Ukko for help, which could well indicate a move to diminish her power by elevating the male sky god above the creator goddess:

> "Ukko, O God, up yonder,
>
> You the ruler of the heavens,
>
> Come here, I need you,
>
> Come here, I implore you,
>
> To deliver me from trouble,
>
> To deliver me in travail.
>
> Come I pray you, hasten here,
>
> Hasten more that you are needed,
>
> Hasten and help this helpless maiden!"
>
> (Rune I)

In a similar manner, our hero Väinämöinen prays to Ukko for rain to bring life to the fields he has sown:

> "Ukko, O God, above,
>
> You, O Father of the heavens,
>
> You that lives high in Ether,
>
> Curb all the clouds of heaven,
>
> Hold in the air your counsel,
>
> Hold in the clouds good counsel."
>
> (Rune II)

Väinämöinen also speaks of Ukko as the prime creator and maker of iron:

> "I know well the source of metals,
>
> I know the origin of iron;
>
> I can tell how steel is fashioned.
>
> Of the mothers, air is oldest,

Water is the oldest brother,

And the fire is second brother,

And the youngest brother is iron;

Ukko is the first creator.

Ukko, maker of the heavens,

Cut apart the air and water,

Before the metal and iron were born."

(Rune IX)

As is often the case, we don't know how many of Ukko's qualities as we have them today are pre-Christian and how many were invented later on or invented by Lönrott in his retellings.

Regardless of his origins and connections, Ukko seems to have been widely worshiped and revered, though he usually only manifested in the form of natural phenomena, which were signs for the faithful. As a god of thunder and rain, he would have controlled weather, so people directed their prayers for rain and good harvests to him. If the rains came, it was a sign of the god's favor. And that was probably all the people really needed from him.

## LOUHI/LOVIATAR

Louhi is the matriarch of the northern land of Pohjola, and a main figure in the epic. The *Kalevala* describes her as a toothless witch with an ugly and horrible visage. She can change her shape and create powerful spells and enchantments, for good or ill, and can also affect the weather and even the course of the sun and moon. She is often the enemy of Väinämöinen and other heroes, and battles with him over the coveted Sampo.

Despite her fearsome appearance, she has various beautiful daughters, the Maidens of Pohjola, who attract the attention

of Finnish heroes, including Ilmarinen and Väinämöinen. But Louhi will not let these daughters go, unless their would-be suitors complete nearly impossible tasks, Hercules-style. Thus, she represents temptation and perhaps the troubles and burdens that can come with it.

She is also spiteful, and at one point late in the narrative, she succeeds in stealing the sun, moon, and fire, and only gives them back when faced with death.

> Louhi, hostess of Pohjola,
>
> Northland's old and toothless wizard,
>
> Makes the Sun and Moon her captives;
>
> In her arms she takes the fair Moon
>
> From her cradle in the birch-tree,
>
> Calls the Sun down from its station,
>
> From the fir-tree's bending branches,
>
> Carries them to upper Northland,
>
> To the dark Sariola;
>
> She hides the Moon, no more to glimmer,
>
> In a rock of many colors;
>
> She hides the Sun, to shine no longer,
>
> In the iron-banded mountain;
>
> Thereupon these words she utters:
>
> "Moon of gold and Sun of silver,
>
> Hide your faces in the caverns
>
> Of Pohjola's dismal mountain;
>
> Shine no more to gladden Northland,
>
> Till I come to give you freedom ..."
>
> When the golden Moon had vanished,
>
> And the silver Sun had hidden

In the iron-banded caverns,

Louhi stole the fire from Northland,

From the regions of Väinölä,

Left the mansions cold and cheerless,

And the cabins full of darkness.

Night was king and reigned unbroken,

Darkness ruled in Kalevala,

Darkness in the home of Ukko.

(Rune XLVII)

She was probably originally the same being as the goddess Loviatar, but Lönnrot made them into two different characters. It's likely that the two names were used in different regions and times but described the same being.

In the *Kalevala*, Loviatar is a blind goddess of disease and death, and is the daughter of Tuoni, a goddess of death herself. Rune XLV of the *Kalevala* relates how she was impregnated by the wind and gave birth to nine children, or rather, nine diseases (here we see the number nine as being significant, just as we did in the Norse myths). Some magical spells in Finnish tradition call for the disease of the afflicted to be returned to Loviatar, who sent it. But other folk traditions say that Louhi is the mother of these diseases, further showing their connection and perhaps that they were the same figure.

Existing descriptions of Loviatar's evil nature could well be Christian-era attempts to rewrite her story and demonize her. Originally, she might not have been a bringer of disease at all. In fact, the name Loviatar might derive from the Finnish *langeta loveen*, a trance state, which would make her nature something more akin to a goddess of an underworld transformation. The underworld of this older, primal cosmology would be a place for the spirit to go for deep soul-level healing, as facilitated by an experienced practitioner in making those journeys. In this way, she might even have connections to the Sámi Noaides or to shamanic-style trance work from farther east. And of course, this practice calls to mind the Seidr magic of the Norse.

In another point that suggests she was not originally a villain, her name might come from the Finnish *lovi*, meaning entry, door, or even vagina. As a goddess of female mysteries and transformation, and perhaps feminine power over sexuality and procreation, we can see why missionaries would want to demonize her and turn her into a malevolent hag that brought death and disease.

Suggestions of such power and divine feminine qualities would have been anathema to the Christian missionaries seeking to impose their new faith over these older female-centered folk beliefs and traditions. Louhi-Lovitar, the goddess of the underworld, was an easy target to demonize and make into a denizen of the Christian hell, an evil witch or spirit that brought the world's ills with her.

Sadly, it is likely this malevolent version of the goddess that ended up in the *Kalevala*, and earlier traces of her are hard to identify.

## JUMALA AND PERKELE

In pagan times, the name Jumala was probably given to a sky god, and similar names are also found among the Baltic peoples for their sky gods, indicating that Jumala was probably a popular deity worshiped across the eastern Baltic regions, as well as Finland. To the east, the Permians of modern-day northwest Russia worshiped a similar god, and two Old Norse sagas refer to a god named Jómali that was honored in that same area. Jómali might have been a Sámi god, as well. In Finland, Jumala seems to have been replaced by Ukko, or at least the god's name changed, if not his role. Eventually, "Jumala" became more of a generic term for any god.

It's also possible that a feminine form of Jumala existed in Slavic belief, especially in the Ural Mountains; this makes sense if the word and its relations were generic terms for any deity. If so, Jumala might have been seen as a goddess. It's also possible that some peoples saw Jumala as genderless or androgynous, not unlike the enigmatic Ymyr at the beginning of the Norse creation story. Could Jumala have been a primal, maybe even prehistoric, non-gendered deity that gradually took on other identities to suit different needs and times?

The meaning of "Jumala" changed yet again with the arrival of Christianity. What's remarkable is that it survived, and that Finnish Christians adapted the word to refer to their own new god. They likely understood that it was a kind of all-purpose word for a powerful deity, and encouraged its use to make conversion more appealing to pagan Finns.

If there weren't already enough meanings for the word, in the *Kalevala*, Jumala can refer both to a god and to the realm of the gods, where it means something like "Thunder Home," which immediately calls to mind Thrudheim, Thor's home. In Rune IX, we read of Väinämöinen offering up a prayer to the supreme god, Ukko:

> Then the ancient Väinämöinen
>
> Raised his eyes to high Jumala,
>
> He looked with gratitude to heaven,
>
> Looked on high, in joy and gladness,
>
> Then addressed omniscient Ukko.

Here, the god Ukko and Jumala are separate, and it seems as if the idea of an all-knowing god is a Christian overlay in the text. Likewise, in Rune XV:

> Now the Sun retires in magic,
>
> Hovers here and there a moment
>
> Over Tuoni's hapless sleepers,

Hastens upward to his station,

To his Jumala home and kingdom.

So even in the old poetry, the word could mean both a god and the realm of the gods.

A bit of trivia: The modern Finnish phrase Jumala siunatkoon sinua, "God bless you," might seem an appropriate response to a sneeze, but Finns will often instead say, terveydeksi, or "for health."

Perkele, on the other hand, means a kind of evil spirit, mainly in the eastern, Karelian languages and dialects. However, during and after Christianization, the name also became associated with the devil. Early Finnish translations of the Bible referred to Satan as Perkele, presumably to drive home the point that the church wanted everyone to avoid him.

The name Perkele has some similarities with Pellervo and Pellonpekko (both gods of agriculture and crops whom we'll meet later), and it is possible that at one time Perkele was a weather god and perhaps a variation of Ukko. The name also seems very close to that of the Baltic god, Perkunas, so when the Christian church set about demonizing this figure, he was probably widely worshiped.

A second bit of trivia: These days, *perkele* is a common Finnish swear word, with a meaning anywhere between goddamnit and f*ck, depending on how it's used. Given the wonderful Finnish language and its mesmerizingly long words, this simple swear word can be combined with other letters and words for added emphasis. In any case, going from weather god to everyday swear word seems quite the fall!

# ILMARINEN

Ilmarinen is one of the main heroes of the *Kalevala*, along with Väinämöinen and Lemminkäinen, though there is little to distinguish him from a god. Indeed, he is a master blacksmith and maker, the greatest in all the lands. He is in some ways an equivalent to the Greek god Hephaestus and the Roman Vulcan. He can create almost anything from any metal, including gold, iron, silver, copper, and brass. Perhaps most importantly, he forges the magical and coveted Sampo (more about that on page 340), which becomes the object of quest and even obsession for several characters in the *Kalevala*.

As we've seen, the word ilma means "air" or sometimes "weather" in Finnish, which speaks to the likely origins of Ilmarinen as a kind of sky god. In fact, Agricola identifies him as such. Ilmarinen might even resemble and have some connection to Thor and the other weather gods, wielding a smith's hammer and being of the sky. He might well be related to Ilmaris, the eastern Sámi god of storms, before he became a "mere" hero in the Finnish epic. Many ancient Finns probably saw him as the creator and builder of the very world and the cosmos.

Rune IX of the *Kalevala* tells us that he first came to Earth to work iron:

> Then the blacksmith, Ilmarinen
>
> Came to earth to work the metal;
>
> He was born on the Coal-mount,
>
> And skilled and nurtured in the coal-fields;
>
> In one hand, he had a copper hammer,
>
> In the other, tongs of iron.
>
> He was born in the night
>
> And in the morning he built his smithy,
>
> He looked with care for a favored hill,

Where the winds might fill his bellows;
He found it in the swamp-lands,
Where the abundant iron hid;
There he built his smelting furnace,
There he laid his leather bellows,
He hastened where the wolves had traveled,
Followed where the bears had trampled,
And found the iron's young formations,
In the wolf-tracks of the marshes,
And in the footprints of the gray-bear.

At first, iron is afraid of him and of his fire, but Ilmarinen calms the metal's fears, telling it that fire will not destroy it, but rather will allow it to transform into greater things:

"Be not frightened, useful metal,
Surely Fire will not consume you,
Will not burn his youngest brother,
Will not harm his nearest kindred.
Come to my room and furnace,
Where the fire is freely burning.
You will live, and grow, and prosper,
You will become the swords of heroes,
And Buckles for the belts of women."

Indeed, Ilmarinen has such great skills that Väinämöinen praises him to Louhi, telling her that his work in crafting the very sky itself is so fine that no one can even see a trace of the smith's marks left behind:

"I will send you Ilmarinen,
He will forge the Sampo for you,

Hammer the lid for you in colors,

He may win your lovely maiden;

Ilmarinen is a worthy smith,

In this art, he is the first and master;

He, the one who forged the heavens

He forged for the air a hollow cover;

Nowhere can we see hammer-traces,

Nowhere can we find a single tongs-mark."

(Rune VII)

Various other songs speak of Ilmarinen's skill, saying that his forge has no windows or even a door. He creates all his own tools from his clothing and can use his knee in place of an anvil, which must hurt!

But for all his skill, he is unlucky in love. He loses his beloved wife to the cursed man Kullervo (see page 367), and later tries to make another woman out of gold, perhaps reasoning that there is nothing he cannot build. But of course, he fails, so he tries to give this metallic woman to Väinämöinen to be his companion instead, which doesn't work at all.

## LEMMINKÄINEN (AHTI SAARELAINEN, KAUKOMIELI)

Lemminkäinen, along with Väinämöinen and Ilmarinen, is another hero of the *Kalevala* who isn't necessarily divine, although he knows magic and uses it to his advantage. And that's the problem; Lemminkäinen is arrogant, impetuous, risk-taking, and ignores advice from his mother on several occasions. And it comes back to bite him on the rear. He is also very handsome and all the young ladies swoon over him, which he loves! This only makes him that much more full of himself. Believing himself as the gods' gift to the ladies, he sets out to win the heart of the beautiful Kyllikki. She wants nothing to do with him, but he persists in pursuing and eventually marrying her, and that only makes what follows more tragic. After their marriage disintegrates, he searches for another bride, a foolish quest that ends in his death ... at least for a while. He's definitely not the most sympathetic of heroes.

Lemminkäinen serves as a warning about the brashness of youth and failing to listen to those around them. His attempts to win gold and glory for himself end in miserable failures, and ultimately cost him his life. It's only because his long-suffering mother cares enough about him that she is able, with assistance, to bring him back from the dead, but not without a stern lecture telling him that he must change his terrible behavior.

Interestingly, Lemminkäinen bears some resemblance to the Norse god Baldr. Both are young, very good looking, and desired by many while being imbued with magic and divine energy. Both have very caring and concerned mothers who try to keep them from harm. And while Snorri depicts Baldr as more of a gentle Christ-like figure, Saxo's account portrays him as a warrior, and one with a bit of an attitude, which as we've seen, might reflect another strand of old myths that haven't survived elsewhere.

Another similarity between Baldr and Lemminkäinen is that both meet their deaths at the hand of a blind man: Baldr accidentally, and Lemminkäinen due to a desire for revenge. Both are pierced by a weapon (mistletoe for Baldr and a viper's fangs for Lemminkäinen) against which they don't have any protection. Their mothers lament for them and try everything they can to bring them back. But while Frigg fails to revive Baldr, Lemminkäinen's mother succeeds, with the help of various gods. She finds pieces of his body in a river and sets about gathering them up so that the gods can stitch him back together. This portion of the tale bears a striking resemblance to the myth of the Egyptian goddess Isis finding the parts of Osiris' dismembered body and reassembling them, though this ancient account probably had

no direct influence on the Finnish version. Rather, it speaks to the universality of certain types of story and symbolism.

Various scholars have speculated that Lemminkäinen's ordeals resemble those of some of the shamans of northeastern Asia. Their spirits travel far and in some cases they are torn apart and have to be reassembled for the shaman to emerge whole. In contrast, Lemminkäinen misuses his power and is filled with bravado, so perhaps his story is a warning. If his death weren't enough to encourage caution, in some versions of the story, he is unable to come back to life.

Indeed, while the *Kalevala* tells one version of Lemminkäinen's misadventures in the north, there are others, including a tale where he makes the journey to Pohjola to attend a celebration and is confronted with the grisly sight of human heads stuck on stakes outside of the hall. It's a scene that seems more at home in a tale from Norse mythology. One of the stakes has no head on it, which might be an ominous sign for the fate of one about to crash a party! In both versions of the myth, Lemminkäinen ends up dead and dismembered. His attempt to barge in on a party where he is not wanted also calls to mind Loki returning to Aegir's feast to insult all the gods and goddesses and nearly coming to blows. In Lemminkäinen's case, fighting actually does erupt, and in most versions, it goes badly for him.

We can't know for sure what strands of story traveled where and wove their way into new tales far from their homeland. Whether the figure of Lemminkäinen was influenced by myths of nearby cultures, or grew up in the imaginations of the Finns themselves, his stories are a reminder about becoming too filled with one's own sense of greatness and entitlement.

One last thing about our brash hero: after his embarrassing defeat, death, and resurrection, his mother chastises him and tells him to return to their farm and get back to work, and hopefully learn some humility. Sorry, Mom!

# JOUKAHAINEN

Like Lemminkäinen, Joukahainen is something of a brat, an arrogant young man who thinks far more highly of himself than he should. He fancies himself as a rival to Väinämöinen, and as you might imagine, things go wrong very quickly when he tries to challenge the old wizard. Against the advice of his mother (naturally!), he boldly strides off south to engage Väinämöinen in a contest of magic, and he quickly learns that he's no match for the old man.

Väinämöinen gets so irritated with him that he sings the poor kid into a swamp, forcing Joukahainen to offer him many things in order to free himself, including marriage to his sister, Aino. Of course, neither Joukahainen nor Väinämöinen ever asks Aino what she thinks of the deal. But that's another whole problem with its own tragic consequences, as Väinämöinen soon realizes, much to his regret.

In myths and poems outside of the *Kalevala*, the rivalry between Joukahainen and Väinämöinen takes many forms. In one version of their story, the two are brothers—sons of a goddess named Ito or Iro (quite possibly Ilmatar)—and are both present at the creation of the world. They're also siblings of Ilmarinen the smith.

Brothers or not, Joukahainen and Väinämöinen usually begin their stories as friends, but always end up as rivals and even enemies, with their conflicts often coming to blows. Indeed, in yet another version of the creation myth, the world is actually created when Joukahainen shoots Väinämöinen with a crossbow and causes him to fall into the ocean. Even though this is quite a different tale from the one found in the *Kalevala*, some of the bigger details are the same, suggesting that, as with the Norse myths, different versions of these stories circulated in different regions and at various times throughout Finnish pagan history.

The enmity between these two might have been based on real-life mistrust, hostility, and conflicts, possibly between the Finns and the Sámi people. Some stories refer to Joukahainen as Lappalainen, a Finnish word for the Sámi people, though in some regions the term is used to describe anyone who lives in the far north. Lappalainen tends to have some negative meanings, and the far north is said to be the land of cold, misery, and the dead. In the minds of the ancient Finns, the people who lived there must therefore have been strange and dangerous. The word found its way into common usage, such that the Sámi were referred to as Lapps, and their homeland as Lapland. However, the Sámi consider these words to be derogatory, and they shouldn't be used now.

In the *Kalevala*, Joukahainen offers up his sister Aino to Väinämöinen, in order to be free of the wizard's trap. But Aino seems not to have been a character in Finnish myth and folklore before the creation of the *Kalevala*. The word means "only," as in an only child, but there is no Aino in the earlier poetry with a capital "A" as a defined character. There are folktales that have similar stories to how she is portrayed in the *Kalevala*, but they are not connected to Joukahainen. It might well be that Lönrott concocted the idea of an "only" sister to Joukahainen and gave her the word as a proper name. It worked, because Aino is now a popular girl's name in Finland!

## KULLERVO

Like Joukahainen, Kullervo is a mortal man, not a god or demi-god, though he is protected by magic to some degree and knows his own share of spells. But on the surface, he is little more than a hot-headed young man, whose impulsive and angry outbursts bring him misery, ruin, and eventually death. His story is the most tragic of all the *Kalevala* tales. But the tragedy of his life has deeper meaning and invites the reader or listener to ponder on the lessons his story imparts.

Kullervo is damned and cursed from the very beginning of his life, though even as an infant, he is already aware and swears vengeance on those who have wronged his family. He grows up without love and endures much pain and abuse at the hands of his supposed caretakers. As he matures, he becomes increasingly bitter and resentful, focusing on getting what he wants without concern for hurting others. He becomes arrogant, selfish, and irredeemable, and even when he tries to do the right thing, it invariably goes wrong.

This myth is quite striking, for it shows the consequences of childhood abuse and neglect. Kullervo is obviously talented, good-looking, and has real promise for whatever he might decide to do, but his past and his horrid treatment at the hands of his abusers mean that he will forever be tainted by their actions. This is a curse far worse than any magic that could be laid upon him.

At the end of his tale, he takes his own life, having lost everything. When Väinämöinen hears about his fate, he laments the loss:

> "O, you unborn nations,
>
> Never nurse your children with evil,
>
> Never give them over to strangers,
>
> Never trust them to the foolish!
>
> If the child is not well nurtured,
>
> Is not rocked and led well,
>
> Though he grows into manhood,
>
> And has a strong body,
>
> He will never know discretion,
>
> He will never eat the bread of honor,
>
> And never drink the cup of wisdom."
>
> (Rune XXXVI)

It's a strikingly modern call to make sure that children are nurtured, loved, and properly cared for, and it is almost unique in northern mythology.

Kullervo's story partially inspired Tolkien to create his tragic hero from the First Age of Middle Earth, Túrin Turambar. He too lived under a curse, and things always went tragically wrong for him. In the end, like Kullervo, he confronts the awful shame of unknowingly having had sex with his sister, and he falls on his sword and kills himself, just as Kullervo does.

## TUONETAR, TUONI, AND TUONELA

Tuonetar and her husband, Tuoni, rule over Tuonela, the Underworld. The two seem to embody evil and the darkness of death, though how much of this was due to Christianization is uncertain. Tuoni is said to be the very personification of darkness, while no surviving sources describe Tuonetar, though some sources suggest that she might be beautiful to look at or hideous beyond comprehension. Both of them have created pestilence, darkness, and monsters.

Tuonela is comparable to the Norse Hel and the Greek Hades, in that everyone goes there after they die; it is neither punishment nor reward for one's deeds in life. That said, it appears to be full of perils and terrible things created by Tuonetar, which Christians might have seen as similar to their own Hell. However, earlier versions of Finnish myth seemed to have portrayed it as a less fearsome place. We are not told what kind of realm it is for the souls who dwell there, and whether it is one for punishment or happiness.

Located in the northernmost part of the world, Tuonela is not easily accessed, and the dead must cross a dark river to get there, either by swimming, crossing a bridge as narrow as a thread, or by being ferried by Tuonen Tyttö ("Tuoni's Girl"), who is a daughter

of Tuonetar and Tuoni. To make matters even more difficult, a black swan guards the river, singing spells of death. Charming.

Once either the dead or the living have entered Tuonela, they are not permitted to return to the land of the living. Only the children of Tuonetar and Tuoni can roam other worlds freely. If someone who is still alive does try to reach Tuonela, they must make a dangerous journey through a thorn-infested forest, and are greeted with a not-so-warm welcome from the creature known as Surma, described as a dog-like creature that has a snake for a tail and can turn victims to stone with its gaze. Surma is a bit like the Greek Cerberus, a three-headed dog who guards Hades, and also resembles Medusa, who can turn mortals to stone with just a look. Surma, of course, also resembles the Norse hound, Garmr. Surma serves Kalma, a goddess of death and decay whose very name means "The Stench of Corpses."

Of course, stories tell of living gods and heroes crossing into Tuonela and trying to return.

The mighty Väinämöinen journeys to the underworld on a quest for three specific magic words, but he is barely able to escape. Here we also see parallels to the story of the Norse god Baldr, who is unable to leave the realm of Hel. While in Tuonela, Väinämöinen encounters Tuonetar, who challenges him with an assortment of magical ordeals. But even so, Väinämöinen escapes. When he returns to the land of the living, Väinämöinen cautions the people to live virtuous lives so that they can avoid Tuonela. But how can one avoid Tuonela if all the dead are destined to go there? Perhaps Christians interpreted the Underworld as a parallel to their own Hell, and transformed the story of Väinämöinen into one of a warning to teach morality.

While Väinämöinen is in the realm of the dead, Tuonetar offers a goblet of beer that is said to induce forgetfulness, so that he will not remember his former life. But on inspection, Väinämöinen finds that this brew is far more horrid than it might have first appeared!

# MIELIKKI

Mielikki is a goddess of the forest, the hunt, and of all those who rely on the forest for their lives, such as by gathering berries, mushrooms, and other wild foods. Her name probably derives from *mielu*, meaning "luck," or "to please," which might indicate her popularity among those who lived close to the land. Mortals prayed to her for successful hunts, sometimes by whistling or singing their praises. She is also a healer, especially of animals, and people with injured or sick livestock would pray to her for their relief. She protects cattle grazing in the forest from wild animal attacks and other misfortune, if she favors those who own them.

She was believed to have played a major part in the creation of the first bear, Otso (or Otho), further showing her strong connection to nature, especially the wilderness. When the great god Ukko cast hair and wool down from the heavens, Mielikki took it and fashioned it into a new animal, the bear. She asked that it be given teeth and claws as protection, and she herself gave it a fondness for honey, which was abundant as a food source in the woodlands. And so, bears love honey to this day.

Some legends said that her beauty was too powerful to be viewed by mortals, and so she hid herself in a cloak and a hat, so as not to overwhelm them. Mortals who saw her might have even thought they'd seen an old man in the distance. Here we see a curious similarity to Odin, who was known to walk about in a cloak and hat, and who, as we've seen, wandered about Midgard for many different reasons. Though the two are probably unrelated, it is an interesting coincidence. Did northern woodland travelers who thought they caught a glimpse of an old man in the sylvan distance actually see Mielikki ... or even Odin?

In other accounts, when hunters prayed to her for a successful hunt, she might appear to them in one of two ways: if their hunt was destined to be successful, she could show herself to them as a beautiful woman (though presumably not too overwhelming!)

dressed in gold and silver. But if the hunt was meant to fail, she would appear as an old hag dressed in rags, an ill omen, indeed! She is said to be the keeper of a key to a chest filled with honey, a gift to the forest spirits (and maybe to bears?). Any mortal that finds this chest would be blessed indeed, and it would guarantee their success and the favor of those woodland spirits. Indeed, the hero Lemminkäinen prays to her with these words:

"Mistress of the woods, Mielikki,

Forest-mother, formed in beauty,

Let your gold flow out abundant,

Let your silver wander onward,

For the hero that is seeking

For the wild-moose of your kingdom;

Bring me here your keys of silver,

From the golden girdle around you;

Open Tapio's rich chambers,

And unlock the forest fortress."

(Rune XIV)

Her status as a patron of hunters and gatherers suggests that she might be a very old goddess, perhaps a survival of a prehistoric figure. Some have likened her to the Norse Skadi, though Mielikki is not limited to the snow and ice of winter. But it is possible that the two have a very ancient common source, assuming that Skadi was always a goddess and not once a god.

Mielikki has several children, including Tellervo, a goddess of the forest, and Tuulikki, a goddess of animals, as well as Annikki, Tyytikki, and Nyyrikki. Their father is Mielikki's husband, Tapio, the great god of the forest, and we now turn to him.

# TAPIO

Tapio, also known as Metsähine or Hiisi, rules over the woodland known as Tapiola, and the ancient Finns revered him as a major god. He shares several qualities with his wife, Mielikki. He is a god of the forest and all its wildlife, as well as hunting and game. He has the power to grant humans a favorable hunt if he so chooses. Hunters saw themselves as guests in his realm and needed to act accordingly. If they took more than their fair share, or wantonly slaughtered the creatures within the woods, they risked his wrath and Mielikki's, as well.

To appease Tapio, hunters would leave offerings at a place called a Tapion pöyta, a "table of Tapio." This might be a simple stump of a tree, or perhaps a bush with a flat(ish) top, on which they could lay offerings, including a portion of the animals that they'd hunted, to acknowledge the gifts of the god and the forest. Those that used the woodlands for activities other than hunting, such as animal grazing, or even gathering, were expected to make offerings to both the god and goddess. It was also a way of appeasing any capricious forest spirits who might be lingering about, waiting to cause mischief! Hunters needed to be very careful to only take what they needed and never kill an unusual-looking or unknown animal, which might be a forest spirit in disguise.

Tapio's appearance is said to be human-like, at least from the front, though his beard might look like wood or bark. From the back, he resembled a gnarled old tree. In this way, he shares a physical similarity with the Green Man in Celtic and English folk belief, though there is probably no direct connection. Rather, his form represents a universal tendency—or even a need—to personify nature in ways that can be better understood.

As with Mielikki, the hero Lemminkainen acknowledges Tapio's presence and dominion over all nature when he praises the god:

"Greetings I bring to the mountains,
Greetings to the vales and uplands,
Greet you, heights with forests covered,
Greet you, ever-verdant fir trees,
Greet you, groves of whitened aspen,
Greetings to those that greet you,
Fields and streams and woods of Lapland.
Bring me favor, mountain woodlands,
Lapland-deserts, show me kindness,
Mighty Tapio, be gracious,
Let me wander through your forests,
Let me glide along your rivers,
Let this hunter search your snow-fields,
Where the wild-moose herds in numbers
Where the bounding reindeer lingers."

(Rune XIV)

For the Finns, the whole world was imbued with spirits and sacredness, which needed to be acknowledged and respected. Tapio and Mielikki were personifications of the objects of that reverence.

## SAMPSA PELLERVOINEN

Sampsa Pellervoinen, sometimes called Pellervo, is a god of agriculture and vegetation, the first to greet the newborn Väinämöinen (remembering that he was born an old man) and make fertile the barren rocks on which he lands after his birth. As the second Rune of the *Kalevala* states:

Pellervoinen, earth-begotten,
Sampsa, youth of smallest stature,
Came to sow the barren country,
Thickly scattering seeds around him.
Down he stooped to scatter the seeds,
On the land and in the marshes,
Both in flat and sandy regions,
And in hard and rocky places.
On the hills he sowed the pine-trees,
On the knolls he sowed the fir-trees,
And in sandy places heather;
Leafy saplings in the valleys.

(Rune II)

He is a fertility god, who is awakened with the coming of
summer to sow the seeds so that they can grow and be ready for
harvest. He is often depicted as a young man with a sack slung
over his neck and shoulder, or perhaps a basket, in which he carries the seeds of all things that grow. As such, he bears some resemblance to the English folk figure John Barleycorn, and even
to the Norse god Freyr, though direct connections with either
are unlikely. Readers familiar with American folktales might
also see him as a kind of Finnish Johnny Appleseed.

Sampsa's sowing happens near the beginning of Lönnrot's *Kalevala*, in the second rune, right after the emergence of
Väinämöinen, and helps set the stage for Väinämöinen's role as
the chief character of the epic. But earlier versions of the story
state that Sampsa sowed the Earth with the help of pieces of the
Sampo, indicating that it had to have been forged first. This is
another example of conflicting old folk tales existing in different regions, which Lönnrot brought together to create a more
unified story, one that quite possibly never existed among the
ancient Finns.

In the folk tales of Karelia, there is evidence that Sampsa was linked to pre-Christian fertility rites. In them, a young woman must go and awaken Sampsa so that he may scatter his seed and water the lands. In some tales, three young women seek out Sampsa to "awaken" him, one each representing winter, spring, and summer (autumn misses out, presumably because by then, the land is already giving of its bounty). Summer is successful, and by awakening him, she becomes pregnant and will give birth to the fruits of the Earth. The sexual imagery here is obvious. That said, in some versions, the woman who awakens him is his mother or sister. One can imagine that various fertility rituals were connected with this myth, and if so, they seem to have been celebrated in mid- to late June, around midsummer, perhaps to coincide with the solstice or a bit later.

And yet, for all the obvious pagan fertility themes, some suggest that the god's name (though not the god himself) might derive from Saint Sampson the Hospitable of Constantinople, a saint in the Orthodox Church who lived sometime before the sixth century, if he ever lived at all. Perhaps the name "Sampsa Pellervoinen" was a Christian reworking of the original god Pellervo, to downplay his explicit fertility aspects? We will probably never know.

## PELLONPEKKO

Pellonpekko ("Pekko of the Field"), or just Pekko, is a god of fields, barley, and best of all, beer! He was prominent in eastern and southern Finland and Karelia, as well as Estonia, where he was praised for being the first to sow barley and to brew the beer made from it. Indeed, in south central Finland, the word *pekko* once meant beer. The god Pekko might be related to the Baltic god of thunder and lightning Perkūnas, but the similarity of names might be coincidental.

In 1551, Agricola wrote that Pekko was worshiped as the god of barley and beer in Karelia, showing that he never lost his grip on the public's imagination, even long after the lands were officially Christianized. In eastern Finland, it's possible that people worshiped him until the eighteenth century, alongside their Christian observances.

Even as late as the twentieth century, the Seto people in eastern Estonia revered him through their folk traditions. Pekko is a symbol of their pride and identity, and the people see him as a national hero. The Setos would create wood and wax effigies of him, named Peko, and store them in granaries, presumably as protection against mice, fungus, and other ravages of the natural world. They would only publicly display these idols at certain times, such as during key rituals and festivals.

The Setos even integrated worship of the beer god into supposedly Christian rituals, such as Pentecost. Young men would rise before dawn on that day and engage in ritualistic fights. Whoever bled first was obliged to host the ritual feast the next year. The people then lit candles in honor of Peko and chanted to him in the hope that he might drink the beer they had brewed. And then, presumably, they all went off to church.

Interestingly, Estonia's official travel website, "Visit Estonia," assures us that the god is now alive and well again:

"Jumalamägi (God's Hill) is an ancient sacred place of the Setos. [...] In the past, the hill was a place of only local significance and it seemed like it was a thing of the past, but in 2007, the village elder and the locals once again started using it as a sacred place. A local sculptor R. Veeber built the Peko statue on the hill. People visit Peko—fertility god of the Setos—before major undertakings for luck and success. They also make sacrifices there. Locals see the statue as a place of positive energy, which is why it is perfect for charging one's batteries."

Peko would no doubt raise a mug of beer to them in gratitude!

# AHTO AND VELLAMO

Ahto ("Wave Host") is a major god of oceans, lakes, and rivers. Vellamo is his wife, and together they dwell in Ahtola, hidden in black cliffs under the sea.

Ahto in the *Kalevala* is somewhat gloomy and jealous of the gods in the sky, who get more attention than he does. If he feels that he's not being properly worshiped or appeased, he might send his water sprites to stir up whirlpools that wreak havoc on ships, quite possibly sending their crews to a watery doom. Ahto is also said to be greedy for the treasures that fall into the ocean and is reluctant to return them. After parts of the Sampo fall into the ocean, he finds them and has no desire to relinquish them, as is proclaimed in the *Kalevala*:

> Where the Sampo breaks in pieces,
>
> Scatters through the Alue-waters,
>
> In the mighty deeps for ages,
>
> To increase the ocean's treasures,
>
> Treasures for the hosts of Ahto.
>
> Nevermore will there be wanting
>
> Richness for the Ahto-nation,
>
> Never while the moonlight brightens
>
> On the waters of the Northland.
>
> (Rune XLIII)

Further, when Väinämöinen loses his kantele (harp) beneath the waters, he laments:

> "But, alas! My harp lies hidden,
>
> Sunk upon the deep-sea's bottom,
>
> To the salmon's hiding-places,
>
> To the dwellings of the whiting,

To the people of Vellamo,

Where the Northland-pike assemble.

Nevermore will I regain it,

Ahto never will return it,

Joy and music are gone forever!"

(Rune XLIV)

Ahto had a good reason for keeping Väinämöinen's kan-tele, for when he heard the music, he was overcome with joy and emotion:

Ahto, king of all the waters,

Ancient king with a beard of sea-grass,

Raised his head above the billows,

In a boat of water-lilies,

Glided to the coast in silence,

Listened to the wondrous singing,

To the harp of Väinämöinen.

These are the words the sea-king uttered:

"Never have I heard such playing,

Never heard such strains of music,

Never since the sea was fashioned,

As the songs of this enchanter,

This sweet singer, Väinämöinen."

(Rune XLI)

While he covets what falls into the ocean, his greed might simply reflect the understanding among fishermen and others that when something is lost at sea, it is likely gone forever and cannot be recovered.

While Ahto can be selfish and brooding, he can be quite generous. Fishermen prayed to Ahto in the hopes of a good catch

and for safe passage. It was up to the god as to whether he would grant their request or not, though he often did. In one story, when a young shepherd whittling by a river loses his grip on his knife, it falls into the water. He cries and laments his loss, and Ahto, hearing his tears, swims to him, offering to retrieve the knife. But the god decides to test the lad. He first recovers a knife made of gold and offers it up, but the boy says it is not his knife. Ahto then returns to the bottom of the water and comes up again with a silver knife. Again, the boy thanks him but insists it is the wrong blade. Finally, Ahto dives and comes back with the boy's true knife, which he gladly accepts. Ahto then gives him the other two knives as a reward for his honesty.

Ahto's name is very similar to that of Ahti, a folk hero who is also called Saarelainen, or "Islander." There might be a connection between the two, but it's not clear, leaving scholars to speculate. As noted, Elias Lönnrot condensed characters from different poems, often into one, perhaps because their stories were similar, or perhaps just because it made the narrative easier to follow. Ahti and another hero, Kaukomiele, might have been combined and folded into Lemminkäinen, but it's possible that Ahti's adventures are very old, dating back to before the year 1000. His stories involve sea voyages, which might be a clue to his connection to Ahto. He is a warrior who goes to sea (not unlike a Viking), and perhaps there is some Viking influence in his identity.

And just as the Vikings would petition Aegir and Rán for aid, a pagan Finn taking a boat might pray to both Ahto and Vellamo and ask for protection. In the following passage, Vellamo is depicted as being wrathful, perhaps even lying in wait for the chance to sink boats and cause destruction and death. So she must be appeased, or at least implored to leave the sailors alone. The great Väinämöinen beseeches her and her husband:

> "Give me of your oars, O Ahto,
>
> Lend your aid, O King of sea-waves,

Guide as with your helm in safety,

Lay your hand upon the rudder,

And direct our war-ship homeward;

Let the hooks of metal rattle

Over the surging of the billows,

On the white-capped waves' commotion.

"Sea, command your warring forces,

Bid your children to cease their fury!

Ahto, still your surging billows!

Sink, Vellamo, to your slumber,

That our boat may move in safety."

(Rune XLII)

It's not surprising that, like Ahto, Vellamo is a goddess of oceans and lakes. Her name might come from or be related to the old Finnish word velloa, which means "the peaceful movement of waves," though she can be anything but peaceful, if the mood takes her. Her name might connect her to Veen Emo (see the next entry), another goddess or spirit of the waters. It's possible that they were different names for the same goddess, invoked in different regions of Finland for the same purposes.

Vellamo is said to be beautiful and imposing, wearing a dress of blue sea foam. Like Ahto, she demands to be appeased. If she is pleased, she can bring good luck and calm seas, as well as the winds needed to speed sailing ships along their way. She is said to keep a herd of sea cows under the water that she sometimes brings to the surface to graze. Perhaps this is a reference to walruses or seals, sprawled out on the rocks before diving back into the ocean.

As with Ahto, fishermen would appeal to her for a good catch and for trouble-free sea journeys. Whether she would grant these requests was apparently entirely up to her mood at the time, a fitting response for the trickery and capriciousness of the sea, as those who lived from it knew all too well.

Even Väinämöinen once sought to appease her and ask that she set aside her unpredictable ways:

> Väinämöinen, ancient singer,
> Long reflecting, spoke these measures:
> "Dear Vellamo, water-hostess,
> Ancient mother with the reed-breast,
> Come, exchange your water-raiment,
> Change your coat of reeds and rushes
> For the garments I shall give you,
> Light sea-foam, your inner vesture,
> And your outer, moss and sea-grass,
> Fashioned by the wind's fair daughters,
> Woven by the flood's sweet maidens;
> I will give you linen vestments
> Spun from flax of softest fiber,
> Woven by the Moon's white virgins,
> Fashioned by the Sun's bright daughters,
> Fitting raiment for Vellamo!"
>
> (Rune XLVIII)

If the great wizard himself had to appeal to her in such a lavish way, she must have been feared, indeed!

Vellamo is said to have many maidens, spirits who dwell in all of the waters:

> "Where the water-gods may linger,
> Where may rest Vellamo's maidens?"
> Then Untamo thus made answer,
> Lazily he told his dreamings:
> "Over there, the mermaid-dwellings,

Yonder live Vellamo's maidens,

On the headland robed in verdure,

On the forest-covered island,

In the deep, pellucid waters,

On the purple-colored sea-shore;

Yonder is the home of sea-maids,

There the maidens of Vellamo,

Live there in their sea-side chambers,

Rest within their water-caverns,

On the rocks of rainbow colors,

On the juttings of the sea-cliffs."

(Rune V)

The spirits of the waters were sometimes known as Ahto-laiset, meaning "those who live in Ahtola." They were also called the "water people," "Vellamo's people," and "People of the Foam." These include minor goddesses, such as Allotar ("wave-goddess"), Koskenneiti ("cataract-maiden"), and Melatar ("goddess of the helm"). Like Ahto and Vellamo, they could help or hinder those who traversed their realm, so people likely appeased them as well before setting out on a water voyage.

## VEEN EMO

Veen Emo (or Veen Emonen, or Vedenemo), the "Water Mother," also known as Vete-ema to the Estonians and Ved-ava to some Slavic peoples, is a goddess or spirit of the water, who can be both benign and terrifying. Legends say that she resembled something like a mermaid, having the lower body of a fish and the upper body of a beautiful woman. Some believed that she was a true goddess, while some accounts suggest that she was the powerful spirit of a drowned woman. It's possible that she was also seen as a personification of the element of water itself.

Belief in her presence was especially strong in Karelia. A Karelian legend says that she is the kindly water spirit of a woman whose husband drowned while out fishing. Filled with remorse, she still waits for him to return, and in the meantime, she offers protection to others on the water so that they will not fall to the same fate.

She was once worshiped and placated by fishermen and those whose lives depended on the sea or other bodies of water, of which there are plenty in Finland. People would pray to her for good catches or for safety from the waters, and they might offer up a portion of their catch to her in thanks. They also placed self-imposed restrictions on the kinds of fish they could catch or how many they could take.

While anyone going on the water might seek to appease her, if they actually caught sight of her while out in their boats it was usually a bad omen, perhaps that she would take someone and drown them. It's possible that she acted rather like a Greek siren, trying to lure sailors toward her and off their courses, unless she favored them. Or perhaps she demanded occasional sacrifices in order to provide a good catch or a successful voyage.

Other tales speak of her as Vendenemo, a grotesque creature that dwells underwater, whether in the ocean or in the thousands of lakes in Finland. This belief might be a result of the degrading and demonization of the pagan gods by Christianity, or it might represent a dual tradition held by people living in different areas. In this version, she more closely resembles a fish with legs, almost a mermaid in reverse, and is responsible for many deaths and disappearances on the waters.

She could also appear as an octopus or squid-like creature. One nineteenth-century legend tells of how a captain tried to find two of his lost sailors at sea. He describes Vendenemo as repulsive, having a human head with tentacles, perhaps like one of H.P. Lovecraft's most famous horrific creations, Cthulhu. This depiction might also be related to legends of the kraken, the monstrous squid of the open ocean that explorers long feared. Indeed, the captain in question only returns home with one of his missing sailors; Vendenemo devours the other whole.

Another tale relates that Vendenemo is actually the daughter of the ruler of Karelia. She falls in love with a man (who in some sources is Väinämöinen), but will not marry him unless he can build a stone castle for her in a single night. Despite the unreasonable request, Väinämöinen is prepared to give it a go. But a sorcerer tricks him in his attempt, and he is unable to finish the task. Vendenemo is bitterly disappointed and flees into the woods, where she transforms into a fish (as one does), and thereafter lives in the waters.

Clearly, she represents a powerful force that is connected to all kinds of water, and the various versions of who and what she is demonstrate the awe and fear that humans have had for the ocean and for other bodies of water for thousands of years. As seen in Veen Emo and Vedenemo, water is both life and death.

## IKU-TURSO (TURSAS)

Iku-Turso, "the eternal Turso," also known as Tursas, is the Tavastian (southern Finnish) god of war and strife. You might notice a similarity in his name to the Norse Tyr and the Germanic Tîwaz. Since Mikael Agricola connects Tursas to war, we can't be completely sure if he was a war god, or if this was Agricola's invention. As is so often the case, this god might have been seen differently in different regions and times. But he almost certainly has a connection with water, as so many Finnish deities and spirits do.

It's possible that his name is also connected to the Old Norse thurs and the proto-Germanic *Þurisaz, both being words for jötunn, though whether this is a direct borrowing or if they simply have a common ancestor is not known. Further, the old

Finnish word tursas means "walrus," so it's possible that there is some link between these animals and jötnar in popular belief. Indeed, Iku-Turso was seen as a malevolent and bearded god or monster of the sea, so some might well have envisioned him as a giant walrus, an animal known to be fierce and dangerous to sailors. Interestingly, the modern Finnish word tursas means octopus, again reinforcing the aquatic nature of this god/being.

Some runes and poems say that he is the father of the nine diseases that are the children of Loviatar, and there seems to be a general agreement about his evil nature. He is another malevolent force lying in wait to take the unwary into a watery doom, the fear of which must have been a constant preoccupation with the ancient Finns in their land of so many thousands of lakes and rivers.

Some traditions suggest that he, under the name Meritursas Partalainen, is the one who makes Ilmatar pregnant. If so, then he is the father of Väinämöinen, which might help explain some of the wizard's great powers. Though thankfully, Väinämöinen doesn't take after his father!

Indeed, the old man must undo the trouble caused by this watery menace. The second rune of the *Kalevala* tells us:

> Väinämöinen, the ancient hero,
> Spies four maidens in the distance,
> Water-brides, he spies a fifth,
> On the soft and sandy sea-shore,
> Near the forests of the island.
> Some were mowing, some were raking,
> Raking what was mown together.
>
> From the ocean rose a giant,
> Mighty Tursas, tall and hardy,
> He pressed compactly all the grasses,

That the maidens had been raking,

And kindled a fire within them,

And the flames shot up to heaven,

Till the lines of hay burned to ashes,

In the ashes of the windrows,

The giant places tender leaves,

In these leaves he plants an acorn,

From the acorn, quickly sprouting,

Grows an oak-tree, tall and stately,

The oak-tree's many branches spread,

Rounds itself a broad corona,

Raises it above the storm-clouds;

Far it stretches out its branches,

It stops the white-clouds in their courses,

With its branches it hides the sunlight,

With its many leaves, the moonbeams,

And the starlight dies in heaven.

Tursas plants an oak to blot out the sun and the sky, and Väinämöinen must kill the tree to bring them back. Later, the two are in conflict again, and Väinämöinen seizes him by the ears, asking him:

"Iku-Turso, son of Old-age,

Why do you rise from the waters?"

(Rune XLII)

Iku-Turso admits that he was trying to deprive the people of the magical Sampo and return it:

Iku-Turso gave this answer:

"I came here with the intention

To destroy the Kaleva heroes,
And return the magic Sampo
To the people of Pohjola."
(Rune XLII)

But he knows that even he cannot defeat the mighty wizard (possibly his own son), and so he offers a bargain:

"If you will restore my freedom,
Spare my life, from pain and sorrow,
I will retrace my journey,
And nevermore show my visage
To the people of Väinölä,
Never while the moonlight glimmers
On the hills of Kalevala!"
(Rune XLII)

Väinämöinen agrees to this and sends him back to his castle deep beneath the sea, commanding of him:

"Iku-Turso, son of Old-age,
Nevermore arise from the ocean,
Nevermore let the Northland-heroes
See your face above the waters."
Nevermore has Iku-Turso
Risen to the ocean-level;
Never since have Northland sailors
Seen the head of this sea-monster.
(Rune XLII)

Väinämöinen banishes this malevolent creature beneath the waves, which seems curious if Iku-Turso is indeed the same god that Agricola writes of. Again, we are probably looking at two (or more) different traditions from pagan Finnish lore. It's possible that belief in Iku-Turso as a god predates Iku-Turso as a sea demon, which likely developed during Christian times.

This ancient god to whom sailors once made offerings in hopes of being left alone might have been downgraded over time, such that Väinämöinen was able to extract a great promise from him. Is he the great wizard's father? Perhaps in some traditions, but not all.

## PÄIVÄTÄR AND KUUTAR

Päivätär and Kuutar are the goddesses of the sun and moon respectively, and some might also have thought of them as twins. Their names derive, quite simply, from the old Finnish päivä, meaning "sun," and *kuu* meaning "moon." As with Norse belief, the sun is a goddess, but unlike Norse myth, the moon is as well. They are feminine personifications of the natural forces. Therefore, it's not clear if they were formally worshiped, or simply invoked by people in times of need. Certainly, sun worship is one of the most ancient of all religious expressions, so there's no reason to think that the pagan or prehistoric Finns didn't engage in it at some point. But whether they made a connection to the specific goddess Päivätär for rituals, we don't know.

Päivätär might also be identical to a goddess named Auringotar, the creator of fire, since both names have the same meaning. As we've seen, gods often had many names. Päivätär and Kuutar were possibly two of the goddesses whose breast milk led to the creation of iron, allowing the smith Ilmarinen to make many wonderful things (see page 281), though this is not certain.

Even with their unclear connections to other deities, we do know that these two goddesses own the silver of the sun and gold of the moon (an interesting reversal of what one might think the colors should be), and they can spin these magical hues into beautiful thread, from which they can make equally beautiful clothing. Sometimes, if one is lucky, one can catch a glimpse of them in the sky doing their work. The girls and young women of Kalevala would sometimes ask them for gifts of gold and silver, perhaps when they were hoping to be married, or needed to present themselves in a showy way.

Some scholars think that these two might have a connection to fate and might also be associated with Ilmatar, in which case the three of them would have some resemblance to the Norse Norns, though how true this is, or if it was something widely believed in pagan Finland, is not known. Other traditions have these same three connected with other goddesses, so there might have been more than three beings together at any one time. This undermines the theory of a possible connection to the Norns, who were always three in number. But the fact that they all weave might well have some significance.

One myth says that a great cherry tree was created by the golden and silver tears cried by the sun and moon. This tree was an axis of the cosmos, and it's tempting to see a connection not only to the Norse Yggdrasil, but also to Freya's golden tears. Again, we are looking at localized traditions that might not have been widely spread beyond a given area, but it is interesting to think that Finnish tradition might have influenced Norse, or the opposite. However, during the period of Christianization, there was likely some attempt to replace them.

Given her association with the sun, Päivätär might also have been a goddess of light and daytime, which would also connect her to her opposite, Kuutar. Interestingly, she is also associated with bees (and other stinging insects). Some surviving spells invoke the protection of both goddesses against being stung, especially for children. Finish belief connects bees with the sun, given that honey is golden, highly prized, sweet, a useful medicine, and beloved of the sacred bear, an animal of great importance in Finnish culture and mythology (as we've seen in Mielikki's entry). The two goddesses might have been invoked in magic

for healing, and as honey was a healing ointment, this seems a logical connection. They were also sometimes called upon for successful hunts or fishing excursions.

That said, the connection with bees might be a post-Christian invention. During the period of Christianization, the Virgin Mary seems to have taken on the role of being associated with daylight, and some Finish poetry and imagery associates Mary with bees. This would seem like an obvious attempt to replace Päivätär, but some scholars have suggested that the bee association might have belonged to Mary first, and that some Finnish pagans adopted the idea for Päivätär to counteract the growing presence of Christianity in their lands. We are probably at far too distant a point in time now to ever know for sure. The pagan Finns might also have seen Päivätär in contrast to Louhi, who ruled over the dark. These goddesses were two sides of the same coin, at least until Päivätär was replaced and Louhi was demonized.

# INTRODUCTION TO THE *KALEVALA*

I am ready now for singing,
Ready to begin the chanting
Of our nation's ancient song
Handed down from past ages.
In my mouth the words are melting,
From my lips the tones are gliding,
From my tongue they wish to hasten;
When my teeth are parted,
When my ready mouth is opened,
Songs of ancient wit and wisdom
Hasten willingly from me.
Golden friend, and dearest brother,
Brother of mine in childhood,
Come and sing with me the stories,
Come and chant with me the legends,
Legends of the times forgotten,
Since we now are here together,
Come together from our wanderings.
Seldom do we come for singing,
Over this cold and cruel country,
Over the poor soil of the Northland.
Let us clasp our hands together
That we may best remember.
Join we now in merry singing,
Chant we now the oldest folklore,
That the dear ones all may hear them,
Of this rising generation.
These are words taught to me in childhood,

Songs preserved from distant ages,
Legends that once were taken
From the belt of Väinämöinen,
From the forge of Ilmarinen,
From the sword of Farmind,
From the bow of Joukahainen,
From the fields of the Northland,
From the heaths of Kalevala.
There are many other legends,
Incantations that were taught to me,
Gathered in the fragrant copses,
Blown to me from the forest branches,
Culled among the plumes of pine-trees,
Scented from the vines and flowers,
Whispered to me as I followed
Flocks in lands of honeyed meadows,
Over hillocks green and golden,
Many runes the cold has told me,
Many lays the rain has brought me,
Other songs the winds have sung me;
Many birds from many forests,
Often have sung me lays in concord
Waves of sea, and ocean billows,
Music from the many waters,
Music from the whole of creation,
Often have been my guide and master.
Sentences the trees created,
Rolled together into bundles,
Moved them to my ancient dwelling,
On the sledges to my cottage,

Laid them in a chest of boxes,
Boxes lined with shining copper.
Long they lay within my dwelling
Through the chilling winds of winter.
Shall I bring these songs together
Collect them from the cold and frost?
Shall I bring this nest of boxes,
Keepers of these golden legends,
To the table in my cabin?
Shall I now open these boxes,
Boxes filled with wondrous stories?
Let me sing an old legend,
That shall echo forth the praises
Of the beer that I have tasted,
Of the sparkling beer of barley.
Bring to me a foaming goblet
Of the barley of my fathers,
Lest my singing grow too weary,
Singing from the water only.
Often I have heard them singing,
That the nights come to us alone,
That the Moon beams on us alone,
That the Sun shines on us alone;
Sing also, Väinämöinen
The renowned and wise enchanter,
Born from everlasting Air
Of his mother, Air's daughter.

# THE CREATION OF THE WORLD AND
# THE BIRTH OF VÄINÄMÖINEN

*Rune I*

At the beginning, there was Ilmatar, the virgin goddess, and the great void and its wind. She grew weary of her endless existence and descended into the waters below, where she was tossed about by the air and waves. In this tempestuous environment, she conceived the child of the wind. Afterward, she floated for seven hundred years (nine human lifetimes), but could not yet give birth. There was no land where she could rest. She began to despair, lamenting ever having left her life up in the ether. She found no relief from her condition, so she called upon Ukko for help, appealing to him to deliver her from her plight.

At these words, a duck appeared in the sky. Like Ilmatar, the bird was weary; she could find no land on which to settle and build a nest to lay her eggs. Seeing Ilmatar's knees above the waters, the duck thought them to be suitable refuge on which to rest for a while. Landing on one of Ilmatar's knees, the duck set about building her nest. She laid seven eggs, six of gold and one of iron. Ilmatar was happy to provide a safe haven for the eggs, but it was not long before the goddess became restless. The water warmed and she felt a burning in her knee, her shoulders, and her very veins. She needed to move, but in doing so, she dislodged the eggs from their resting place, sending them tumbling into the primordial sea.

They broke, but were not destroyed, for out of them came the very forces of creation. They were transformed in wondrous beauty to make the sun from the yellow, the moon from the egg white, the stars from the motley, and the Earth from the shells. And so was the world made, and then the years passed quickly under the light of the new sun and the new moon. The yolk of the iron egg became a cloud of thunder.

And yet, the daughter of ether still swam in the sea. After ten more years, she lifted her head from the waters, and began to create and shape the materials before her: hills, rivers, bays and inlets, rocks, reefs, islands, forests, and land. And for many more long years, she engaged in this work, while the child inside of her grew into an old man. He was named Väinämöinen, and he longed to see the sun and the moon. He implored these two celestial bodies and the Great Bear among the stars to release him from his dark prison, but none would offer their assistance. His patience came to an end, and he forced his way out of his dark world.

He plunged into the ocean and swam in all directions to observe his new surroundings. He rested in the ocean for seven years and then during the autumn of the eighth, he came ashore, planting his right foot on solid ground and then his left. He beheld the sun and the moon, and the Great Bear in the sky, and thus he was delivered into our world. He was already old and wise, an enchanter and reciter of runes. But he saw that the land was rocky and barren, and wondered how he would make it verdant and abundant.

## VÄINÄMÖINEN'S SOWING AND THE CHALLENGE OF JOUKAHAINEN

*Runes II and III*

Väinämöinen long worried about how he would farm this land and make it produce the bounty of the Earth. The god Sampsa Pellervoinen was aware of Väinämöinen's distress and came to him. He began to sow the seeds for many trees, which soon grew in abundance: birch, spruce, willow, oak, rowan, juniper, and more. But one oak among them grew especially tall, so much so that it began to block out the sun, and Väinämöinen knew that he must chop it down to preserve the sun's life-giving light.

He appealed to his mother, Ilmatar, asking her for the strength of the very ocean itself to undertake the task. The goddess heard his prayer and at once, a tiny man emerged from the sea. He wore a hat, boots, and gloves all made of copper, but he was only the size of a finger, and Väinämöinen wondered what use he would be. In answer, this miniature man began to grow, and soon he touched the heights of the clouds themselves. He drew out an axe and struck the oak, creating a fire and sending it crashing to the ground below.

Väinämöinen took up his own axe and cut other trees to make a clearing for fields that could be farmed, though he left one birch. An eagle flew by and asked him why he had left this tree when he had felled so many others. Väinämöinen answered that this tree was for the eagle, a place for him to rest during his travels, and a place where the cuckoo could alight and sing its song to the delight of all.

The eagle was well pleased with this generous offer and gave as thanks a spark that grew into a great flame to burn the trees that Väinämöinen had felled. The fire reduced them to a fertile ash, which Väinämöinen spread over the fields. Väinämöinen then sowed barley in those fields, worked his magic over them, and prayed to the great god Ukko for rains to nourish the seeds and make them grow. And he prayed to Mannu, the Earth goddess, to make the land fertile that the barley might grow strong and full of flavor. And in response, Ukko sent rain, and Mannu made the grain good. Väinämöinen was delighted and he called to the cuckoo, inviting him to sit in the birch tree and sing a sweet song in hopes that the land would yield its bounty.

Thus, Väinämöinen gained much renown as a wizard, a wise sage, and a singer of magic runes. He lived in Väinölä, also known as Kalevala, and sang of all the things from the creation until his own age. Such was his fame that word of his power and wisdom traveled throughout the lands, reaching as far north as Pohjola. There, a young man named Joukahainen heard of Väinämöinen and his singing skills. But Joukahainen fancied himself as the greatest of rune singers, and desired to challenge Väinämöinen to see who truly was the finest. His family learned of his boastful intent and tried to stop him, but he would not heed their warnings, thinking that his own desire was more important than theirs. He set off in search of Väinämöinen, riding in his sleigh drawn by a steed that breathed fire out of its nose and shot flames from its hooves.

Joukahainen rode for three days, coming at last to Väinölä. As he traveled onward, he saw another sleigh approaching him from the opposite direction. But the vain young Joukahainen did not try to get out of its way, and crashed his own sleigh into this stranger's, damaging them both and entangling their horses. The other driver became furious and demanded to know who this young upstart was. Joukahainen gave his name, whereupon the other traveler revealed that he was none other than Väinämöinen. The younger man was delighted that he had met his rival so easily, and boasted that while Väinämöinen might know much, young Joukahainen knew even more.

Now, Väinämöinen demanded that this young man tell him of this knowledge. Joukahainen bragged that he had traveled far to the north and south and knew all about the land and its creatures. Väinämöinen countered that a child knew as much, and this was not the knowledge of a man. He asked Joukahainen to speak of the creation of the world. Joukahainen bragged that he recalled when the world and everything in it was created.

Väinämöinen knew that this upstart was lying, and it made him angry. He knew Joukahainen could not have been present for the creation of the world. Upset and humiliated, Joukahainen demanded that they fight one another instead, if they could not compare their knowledge. Väinämöinen refused, again calling him a useless child.

Joukahainen cursed Väinämöinen, threatening to turn him into a pig and shove him into a pile of manure. Väinämöinen had finally had enough and began to recite a spell that made the very land around them rumble. Joukahainen's sleigh was cast

into a pond and changed into nothing more than logs, while his horse turned into rocks. His whip turned into lightning and vanished, and he began to sink into a bog that appeared beneath his feet. Joukahainen pleaded for his life, offering Väinämöinen a hunting bow, a boat, and even his fields if the old wizard would free him. Väinämöinen rejected all these gifts and the gold that Joukahainen next offered. So Joukahainen offered his sister, Aino, to Väinämöinen to be his wife, and Väinämöinen happily accepted. He brought back Joukahainen's sleigh and horse and let him go free. Humiliated, the young man returned to his home in the north.

## THE TRAGIC FATE OF AINO

*Runes IV and V*

Joukahainen went home, deeply regretting his brash behavior. Arriving at his family's farm, he smashed his sleigh in anger and went to tell his parents what had happened, including his foolish promise to give Aino to Väinämöinen as a wife. While Joukahainen's mother was delighted at the news and the prospect of having the great wizard as a son-in-law, Aino began to cry. She didn't want to marry an old man, leave her home, or cover her hair in the manner of a married woman. This was not her choice, and she would cry for the rest of her life if forced into it.

But her mother scolded her, and told her that Väinämöinen was a prestigious man, and that Aino should be glad to marry him. Did she want to spend her whole life on the farm? Aino had no answer.

In time, Väinämöinen journeyed to Pohjola to meet Aino. He found her in a forest, where she was making branches into sauna whisks. He beheld her beauty and was overjoyed. He began courting her at once. He introduced himself and asked her to present herself for him and him alone, since he was to be her husband.

But Aino was ever more bitter upon meeting him; he was even older than she had feared! She refused to do anything for him, tearing off her adornments and running home in tears. Her family asked her why she cried so. She told them that she had just met Väinämöinen, and that she never wanted to see him again. She pleaded with her mother to let her stay on the farm.

But her mother would not hear of it and demanded that poor Aino go and dress herself beautifully, that she might please Väinämöinen. She was to put on belts of gold, and skirts of deep blue, woven by the moon herself. Aino was to plait ribbons in her hair, and wear pearls and gold and make her family proud. But the young woman wanted none of this, and wished that she was still a child, or that she could live in the sea among the fish.

Still, the next morning, she dressed as her mother commanded, but she did not come to see her mother. Instead, she wandered into the wilds for three days, through forest and past bogs, until she came to the shore of the sea. In the darkness before dawn, she gazed out to the ocean and saw what she thought to be three young women bathing. Eager to join them, she removed her jewels and all her clothes, and waded into the water. She swam to a rock, but as the sun rose, the rock sank and she with it. And so she drowned.

Four animals—a wolf, a rabbit, a bear, and a fox—saw what had happened, and they chose the rabbit to tell Aino's family about her fate. When the little animal did so, Aino's mother wept bitterly. She regretted forcing her daughter to marry old Väinämöinen and would ever after advise others to respect their children's wishes. She cried so much that her tears became a river, from which rocky outcroppings emerged, and on them were hills where there soon grew birch trees. Three cuckoos came to the trees and sang, one for the loss of Aino, one for Väinämöinen, and one for Aino's mother. Aino's mother listened to them so that she would never forget her daughter and her loss.

Now, Väinämöinen also felt deep remorse for Aino's sad fate, and even sailed out into the sea in the hopes of finding her. One time, he reeled in a salmon, but it slipped from his hands and wriggled back into the water. As it swam away, one side became as a young woman's and raised a hand to him, as if saying goodbye. Aino had indeed come into the service of the goddess Vellamo, wife of Ahto. Aino had gotten her wish to live among the fish of the sea. Väinämöinen never saw her again.

## JOUKAHAINEN'S ANGER AND VÄINÄMÖINEN'S ADVENTURE IN POHJOLA

*Runes VI and VII*

Joukahainen was furious over his sister's presumed death. He blamed Väinämöinen and wanted revenge. Joukahainen's own mother had warned him against the path of revenge, saying that to kill the great Väinämöinen would be to rob the people of his majestic singing and all their joy, but the young man cared not. His heart was set on killing the one he blamed for Aino's fate.

One day while searching for Väinämöinen, he journeyed to the seaside, and out on the waves, he beheld an astonishing sight: Väinämöinen was riding toward Pohjola, but not on land. His horse galloped over the waves as easily as it would over hill and dale, and water seemed to touch neither the wizard nor his horse. But Joukahainen cared not for this remarkable feat, and drew his bow, ready to strike down the man he held responsible for Aino's tragic fate. His arrows were laden with venom and could cut down even a mighty magician like Väinämöinen.

He let loose an arrow, then a second, and a third, which did not hit the man but instead, his poor horse. The steed buckled, and Väinämöinen was thrown into the sea. Joukahainen rejoiced, thinking that justice had been served, and that the waters would take the old wizard down to his well-deserved fate.

The waters did indeed carry away Väinämöinen, and he despaired of ever seeing his home again. Yet the ocean did not drown him. He drifted for many days, with no sight of land. His will to live began to fade, for he saw no way out of his plight. But it was not the end for him.

An enormous eagle from Pohjola flew overhead and, spying the great wizard, it swooped down, asking him how he'd come to be so far from shore. Väinämöinen answered that his horse had been taken out from under him. Now he drifted aimlessly toward his doom, for without food or water, he would soon die if he did not drown first. The eagle told him that it would rescue him and offered his back for Väinämöinen to climb up upon. The bird remembered the kindness that Väinämöinen had shown in leaving a birch tree for birds to rest in, and in gratitude, it would now bear him to Pohjola, as he intended. And so, Väinämöinen was saved.

The eagle kept his word and took the great wizard to Pohjola, leaving him safely on the ground. Väinämöinen stayed in that place for days, bemoaning his fate, and wondering how he would ever return home. For Pohjola was ruled by the powerful sorceress, Louhi, and all under her rule feared her, even her own family. What's more, she was determined to staunchly defend her kin from any outside suitors or troublemakers, and that included Väinämöinen.

It happened that while Louhi was out one day, she heard a man weeping. She followed the sound and found Väinämöinen in his pitiful state. She offered to take him back to her home, and once there, she gave him food, healed him, and saw to it that his clothing was mended. But she did not do this simply out of kindness. She knew that Väinämöinen longed to go home, and so she pressed her advantage.

She asked him what he would give her if she returned him to his own lands. He offered her plentiful silver and gold, but she had no use for these things. She wanted instead for him to craft the Sampo, a magical object that would give its possessor unlimited wealth and plenty of all kinds, never ending. She had the knowledge of how it was made, but not the smith's skills to make it herself. She asked if he possessed the means to create this wondrous object, crafted from the quill of a swan, the milk from a barren cow, a tuft of a lamb's wool, and a single grain of barley. If he could do this for her, she would not only take him home, but offer up her most beautiful daughter in marriage.

But Väinämöinen, for all his skill, could not craft the Sampo. He told her it was beyond him, but there was one who could: the blacksmith, Ilmarinen. Ilmarinen had created the very heavens and the sky above at the beginning, and his work held them up to this day. He, of all beings, would be able to make the wondrous object, Väinämöinen said. If Louhi would take him back home, Väinämöinen would send Ilmarinen to make the Sampo for her.

His words delighted Louhi, and she agreed to equip Väinämöinen for the home journey. She gave him a fine sleigh and an excellent steed, and she sent him on his way. But she left him with a warning. He was not to look up on the homeward journey or bad luck would befall him. Väinämöinen promised to heed her warning, and with enthusiasm, he set off for home.

## THE RAINBOW MAID OF POHJOLA

*Runes VII to IX*

Väinämöinen was delighted to be on his way, free of Louhi and of Pohjola, which he thought was a miserable land, most unsuitable for him. So happy was he that he forgot her warning and happened to glance up once. He saw a magnificent rainbow in the sky, and on it the wondrous Maid of Pohjola sat. She was the daughter of Louhi, and she was dressed in brilliant white, while weaving cloth of gold and silver. This glorious sight captivated Väinämöinen, for it was she that Louhi had offered to him if he could convince Ilmarinen to craft the Sampo. Väinämöinen was so entranced that he completely forgot his promise to the maid's mother and decided that he would try to woo her then and there.

He slowed his horse and called out to her, inviting her to join him and come with him back to Kalevala, where she would be welcomed and honored. But she only laughed at him and said that she desired to stay where she was. She would remain a maiden, for the birds had told her that such a girl was always treasured in her family's home, but as a wife, she would be so much less. A true daughter was loved much more than a daughter-in-law. No, she would not join him. Väinämöinen countered that these birds spoke foolishly to her. A maiden would always be seen as a child, while a wife was a true woman. He had power and prestige and would be an excellent husband for her.

But the Maid answered that first, she needed to see his quality and suitability for her. He must slice a horsehair using a knife with no blade. And then he must steal an egg from a bird using an invisible snare. For a man like Väinämöinen, these were not difficult tasks, and when he had accomplished them, he came back to her. She then bid him to draw bark from stone and take a sliver of ice from a larger ice block without damaging it. Again, he did these things easily. But again, she resisted, asking for a man who could use his magic to craft a boat from nothing and then set it in the water without ever touching it.

Väinämöinen set about the work. As he labored to bring forth the boat, an evil spirit possessed his axe, and when he struck with it, it deflected and cut him instead. The cut was deep, and try as he might, he could not heal the wound. Louhi's promise of bad luck had come true. He knew he needed magic to save himself, but he did not know the spell to do so. He stumbled back to his sleigh and made his way to a nearby village, where he found an old man who could work a healing spell for him.

But the man said that Väinämöinen must sing about the origin of iron, so that the damage from the axe could be mended. This Väinämöinen knew, and so he sang of how Ukko had rubbed

his hands together and made the three mothers of iron. As they wandered in a cloud, milk from their breasts fell to the Earth, and this was how iron was first made. Iron desired to know its brother, fire, but in the meeting, iron was almost burned, so it hid itself in a swamp.

It happened that Ilmarinen, that great smith, found iron, and promised to help it make wonderful weapons. But iron did not want to be used in such a way. Instead, Ilmarinen began creating many useful tools. As he worked the forge, a hornet had added a viper's venom and blood to the tempering water. Ilmarinen knew this not, but when he sought to temper the iron, the metal became filled with rage and tried to destroy the forge. After that, it slew fire and became a weapon, and ever since, blood has been spilt by iron.

Väinämöinen ended his tale, and now the old man understood where iron came from. He recited a spell to stanch the blood and invoked Ukko to press his thumb into the wound to stop the flow. The wound was sealed, and the man placed an ointment on it, which he had made from an oak tree's sap. He sent the pain from the wound to a place called Mount Anguish, and there it would afflict the stones, rather than Väinämöinen. And so Väinämöinen was healed.

## THE FORGING OF THE SAMPO

*Rune X*

Now that Väinämöinen was fully recovered, he gave his thanks to the old man, prepared his horse and sleigh, and set out again for his home. He thought about how he had broken his promise to Louhi when he looked up and saw the Maid, and this weighed on his mind. He also knew that he must ask Ilmarinen to journey north to Pohjola and forge the Sampo for Louhi, but he was as yet unsure how he would convince him to do so. It is far easier to promise something in the moment than to put it into action. He knew he would need his magic.

At last, he returned to his homeland, and he set about his task at once. Using a mighty spell, he brought forth a gigantic spruce that grew and grew until it touched the very sky, and even the moon and the stars. There was nothing else like it. Then he went to visit Ilmarinen who, as usual, would be at work, alone in his forge.

Ilmarinen was a smith of incredible skill who worked hard each day, so much so that he was always covered in dirt and soot. He was so busy that he had no time for other diversions, such as seeking a wife, and Väinämöinen knew that he could use this fact to his advantage. He came to Ilmarinen's forge that night, where the blacksmith was toiling away. Väinämöinen called out to him in greeting and said that he brought good tidings and the potential for more work: "If you will travel to Pohjola in the north and there forge the Sampo for Louhi, she will offer you her beautiful daughter, the Maid of Pohjola, in marriage."

But even though the offer was tempting, Ilmarinen refused, saying that Pohjola was a dark and dangerous place, cold and unwelcoming. He would not travel there for any reward, not even the hand of the Maid in marriage.

Väinämöinen would not be discouraged. He told Ilmarinen of the great spruce tree, a wondrous thing that was so tall that it reached into the sky and brushed the moon and the stars. There was nothing else like it (of course there wasn't, for he'd created it himself). Ilmarinen was skeptical and refused to believe Väinämöinen unless he could see the spruce with his own eyes. So Väinämöinen agreed to take him to the tree, so that he might behold its wonder.

They went to it, and Ilmarinen was indeed impressed. Väinämöinen suggested that he climb up so that he might see all the lands around them. Ilmarinen agreed and scaled the tree. But once he was up high enough, Väinämöinen tricked him by calling up a magical wind. It caught Ilmarinen in its grasp and

lifted him into the air, carrying him north, all the way to Pohjo-la. It set him down at Louhi's farm, gently and quietly, such that even her guard dogs heard nothing. He might have slipped away unnoticed, but Louhi was outside and greeted him. She asked him if he was the famed smith, and if so, she had been waiting to meet him.

Ilmarinen was angry with Väinämöinen for tricking him, but he greeted Louhi in kind and told her that he was indeed that very same smith. Meanwhile, Louhi told her daughter to dress in her finest clothes, and they welcomed Ilmarinen and gave him food and drink of the best quality. While he gratefully ate, she asked him if he could indeed forge the Sampo. He told her that he could, because he had already made the sky. And yet, there was a problem. The Sampo existed only in the imagination; no one had yet managed to make it. But the more he learned of it from her, the more Ilmarinen decided that he had enough skill to create it. Despite having told Väinämöinen that he would nev-er go to Pohjola or try to forge the Sampo, he now accepted the challenge and wanted to set to work straight away.

But there was another problem: Pohjola had no forge or even bellows that would allow him to do the work. So Ilmarinen searched for some time for suitable parts. Eventually, he found a stone that bore the colors of the rainbow, and this he would use for part of the forge. Then he discovered material to make a proper bellows and was ready to begin his work. He made the fire and brought forth those materials that he needed to make this marvelous object: the swan's quill, the lamb's wool, a grain of barley, and the milk of a barren cow. He placed all of these into his furnace, and he called for servants to help work the bellows and feed the flames.

As the fire raged, Ilmarinen could see something start to form. It was a beautiful bow made of gold, but this was not what he wished to create. Saying that this bow would only kill and bring evil, he threw it back into the flames and destroyed it. The laborers operated the bellows again. Soon, another object took shape, and Ilmarinen could see that it was a ship. But it was a war ship and would also bring only death and destruction, so he cast it into the furnace as well. A third time the bellows blew, and yet again, an object formed in the heart of the flames. This time, it was a plough of gold, but Ilmarinen determined that it would not obey its master's hand and would ruin all other fields than its master's. So, he snapped it in half and consigned it to the flames.

Just as he was about to concede that the Sampo was beyond his skill, the winds blew and the air changed. The furnace grew hotter, and sparks and flames flew all about. Smoke drifted into the sky and darkened it. Again, an object began to take shape in the fire. But this time, something was different. Ilmarinen leaned in once more for a better look, and he beheld something new, something wonderful: the Sampo! He knew it must be this wondrous object, for it was like nothing he or anyone had ever seen before.

He took the Sampo and created a mill for flour on one side of it, and a mill for salt on another side, and finally, a mill to make gold on another side. He created a lid covered in stars to rest atop it and then stepped back to behold his handiwork. He'd done it. He'd created the Sampo!

Of course, Louhi was overjoyed that he had accomplished so great a deed, and that the Sampo was hers. She took it at once and went into the mountains, where she hid it, storing it behind nine locks in the stone, so that no one could ever find it or take it from her. Then she returned to her farm, where Ilmarinen still waited.

He had done what she asked and proven his skill both to her and to himself. He spoke to the Maid, telling her that now that the Sampo was done, it would bring riches and prosperity to her and her family.

He asked her to marry him, but she didn't want to, even now. She did not wish to leave her home and her family and travel to a strange land to live among people she didn't know. She wanted to wait a while longer, until she was older. So, she refused him, leaving him disappointed and downcast. But he respected her wishes and decided that it was time to go home, for he had never wanted to come here anyway.

Louhi was happy that the Maid had chosen not to go with him. She kept her daughter and had possession of the Sampo. Still, she showed Ilmarinen gratitude by preparing good food for him and then offering him a fine boat as payment for his work. She called up a wind to carry the boat and he sailed back home with ease.

## THE LIFE, DEATH, AND REBIRTH OF LEMMINKÄINEN

*Runes XI to XV*

In another part of the land, there dwelled a young man named Lemminkäinen. He was a fisherman who lived with his mother on an island called Kaukoniemi. Lemminkäinen was a handsome man, who attracted many young women to him, but he was also reckless and overbearing.

It so happened that a beautiful young woman, Kyllikki, also lived on the same island, and she had many suitors who would come to her, trying to woo her and ask for her hand in marriage. But Kyllikki always refused them, saying she would not leave her home to face unknown dangers in other lands. Some said that even the moon and the sun sought her for their sons, but still she resisted. It was only natural that the handsome, yet arrogant, Lemminkäinen would want to try to win her heart for himself. But his mother cautioned him not to try. Kyllikki came from a wealthy family, his mother said, and they would have no interest in a poor fisherman like Lemminkäinen.

But the young man paid his mother no heed, thinking that his good looks would be enough to convince Kyllikki that he was the man for her. His mother again cautioned him, saying that his arrogance might bring disaster to them in the form of vengeance from other angry suitors. And yet, Lemminkäinen ignored her. He journeyed to Kyllikki's village, but he didn't try to woo her right away. Instead, he worked in the fields, tending sheep, and at night he would dance in taverns with other young ladies. His goal was to make Kyllikki jealous, but it did not work.

He tried many things to impress her, but always she resisted and told him to leave her alone. After some time, he grew frustrated. One day, when a group of people gathered to dance, Lemminkäinen rode to them in his sleigh, took Kyllikki in his arms, and lifted her up, placing her in the sleigh and speeding off. She was furious and began to cry, telling him that her brothers would come for her. But Lemminkäinen ignored her, telling her that she would never need worry in his company, for while he was not wealthy, he had a mighty and magical sword, by which he would become rich and powerful.

Kyllikki told him that if she were to marry him, he must promise never to go to battle, not even to try to gain the spoils of war. Lemminkäinen agreed but asked her not to run away if they were indeed married. They arrived at his home, and Kyllikki was saddened to see such a poor and run-down house. Lemminkäinen promised he would build something far better for her. Lemminkäinen's mother was thrilled to see that Lemminkäinen had convinced Kyllikki to join him, and insisted that he provide for her properly.

And so, Lemminkäinen and Kyllikki were married, and they did indeed keep the promises they had made to each other, at least for a few years. But one day, Lemminkäinen went out on fishing business and did not return that evening. Kyllikki thought that he had broken his vow at last, so she set off for her home at once, and she enjoyed the company of other villagers there, dancing with them. When Lemminkäinen did return, he was angry that she had broken her vow, and he said to his mother that in return, he would set off to fight in Pohjola. Kyllikki

learned of this and begged him not to go, saying that she'd had a dream in which the whole of their house was consumed by fire, and she knew it would happen if he left.

But Lemminkäinen was angry and would not hear her, saying that because she had broken her vow, he didn't believe her words or her dream. He would go to Pohjola and win gold and renown there. He bid his mother to bring to him his battle gear, though she did not want to. She implored him to abandon this mad quest and to think of his wife. But Lemminkäinen responded that he had no wife. His mother told him that powerful sorceresses lived in Pohjola and if he fought them, he could not possibly win. Lemminkäinen threw his beard comb against a wall and told her that she would know he had died if that comb ran red with blood.

So, he set off to Pohjola, wearing his chain armor and equipped with his magical sword. When he drew near to that cold land, he chanted magical spells, asking for help from the gods and the spirits of the woods and water. He implored them to protect him from the magic and weapons of any enemies he might encounter. And saying this, he rode onward in his sleigh.

A few days later, he came to Louhi's house. Using his magic, he kept her dog quiet and peered into the home, where he saw the great magic-workers singing their spells. With his own magic, Lemminkäinen stepped through the wall and into the house. Flames flew from his eyes. He commanded the singers to be silent, and he threw rocks into their mouths to shut them up. As they fled, he changed some into river foam and some into rocks. But one old blind man, Märkähattu, he did not change. When the old man asked him why, Lemminkäinen said it was because the old man could do no harm now. But Lemminkäinen did know of the terrible things Märkähattu had done in his long life and didn't want to even see him.

Märkähattu ran from the house to the Tuonela River, the dark water that borders the dreaded land of the dead. He was angry and began to think about having revenge for Lemminkäinen's insults. But the young man cared not. He called out to Louhi, demanding that she offer him her most beautiful daughter as a wife. Louhi told him that he already had a wife, and that she would give him nothing.

Lemminkäinen insisted that Kyllikki was unworthy because she had broken her vow, but one of Louhi's daughters would be worthy of him. And again, Louhi refused, calling him worthless. But she made him an offer: at the end of a field filled with evil spirits there was a magical elk, which no one could catch. She bid him to capture the animal and return to her, and then she might reconsider.

So Lemminkäinen went to obtain skis from a man called Kauppi, but Kauppi warned him that this elk was not what it seemed, and no good would come from trying to capture it, only pain. Of course, Lemminkäinen in his arrogance didn't believe the man, and proclaimed that there was nothing he could not hunt and catch. But what he didn't know is that the elk was merely a statue made by the evil spirits of the field. It was merely a tree stump and branches arranged to look like an animal. When the spirits heard of Lemminkäinen and his arrogance, they decided to deceive him. They enchanted the wooden elk to make it run and find Lemminkäinen. Off it went, while Lemminkäinen himself ventured out in search of it.

Hearing that the elk had caused trouble in a village, Lemminkäinen headed there, found the strange creature, and locked it in a pen made of oak. But this pen could not contain the elk, and it broke free, racing into a nearby forest. Lemminkäinen wanted to follow it, but one of his skis broke, and his pole split in half. In anger, Lemminkäinen prayed to Tapio and Mielikki to lead him to the beast and to Tellervo to alert the forest spirits to his need. The gods answered his prayers, and the forest spirits drove the creature back to Lemminkäinen, who threw his lasso over its neck and then pet it on the back to calm it down.

He led the elk back to Louhi and demanded that she honor her word. But Louhi was not yet ready to part with a daughter, and she told Lemminkäinen that first, he must retrieve the horse with a fiery mane, a magical animal that resided with the evil spirits. So again, Lemminkäinen went out, and he soon found the horse and used his magic to subdue it. He jumped up on its back and rode it back to Louhi in triumph.

Again, he demanded that she allow him to marry one of her daughters, and again, Louhi refused, telling him that first, he must launch an arrow into the swan of the Tuonela River and kill it. Since this river crossed into the realm of the dead, Louhi was certain that Lemminkäinen would fail, and she would be rid of him.

But the arrogant young Lemminkäinen would not be dissuaded. He departed for the river, his bow and arrows ready. Yet he had forgotten that the old man, Märkähattu, was waiting for him, eager to repay his insults.

Märkähattu heard Lemminkäinen approaching the river and used his remaining meager magic to call up a water viper. The snake struck at Lemminkäinen and bit into his chest. Its venom worked its way to Lemminkäinen's heart, and the young man knew no magic to stop it. With his body tortured in agony from the venom, he died.

Back home, Kyllikki wondered what fate befell him. Her question was answered when one day, she saw his comb flowing with blood, and she knew that he was gone. Lemminkäinen's mother cried bitterly at the news, but soon resolved that she must find her son's body. So, she made the long and dangerous journey to Pohjola and came at last to Louhi and demanded to know where Lemminkäinen was.

Louhi lied and said that she knew nothing of this young man, and that perhaps he'd been eaten by a wolf. But Lemminkäinen's mother became angry and accused Louhi of lying. She demanded to know where Lemminkäinen was, or she would find where Louhi's precious Sampo was being made and destroy it. At that, Louhi admitted that she knew Lemminkäinen, and that in his arrogance, he had demanded one of her daughters in marriage. So, she had sent him to the river of Tuonela to shoot its fabled swan.

His mother left Louhi and went to the river but could find no sign of Lemminkäinen. She looked under rocks and by trees, she wandered the woods and bogs, but still found nothing. She begged the sun and the moon to tell her, yet they remained silent. Despairing, she made her way to Ilmarinen's forge, and she asked him to fashion for her a rake of iron of enormous size, with tines six hundred feet long. Ilmarinen did as she asked, and then she returned to the river and asked the sun for her help. The sun shone brilliantly on the land, enough to make its people weary and leave the old woman alone.

Now, Lemminkäinen's mother waded into the river and began to rake. At first, she retrieved his shirt, and then his boots and hat. Finally, she brought up his body, though it was missing one arm and his head. She cried in agony and vowed that she would find some magic to bring him back to life.

A raven nearby saw her efforts and told her that she would never succeed, and that she should let his remains float on to the land of the dead. She ignored the bird and raked for the rest of her son's body, finally collecting the missing pieces.

She prayed to the gods and goddesses for help, and they answered. Suonetar attached the veins, Ilmatar sewed the limbs back onto the body, and Ukko restored the muscles to the bones. Lemminkäinen's body was repaired, yet there was no life in it. So, the mother called to a bee and bid it fly to the heavens and fetch balsam and honey. The bee did as she asked, and out past the moon and stars, it found honey in a golden caldron and balsam in a pan. Taking as much as it could, it returned to the old woman.

She thanked the bee and then took these unguents and spread them on her son's body, commanding him to live again. And it was so. Lemminkäinen awoke, saying that he had slept for a long time. His mother scolded him, saying that it would have been much longer if not for her! She demanded to know what had happened. Lemminkäinen confessed that a blind man had thrown a viper at him, which had bitten him in the chest, and he did not know the magic to undo its deadly bite.

His mother scolded him again, proclaiming him to be worthless. Lemminkäinen had bragged about being able to defeat enemies in Pohjola and win gold, and yet he could not counteract snake venom with a simple spell! She told him that the viper itself had come from the spittle of an ogress, and if he'd known that, he could have saved himself.

Lemminkäinen lived once more, but he was humiliated. He'd failed to win gold or one of Louhi's daughters. His mother demanded that he return home at once and be grateful that he was alive at all.

## VÄINÄMÖINEN'S JOURNEY TO FIND THE LOST RUNES

*Runes XVI and XVII*

Väinämöinen desired to go sailing, but he needed wood for a new boat. Sampsa Pellervoinen, who had helped him clear trees so he could sow the lands, offered to help him find the wood he needed. Sampsa took his golden axe and wandered the land. He found an aspen that he deemed suitable, but the tree warned him that if he used its wood, the boat would sink, since it was beset with worms and small things gnawing through it. So Sampsa continued his search. He found a pine that seemed appropriate and prepared to chop it down, but the tree advised that it was a home for ravens that nested in it and raised their young, and thus it served a purpose already. So Sampsa left the tree behind and journeyed on until he found an oak, which told him that it was strong and would make a fine boat.

So Sampsa felled the oak and took it back to Väinämöinen, who set about constructing the vessel he desired. He used no servants, metal, or labor to make this boat, only his own music and magic. But he saw that in making it, he needed three more runes to complete the task, runes that would hold the boat together and make it safe for traversing the ocean.

But where would he find these? He realized that his best chance was to go to Tuonela, the land of the dead. But this was a treacherous place for the living, and Väinämöinen knew he would be putting himself in danger. Nevertheless, he set out on a long journey, taking several weeks to cross the land, its hills and forests, until at last he came to the great river. There he saw the Maid of Tuoni washing clothes in the water. He called out to her, asking her to ferry him across to the other side.

She answered that she needed to know why he wanted to cross, since he was not yet dead. Väinämöinen tried to deceive her, saying that he was indeed dead, killed by iron. She did not believe him, seeing that he had no blood on himself or his clothes. Väinämöinen then said that he had drowned. She wanted to know why his clothes were not wet, if that was the case. He told her that fire had burned him, but she replied that his beard showed no signs of fire. She then warned him not to lie to her again. At last, he confessed that he needed three runes to complete his magical ship, and that he would likely find them in Tuonela.

She told him that his wish to enter the land of the dead was a fool's errand, for when anyone crossed over, they did not return. But Väinämöinen sought the lost knowledge of creation in those runes and told her he had no fear. She agreed to ferry him across but warned him that he would face great sorrow in going to the land of the dead without first dying.

Once on the other side of the river, Väinämöinen walked onward into the gray, twilight land before him. It was quiet and lifeless, and before long he saw in the distance the great home of Tuoni, the god of death. Väinämöinen strode up to the door and let himself in. At once, Tuonetar, the lady of Tuonela, came to him, but when he tried to speak, he could not. And now he began to feel afraid. She brought him a large tankard of drink, but it contained nothing fit for a mortal. In it was a mass of frogs and worms. She bid him to drink of it, but he would not.

Now, he was able to speak, and he told her why he had come, but she rejected his plea, saying that Tuonela did not yield its dark secrets or its magic to the world of the living. For his arrogant presumption, she said, he would have to remain in Tuonela forever. She tried to make him fall into a sleep, placing him on a bearskin bed, but Väinämöinen knew if he did so, he would never wake and would indeed be trapped there forever. With quick thinking, he shape-shifted into a snake and slithered away. He lunged back into the river and swam through the net that was stretched across it to keep the souls of the dead from escaping. And so, against the odds, Väinämöinen freed himself from the dreaded land of Tuonela. He had learned not to test the mighty powers of the dead and their gods, and ever after he warned others to do good deeds in their lives, lest they suffer the fate of sleeping on hot coals, covered by vipers in a terrible eternal sleep.

Yet he had not acquired the runes he needed to complete the boat. He discovered that he might learn these runes from the mighty wizard Antero Vipunen, but that rune master had been dead for a long time. Still, if he could go to Vipunen's burial place, Väinämöinen might be able to speak with him and gain his knowledge. Once again, he went to Ilmarinen and asked him to forge new tools: a steel shirt, along with gloves and shoes made of iron. Ilmarinen did so, but warned Väinämöinen that he would not get any answers from that old, dead wizard.

Väinämöinen paid him no heed and set out. The journey was long and arduous, but at last he came to where Vipunen rested for eternity. He was not buried in a proper grave. Rather, earth covered his body, and trees sprouted out of it. Väinämöinen had to chop each of them down in order to reach the corpse. Opening Vipunen's mouth a little, he pushed an iron rod inside and pried it wide open, commanding the old wizard to rise. Vipunen did so with great pain and tried to bite the iron rod stuck in his mouth. Väinämöinen fell in, and Vipunen swallowed him.

Väinämöinen thought quickly and used a spell to make a boat out of his knife. He sailed through the dead wizard's innards, but he could not escape. So, he came to a stop in Vipunen's stomach, and there he created a forge from his armor, which he worked for days, throwing off sparks that at last burned the dead wizard's tongue.

Vipunen demanded to know who Väinämöinen was, threatening him with legions from Tuonela and iron warriors if Väinämöinen did not vacate the body at once. But Väinämöinen defied him, saying he would stay inside for as long as he wished. He would make bread from Vipunen's liver and soup from his lungs, and furthermore, he would move the forge into the dead man's heart if Vipunen refused to give him not only the runes he needed to complete his boat, but also the rest of his vast knowledge. Väinämöinen said that these spells must not die or lie forgotten in the ground.

Finally, Vipunen relented and sang the stories of creation and the dawn of all things. It was the finest singing Väinämöinen had ever heard, and Vipunen's knowledge was second to none. For several days and nights, the dead wizard sang, and Väinämöinen committed it all to memory. It was said that even the moon and sun listened to this wonder, and that the waters of the ocean and river ceased their movements, so that they might listen.

When Väinämöinen had heard it all, he commanded Vipunen to open his mouth and free him. The dead man did so, and out came Väinämöinen, landing in a nearby meadow. He at last had everything he needed, so he returned home and told Ilmarinen the news.

Väinämöinen took the runes he had learned and completed his boat, using nothing more than magic. And in so doing, he satisfied one of the Maid of Pohjola's requirements: that he build a ship with magic alone and launch it into the water without ever touching it.

# THE RIVAL SUITORS AND ILMARINEN'S WEDDING

## Runes XVIII to XXV

Väinämöinen understood that he had satisfied the demand that the Maid of Pohjola had set for him in order to woo her and marry her. He now had a boat made by the lost runes. So, he set his mind upon her once again and decided that he would return to Pohjola and try to court her yet again. But there was a problem, of course; the Maid was already set to marry Ilmarinen, because he had made the Sampo for Louhi.

But Väinämöinen was not about to let that little inconvenience stop him! He adorned his new magical boat with silver and gold and put up a colorful sail. He then pushed out to sea, intent on journeying at once to Pohjola to press his suit. But as he sailed near one point of land, Ilmarinen's sister, Annikki, stood nearby with her laundry. She recognized him and called out, asking where he was going.

Väinämöinen stammered and lied, saying he was going fishing. But Annikki mocked him, telling him she did not believe him. He had no nets or other equipment to catch fish. Väinämöinen lied again, saying that he was going off to war, but again Annikki called his bluff, saying he was not equipped for battle. Väinämöinen tried now to woo her, but she threatened to overturn his boat, so at last, he confessed that he sailed to try to court the Maid.

Hearing this, Annikki left him and went back to Ilmarinen working in his forge, where she asked him to make her a ring, a belt, and earrings of gold, and then she told him about Väinämöinen's plans. Ilmarinen was furious and resolved that they must act quickly.

Annikki used her magic to prepare a sauna for him, one that would enhance his appeal and invite the Maid to love him. She prepared the wood and rocks and used special water from a sacred well. Meanwhile, Ilmarinen made the things she had asked for and gave them to her. When he was done, he entered the sauna, covered in dirt and grime, as he often was. He spent time cleaning himself, and when he emerged, she barely could recognize him. He was handsome and appealing, and she was pleased with the results.

He dressed himself in his finest clothes, and they prepared to set off for Pohjola in his sleigh. Along the way, he happened to catch sight of Väinämöinen out at sea and called out to him. When Väinämöinen answered, Ilmarinen proposed that they let the Maid make her own choice between them, and that whoever she chose, they would remain friends afterward. Väinämöinen agreed, and they bid each the other farewell as Ilmarinen and Annikki rode on.

Meanwhile, their journey was already known to Louhi, who'd heard that a fine sleigh and a magnificent boat were on their way. She knew who they were, so she went to her daughter and told the Maid to make herself ready. It was time to choose, Louhi said. Louhi wanted the Maid to marry Väinämöinen, because his boat was beautifully arrayed in gold, while Ilmarinen's sleigh was much more plain. When they arrived, Louhi said the Maid should offer a drink to the suitor she preferred.

But the Maid was angry and said that she would never marry a man as old as Väinämöinen! She reminded Louhi of Ilmarinen's great gift of the Sampo, and that she intended to marry him. Louhi and the maid argued, and at that moment Väinämöinen strode in. He bowed and told her that he had created the boat she had asked for, entirely with magic. He asked her to marry him. But the Maid dismissed his announcement, saying that sailors were of no interest to her.

Then Ilmarinen walked in. Louhi offered him a drink, but he refused, saying that he would take nothing until he'd had a chance to see the Maid. At this, Louhi became angry and told him that he would not marry the Maid unless he could plough a field filled with vipers. Only an evil spirit had been able to do it thus far, and she knew that Ilmarinen would certainly fail.

Later that night, a saddened Ilmarinen snuck into the Maid's bedroom and the two conversed in a way that Ilmarinen had never done before with a woman. He asked her what he should do, for what Louhi asked of him was impossible. To his surprise, the Maid took his hand and told him not to worry. She told him to make a golden plough for himself, and with this, he would be able to plough the viper-filled field.

Ilmarinen was heartened by these words and went to the forge. As she had instructed, he made himself a golden plough, along with some iron gloves and a shirt for extra protection. When he was ready, he went to the field and announced his intention to the vipers. He set to work, and sure enough, he was able to plough the field and emerge unharmed. He even brought back some dead snakes and threw them on the ground before Louhi's house.

He demanded to be able to marry the Maid, but crafty Louhi still would not yield. Now she wanted him to fetch the Bear of Tuonela for her. So, he did, but he knew that Louhi was making each task harder so that he would fail.

Then Louhi demanded that he catch and bring her a giant pike from the Tuonela River, but without using nets or hooks. The Maid offered him encouragement and told him to go and forge a giant eagle for himself, a bird of iron and copper. He did so, and he flew on its back to the river, where he saw the pike. The fish was terrifying, a gigantic monster with enormous sharp teeth. The eagle clutched at it with equally sharp talons, but it escaped more than once, even dragging Ilmarinen and the bird under the water. But at last, the eagle was able to grasp it tight, and pull it from the river.

Ilmarinen cut off its head and took it back to Louhi, telling her she could use it as a chair, if she wished. Once again, he asked to marry the Maid, and this time Louhi consented.

The couple made their wedding plans, envisioning a celebration that would last for several days. They invited people from all over Kalevala and Pohjola, but there was one notable omission: Lemminkäinen was not invited. Louhi knew that since he had once tried to woo the Maid, he would likely cause trouble if he showed up.

The celebration would be so grand that Louhi ordered a new home be built to hold everyone who would attend. It was said that the roof was so high that if a rooster sat on top of it and crowed, no one below could hear the sound.

Louhi worried that there would not be enough ale for the feast, for she had never learned the art of brewing. An old man heard her lament and told her a story about how ale had been created. He spoke of barley and hops and water, and how Osmotar, the goddess of brewing, had combined them and with the help of the sparkling maid, Kalevatar, made the drink that they all valued so highly. He spoke at length of their process, and now Louhi knew exactly what to do.

And so the preparations continued. The guests arrived and they dined on fine pork and salmon and excellent ale brewed by Louhi herself. Väinämöinen was there, for true to his word, he was still Ilmarinen's friend. And as he drank, he sang for the guests, and they were delighted. The feast lasted for days, with each guest coming forward to congratulate the Maid and Ilmarinen, and offer advice on how they should best live. Some of this advice was cheerful, some somber, but they listened to it all. The Maid was advised to treat her husband well, to be kind to visitors, and to keep a good home. Ilmarinen was advised to treat the Maid well, to keep good company with her, and always be on her side, no matter what.

The time came at last for them to depart and go back to Ilmarinen's home. The Maid was sad, though many tried to cheer her. The couple journeyed for three days until they came at last to Ilmarinen's house, where there were many people waiting for them who could not attend the wedding. They celebrated again, with yet more food and drink. Väinämöinen had journeyed with them, and he once again sang for them to celebrate their marriage and entertain all.

# LEMMINKÄINEN'S SECOND ADVENTURE

*Runes XXVI to XXX*

Lemminkäinen was bitter and resentful over not being invited to the great wedding of Ilmarinen and the Maid. Worse, he had made a fool of himself and gotten himself killed on his previous adventure. Now, he was back on his island home, Kaukoniemi, with his mother. He plowed the fields all by himself, thinking of the grand celebration taking place in Pohjola. At some point, he'd had enough of his sorry situation. He stormed back home and called to his mother to prepare a sauna so that he could clean himself properly. Then he called for his weapons and armor, for he had decided to go to the wedding ceremony.

His wife, Kyllikki, warned him not to go, and his mother agreed. She reminded him that he had not been invited and would not be welcome. He might face armed men if he boldly tried to barge in. Also, it was still dangerous to journey into the north, for the land was full of magic and unknown creatures. But Lemminkäinen could not be dissuaded, and after cleaning and arming himself, he once again set off for Pohjola.

On his journey, he saw a flock of black-colored grouse. The sound of his horse's approach startled them, and they flew away. As he rode past where they had been, Lemminkäinen noticed that some of their feathers had fallen off and were lying on the ground. He was quick to snatch them up, knowing that grouse feathers could be used in magic. Confident that this was a good sign, he urged his horse onward.

Sometime later, he faced his first true challenge. His horse stopped and refused to move. Wondering what had disturbed the animal, Lemminkäinen ventured forward on his own to have a closer look, and he beheld a river of fire. In that river was an island which also spouted fire, and on the island was an eagle whose beak shot forth flames, while its wings gave off crackling sparks. This was a danger he'd not expected!

But he remembered the grouse feathers and took them out. Concentrating on his magic, he rubbed the feathers between his palms, and out of them a flock of black birds emerged. Lemminkäinen directed them to fly into the eagle's mouth. As they did so, they quelled the fires long enough for Lemminkäinen to continue.

Pleased with himself, he soon encountered another fiery obstacle: a ditch filled with burning rocks that blocked the road for as far as the eye could see on both left and right. And yet, Lemminkäinen felt no fear and used his magic to conjure a mighty blizzard so icy and cold that it calmed the rocks. He then fashioned a bridge of ice to cross the ditch, and he continued on his way.

As he neared Pohjola, he could see the gate to that cold and dark land in the distance. But between him and his destination were a bear and a wolf. Again, Lemminkäinen knew what to do. He retrieved some lamb's wool from his pouch. Rubbing it between his hands, he blew it into the air in front of him, and the wool became a flock of sheep. The bear and the wolf attacked the animals, leaving the way open for him to pass unhindered.

But he was soon beset with another trial, this time near Louhi's farmyard. He saw a palisade, a fence made with metal stakes that stretched as far into the sky as he could see, and he knew that they also reached far underground. Snakes and spears guarded the structure. Once again, his mother had been right about the dangers he would face. Still, he drew his sword and advanced. The worst of the snakes had a thousand tongues and a hundred eyes, and it slithered toward him, hissing and threatening to bite.

Lemminkäinen once again relied on magic, singing a spell that his mother had taught him. Recognizing the snake as a relative to an evil water spirit and an ogre, he sang and commanded it to retreat. And so it did. Pleased with himself, Lemminkäinen now felt worthy to join the wedding ceremony.

Arriving at Louhi's house, he burst in and asked Sariola, the house's master, if he would serve ale to a guest. Sariola said yes,

but only if Lemminkäinen conducted himself well and sat by the kitchen door, as an uninvited guest. The young man was furious and insisted that he would never take such a humiliating seat. Sariola brought him a mug, but when Lemminkäinen looked in, he saw that it was filled with worms and lizards. He threw them on the floor and killed them, again demanding ale. Sariola called up his own magic to set a puddle of water on the floor, telling Lemminkäinen to drink from that instead.

Lemminkäinen was enraged. He conjured a bull to drink the puddle. But Sariola sang, and a wolf appeared to attack the bull. Lemminkäinen himself sang and created a rabbit to distract the wolf, while Sariola sang up a dog to kill the rabbit. Lemminkäinen created a squirrel to bother the dog. And so it went, with each man singing new animals into existence, until Lemminkäinen conjured a hawk to devour Sariola's hen.

The master demanded that Lemminkäinen leave at once, but he refused. So Sariola took up a flaming sword and challenged the young intruder to a duel. Taking their quarrel outside, it ended quickly, for Lemminkäinen was the superior fighter, beheading his opponent. Taking Sariola's head in his hands, he placed it on a stake. Satisfied with his superiority, Lemminkäinen barged back into Louhi's home, demanding water to wash the blood from his hands.

But he did not count on Louhi—who was none other than Sariola's wife—being there. She was outraged and called for her best warriors to attack Lemminkäinen. He knew he could not face them all, so he fled from the house. But outside, he saw no sign of his horse, and her men were closing in. Using magic once more, he transformed himself into an eagle and flew off, all the way back to his home.

Upon arriving, he lamented to his mother about what had happened. She scolded him yet again, telling him that she'd warned him of these very dangers, but he'd chosen not to listen. And now, Louhi's men were coming for him. She told him to flee to Saari, known as the Island of Refuge, a land beyond the nine seas. Lemminkäinen's father had hidden there once during a war. Lemminkäinen realized that she spoke the truth, so he packed up and set off in a boat.

He sailed for a long time before coming to the island, and once there, he found the inhabitants quite welcoming; it was indeed a place of refuge. But he soon reverted to his old ways and began trying to charm every young woman who lived there. This did not sit well with the locals, and before long, the men were threatening to kill him. And so, the Isle of Refuge became an island of new dangers and threats. Lemminkäinen had no choice but to leave. While he sailed away, a storm blew up and tossed him about so much that the boat capsized and sent him hurling into the ocean. He kept his wits and made his way to shore, where he found another boat, and set off once again for his own island home.

But once he arrived, he found that his mother's house had been burned to the ground, and there was no sign of her or Kyllikki. Lemminkäinen was overwhelmed with grief, for he knew that Louhi's men had come looking for him. He wept bitterly, and he was determined to take revenge on Louhi for sending an army to destroy his home and family. He once again vowed to go to Pohjola. But Louhi heard of his vow and determined that she would have no more of his insolence. She froze the sea so that he could not make the journey. He had no choice but to return home once again.

Arriving home, he beheld the ashes and ruins of his family house, but this time, he noticed that there were footprints leading away into the forest. He followed them and soon found his mother. He was overjoyed to see her, and he vowed to build a new and better home to replace the one that they had lost.

# THE TRAGEDY OF KULLERVO

*Runes XXXI to XXXVI*

Once, there was a family with three sons in Pohjola that was beset by a series of misfortunes. An eagle snatched up and carried off one son, taking him all the way to Russia. A hawk swooped down and captured another son, Kalervo, and took him away to Kalevala. Their third brother, Untamo, was not taken, though as he grew up, he became more and more a problem-maker. When he grew into a young man, he was sometimes able to meet Kalervo, but the two brothers didn't like each other, and would take actions against one another. Untamo would try to fish in Kalervo's water, but Kalervo would seize all the fish caught in the nets and take them for himself. Kalervo once tried to use Untamo's fields, but Untamo sent a sheep to eat all the grain before it could fully ripen. In retaliation, Kalervo sent his dog to kill the sheep. And so it went.

Finally, Untamo sent his henchmen to kill Kalervo and burn his village. They murdered Kalervo and his family, and they destroyed their home. Untamo took Kalervo's three-month-old son, Kullervo, back with him, but Kullervo was full of spirit. Untamo thought that he would one day make a good servant, but he overheard the baby beginning to plot revenge for the murder of his family! Untamo knew that he had to get rid of Kullervo, so he forced him into a barrel, sealed it up, and threw it into the ocean. But three days later, he sailed out to the barrel to find that Kullervo was sitting on it, fishing.

Untamo ordered his servants to build a huge pyre. He seized Kullervo and threw him into the flames. Again, he returned three days later to find Kullervo, completely unharmed, sitting among the ashes and hot coals and poking at them. Untamo seized the baby and hanged him from an oak tree by the neck, but when he returned three days later, he saw Kullervo drawing pictures on the tree bark with a piece of flint.

Untamo knew now that the child could not be killed, so he decided to keep him at home and raise him as a servant. When Kullervo was older, Untamo told him to look after his own baby, but Kullervo did no such thing and the infant soon died, after which Kullervo burned the cradle. Untamo tried to put him to work with hard labor, making him cut down trees. Kullervo insisted on having a new axe for the task, and after receiving it, he went to the forest and cut down some trees with it, but soon decided he'd had enough. He whistled to call up evil spirits to do the rest of the work for him. Kullervo then cursed that land, so that no more trees would grow there.

Everything Kullervo did brought misery, so Untamo decided to sell him to the blacksmith Ilmarinen to work as a servant. Ilmarinen and his wife, the Maid of Pohjola, soon became unhappy having him around. The Maid told Kullervo to go and mind the cows. The bread she gave him had a rock baked into it, and she warned him not to eat it before taking the cows into the forest. She prayed to Mielikki, goddess of the forest, and to the forest god Tapio's daughters, as well as his son, Nyyrikki, to protect her herd from any dangers, such as wild animals or being led astray. She also asked Otso, the great forest bear, to either sleep or to wander off when he heard their cowbells ringing. Then the Maid sang a song to ensure that her cows would produce much milk.

Kullervo went out with the cows, but of course, he was not good at his job and spent his time feeling sorry for himself. He took the herd to the woods and then cut open his bread. He found the rock inside, and it broke his knife as he cut. This was his only possession that had once belonged to his father. Kullervo became furious and wept. He began to plot revenge against the Maid. He drove the cattle away into a swamp, where they got stuck. He called for wolves and bears to come and devour them. Then using magic, he changed the bears and wolves into cows and sent them back to Ilmarinen's home, telling them to attack the Maid when she came out to milk them.

When they arrived at the yard, the Maid happily came out to milk them, but the beasts changed back into their true forms and attacked her. She begged Kullervo for her life, but he would not save her, telling her she had condemned herself. She prayed to Ukko to send an arrow down to kill Kullervo, but he used magic to direct the arrow to strike her instead, killing her. He then fled back into the forest with its malicious spirits, where he again lamented his sad state. Others had safe homes and families who loved them, he cried, but he had nothing. Remembering Untamo and his cruelty, Kullervo decided it was time to seek revenge for those wrongs, and he resolved to return to Untamo's village.

But along the way, he met an old woman adorned in blue, who told him that his parents were still alive. They lived in hiding in a fisherman's hut not far from Pohjola, near a river. She told Kullervo that they had other children, a son and two daughters, his siblings. Filled with relief and excitement, Kullervo set off at once to try to find them. He searched far and wide for days, and at last found the hut. When he entered it, his own mother did not recognize him, but when he told her who he was, she was overjoyed and welcomed him with many hugs and tears.

But she also told him that one of his sisters was missing. She had gone to pick berries in the forest but never returned. When the mother had called out for her, she heard a voice from the hills answer, saying that she would never see her daughter again. Kullervo tried to be a good son to his father and mother, but he found that time and again, his temper and carelessness got in the way, and he created problems even when he did not mean to.

Winter came, and his father sent him on an errand to pay taxes. On his way home, he saw a young woman on skis and asked her to join him on his sleigh. But she would have none of it and cursed him, saying that he and his horse could both die, for all she cared. Kullervo scowled but carried on, seeing another young lady farther up, but she, too, told him to leave her alone.

He encountered yet another lady nearer to home, and seized her, throwing her into his sleigh. She threatened to kick his sleigh and make a hole in it. He laughed, and showed her his wealth and fine clothing, flattering her and winning her over. And so they spent the night together.

In the morning, she asked who he truly was, and he admitted that he was the son of Kalervo, a foolish man. The young lady was horrified, for that was her father's name as well. And so they learned that they were brother and sister, and had lain together. She was the missing daughter whom her mother searched for. But now, she was overcome with guilt and anguish. She ran from the sleigh and threw herself into the icy waters of a river, letting its currents take her away to Tuonela.

Kullervo, wishing he'd never been born, returned home and confessed to his parents what had happened. Now he only wanted to die fighting against his hated Untamo. His mother begged him not to go, but he cursed his parents, and his father cursed him in turn. Kullervo set off, but on his way back to Untamo's lands, he received word that his father and other sister had died. He cared not. But when word reached him not long after that his mother had also died, he was filled with grief. He ordered a servant to wrap her in silk and place her gently in a grave. He would avenge her by killing Untamo.

And so, he came to Untamo's lands and did what he had sworn. He killed Untamo and his family, and burned their homes to the ground. But this act did nothing to quell his rage and suffering. He returned to his family's home, which was now empty. He felt no peace, and he cried bitterly. A few days later, he went with his dog into a forest and came to the point in the river where his sister had taken her own life. It was said that the grasses and flowers still wept for her loss.

Kullervo drew out his sword and asked it if it would like to taste guilty flesh and blood. It answered saying that of course it would, for it also tasted the flesh and blood of the innocent. So Kullervo set the hilt of the sword into the ground and leaned his chest against the point of the blade. Then he pushed himself forward, thrusting the sword's point into his heart. And so, he died, beset with guilt, fury, and shame.

When Väinämöinen heard of the young man's tragic life and fate, he was most sorry for it. He said that no one would ever grow up to be honorable or wise if they had no love or care.

## ILMARINEN AND THE GOLDEN BRIDE, VÄINÄMÖINEN AND THE FIRST KANTELE

*Runes XXXVII to XLI*

Ilmarinen was overcome with grief over the death of the Maid and wept bitterly. So sad was he that he began to look older and more haggard. At night when he would reach for her, there was nothing there, and his sadness only became worse. But after some time of suffering, he came up with an idea. He went out in search of gold and silver, taking the gold from the ocean and silver from the mountains. Gathering these metals together, he set them in his forge and began to work the bellows.

As he worked, drawing upon all his skill, he saw a shape begin to emerge in the flames, something so wonderful and strange that his servants were struck with fear. The shape was that of a beautiful woman, with silver skin and lustrous, golden hair. Ilmarinen labored hard to complete her shape, forming her body and her face until each had been crafted to absolute perfection. It was the most beautiful thing he had ever made. And yet, there was no life in her eyes, and she spoke no words of comfort to him.

Nevertheless, he set to cleaning off the magnificent figure, washing it clear of all the soot and impurities of the forge. And still the statue said nothing to him, even when he laid it down in his bed for the night. The dark came, and he reached out to the gold and silver woman, but it offered no comforting touch, no warmth against the cold. Ilmarinen had to cover himself with extra blankets to keep warm, for the statue could do nothing for him.

When morning came, Ilmarinen realized that for all his skill, he had not created a living being, and that this silver and golden statue, beautiful though it was, would never bring him the comfort he desired, nor ease his loneliness. He thought of Väinämöinen, and how he had struggled to find a woman to be a good companion, so Ilmarinen decided to give him this statue as a gift of their friendship.

But when he presented it to Väinämöinen, saying that she would be a good companion for him, the old wizard asked why the great smith was giving him a ghost made of precious metals. Ilmarinen said that Väinämöinen should marry her and be happy. But Väinämöinen merely shook his head and told Ilmarinen to either melt down the statue or take it away to another land, where someone rich might appreciate it more. It was not real, and never would be, and both of them would never be anything but cold and lonely with such a companion.

Meanwhile, Väinämöinen thought about Louhi far in the north enjoying possession of the Sampo. Its magic produced everything she could want: salt, flour, and riches. She and her people were most happy. But why should she have it? She had not made it, Ilmarinen had. To whom did it rightfully belong? Should not the people of Kalevala be the ones to enjoy its bounty, and not the people of Pohjola? Väinämöinen spoke of his concerns to Ilmarinen, and they both agreed that it was time for the Sampo to be brought back to its maker.

Ilmarinen knew that retrieving the Sampo would help distract him from the grief that still gnawed at him over his wife's death, so he set to work crafting a new sword for Väinämöinen and a belt and armored shirt for himself. And when they were ready, they set off for Pohjola.

On the way, they traveled along the coast, and they heard a strange sound coming from near the ocean, like the moaning of a plaintive lament. They went to find its source, and there they

saw a beautiful and magical ship that cried because it had never had the chance to sail at sea. The two men left their horses and resolved to travel to Pohjola by sea on this wonderful ship instead, which would take less time than traveling over land. Väinämöinen began to sing a magical spell, and as he did, the ship was outfitted with a crew of young men and women who helped to row the ship and speed it on its way.

It so happened as they sailed past one headland, they saw Lemminkäinen building a new boat of his own. Seeing them, he called out, asking where they were going. Väinämöinen had the crew row closer to shore, and he told Lemminkäinen that he and Ilmarinen were sailing to Pohjola to bring back the Sampo. Lemminkäinen was enraged at the thought of his misadventures in that northern land, and asked if he could go with them, for he was still furious that men of Louhi had destroyed his home. They allowed him to come aboard, and he brought some of the wood he was using for his own boat with him, thinking it might be useful later. They all then set off.

Soon, the crew began to encounter dangers. They sailed toward a part of the sea that burned with a magical flame, one that might consume the boat. But Lemminkäinen sang a spell and the fire diminished, while Väinämöinen changed the direction of their ship to sail around where the water had burned.

All was well for a time, until the ship ran aground, but there was no island or rock beneath them. Lemminkäinen glanced over the side and was astonished to see a gigantic pike, a fearsome fish that could devour them all. Lemminkäinen drew out his own sword and tried to attack the creature, but he slipped and fell overboard. It was only quick thinking from Ilmarinen that saved him, as the smith pulled the young man by his hair out of the water.

Ilmarinen mocked him and then drew his own sword to slice at the pike. But it went badly for him, and he broke his blade. Väinämöinen cursed, telling them that the two of them together did not even make up one half of a man, much less a whole one.

He drew his own sword and stabbed the monstrous fish, splitting it in half. Part of the fish sank, which freed the boat, while the head of the beast landed on board.

Väinämöinen and the rest of the crew decided to steer the ship to the shore, where they could look at this strange creature more closely. Once on land, Väinämöinen again drew out his sword and cut open the fish's head, slicing it into pieces, so that they would all have a good meal. After they had eaten, Väinämöinen looked at the bones of the skull, and an idea came to him. Using the monster's jawbone as a body, and its teeth as pegs, he created the first kantele, a harp that would bring joy to all those who heard him play it. He created strings from the tail hairs of a horse and then offered it to others to try, but none could produce a pleasing sound from it. Each sounded worse than the last, and many said that he should destroy it by throwing it back into the ocean.

But the instrument spoke then, begging not to be discarded. The reason it did not sound well was that it needed to be played by the one who had fashioned it. So, Väinämöinen sat down, placed the instrument on his lap, and began to play, plucking the strings as if it were the most natural thing to do. And the sounds that he created were joyous, enchanting, and magical beyond words to describe.

The animals of nature—elk, squirrels, even wolves—all ceased their daily activities and drew near to the sound. Bears came, too, knocking over fences and other barriers to hasten to Väinämöinen. Tapio, the great god of the forest, and all his family adorned themselves in their finery and came to listen. The goddesses of moon and sun, Kuutar and Päivätär, who were busily weaving gold, dropped their spindles, so overtaken were they by the enchanted sounds.

And now many birds—hawks, eagles, ducks, and more—flew to Väinämöinen to hear the master singer weave these new musical spells. Fish swam closer to the shore in order to catch some of the sounds that the old wizard produced, and even Ahto, the god of the sea, came to Väinämöinen, proclaiming that never had he heard such music. Along with him came Vellamo, who was so enchanted that she fell asleep.

And still Väinämöinen played on, for the rest of the day, and into the next, and there were none who heard the music that were not overcome with joy and happiness. And Väinämöinen himself understood just how special this instrument was and what he could do with it. As he played, he began to cry, and his bountiful tears fell from his face and rolled out to the ocean. And it was said that a duck named Scaup went to fetch them, for once they had rolled into the waves, they became pearls.

And thus did Väinämöinen enchant the whole land, the people, the animals, and even the gods with the magic of his music.

## THE THEFT OF THE SAMPO, AND THE SECOND KANTELE

*Runes XLII to XVIV*

After Väinämöinen's magnificent playing had enchanted all around him, he and his companions knew that they must return to their journey and travel to cold Pohjola to try to take the Sampo from Louhi. So they and their crew set out once again over the ocean, and continued traveling north.

After a long journey, they found a suitable shore to bring the ship in safely. They set foot on land and asked their crew to remain behind while they made straight for Louhi's home. They did not wait outside, but rather, they burst in. Louhi was angry when she saw them and demanded to know why they had come to her uninvited.

Väinämöinen answered truthfully, saying that they had come to take a portion of the Sampo, for the people of Kaleva-la also deserved its wealth and abundance. But Louhi became furious, saying that it could not be divided and that it rightfully belonged only to her. It would stay with her, she insisted, safely locked away in the mountain where she kept it. She demanded that they leave at once.

Väinämöinen would not be intimidated. He told her that either she would divide it so that all could share in its riches, or he and the others would take the whole Sampo, and she would be left with nothing. Louhi was not frightened by Väinämöinen's threat, and she raised her voice, commanding that the fighting men of Pohjola bring their weapons and attack these three who so brazenly demanded what was rightfully hers.

But Väinämöinen knew what to do; he drew out his kantele and started to play. The music was beautiful and enchanting, of a kind never heard in the land before. It flowed out of Louhi's home and across the landscape. All who heard it were brought under its remarkable spell, and many began to laugh and even weep with joy. But as Väinämöinen continued to play, the music did something else; it made everyone who heard it fall into a deep and peaceful sleep. Väinämöinen ceased his playing and took out a balm from his pouch, which he spread over their closed eyelids, ensuring that they would all stay asleep for some time.

He knew where the Sampo was, and he beckoned Ilmarinen and Lemminkäinen to come with him, so that they could set about freeing it. Indeed, it was kept in a mountain of copper, behind nine locks, and no one save Louhi could open them. But Väinämöinen knew a way. Once again, he sang a magical song, and as he did so, Ilmarinen applied grease to the locks. Then Ilmarinen opened them with a combination of his skill and Väinämöinen's magic. They made their way to where the precious object was, but there was a problem. It was set into the ground so deeply that it was very difficult to move.

Lemminkäinen boasted that he would be able to easily move it, but though he tried pulling on it to dislodge it from the ground, it didn't move at all. The three soon came up with another idea and went to fetch a giant ox. They harnessed it and tied a rope around the Sampo. After much tugging and pulling,

the mighty beast was able to loosen the precious object from the ground. Elated, the three of them carried it back to their ship, and with the help of the crew, they pushed the vessel back into the ocean water and set off.

Väinämöinen prayed to Ahto for safe passage across his domain, and the crew began to row with some vigor. Before long, they were well out to sea. Ever the braggart, Lemminkäinen wanted to sing a song of victory, but Väinämöinen cautioned him that it was too soon to boast about their success, for they were not home yet. Further, if everyone sang, they would not row as hard, and the boat would begin to slow its pace.

And so, they rowed on for two days, and with no sign of pursuit, Lemminkäinen once more wanted to burst into song. But again, Väinämöinen urged caution. Still, the young man would not be dissuaded and began singing, badly, at the top of his lungs. His voice was lifted into the air and carried along the winds. A flying crane heard it, and startled, it flew over Pohjola, calling out. Its voice was loud enough to wake the sleeping people of Pohjola, including Louhi. At once, she began to check on all her possessions, and while her herds and her riches were there, she ran to the mountain in panic, staring in horror when she saw that the nine locks were open and her precious Sampo was gone.

She was furious and terrified, for she knew her own powers would begin to diminish without the Sampo nearby. She began singing a song to the natural powers, asking Ututyttö, the Maid of the Mist, to bring a thick fog down over the ocean to hinder Väinämöinen and the others. She called out to Iku-Turso, the dreaded creature of the deepest ocean, to rise up and sink the ship. She even called upon Ukko to create a terrible storm that would send waves crashing against the ship and bring it to ruin.

And her prayers were heard. Ututyttö sent a fog over the ocean with her breath, a fog so dense that it formed a wall and stopped the ship from moving at all. For the next three days, the crew was trapped in the open ocean. But Väinämöinen grew restless and angry, and using his sword, he was at last able to cut through the fog and disperse it, allowing them to continue.

After they had escaped Ututyttö's fog, a new danger came to them, for Iku-Turso raised its head out of the waters and threatened the ship. But Väinämöinen was determined and fearless. He grabbed the monster by its ears and demanded to know why it troubled them. Iku-Turso howled in pain and admitted that it was trying to hinder their passage, but it promised to leave Väinämöinen and the others alone, if he would let it go. Väinämöinen released his hands and cursed the creature. It returned to the dark depths of the ocean and has never been seen since.

But Louhi's final prayer, to Ukko, also had its intended effect, and the great god brought down a terrible storm of winds and waves. So fierce were these that one took hold of Väinämöinen's kantele and washed it overboard, sending it plunging into the depths of the ocean. Väinämöinen was heartbroken to lose his instrument and he cried bitterly. It is said that this kantele became a beloved possession of Ahto from that time.

Ilmarinen panicked because he was not fond of the sea, and he now feared that the ship would soon be torn apart, and they would all drown. But for once, Lemminkäinen rose to the challenge. He took the extra planks of wood he'd brought from his own boat and used them to strengthen the sides of their ship. His plan worked, and the ship stayed afloat as the storm gradually subsided. He then climbed the mast to look out over the ocean and saw in the distance a terrible sight: a mighty ship filled with one hundred of Pohjola's strongest warriors.

This was a foe they could not fight against, so Väinämöinen ordered the crew to row as hard as they could. Ilmarinen and Lemminkäinen joined them to help. But for all of their efforts, they could not escape from the warship bearing down upon them; it drew ever closer.

Väinämöinen had an idea. He drew out a piece of flint and threw it over his shoulder into the ocean. As he did so, he called out, commanding the flint to grow into a large reef that would rise up, block the ship, and break it apart. And as he shouted, the flint did just that. It grew at a fantastic rate out of the ocean, too quickly for the Pohjola ship to change directions, and it crashed into the reef with a terrible force, splitting in two and sending the hundred warriors into the water amid its ruins.

But Louhi was also on the ship, and she would not be denied. She transformed herself into a huge eagle with vicious talons. She gathered up the warriors on her back and flew toward Väinämöinen and the others. She landed on the mast of the ship, causing it to sway in the water.

Väinämöinen addressed her, asking if she was willing to split the Sampo into parts, for he and the others would be willing to share it if she would do so. Louhi shrieked back that she would never divide it; it was hers and hers alone. Lemminkäinen drew his sword and hacked at her, managing to slice off all of her talons save one. Louhi landed on the ship's deck then and tried to grasp the Sampo with her only remaining claw, but instead she pushed it into the water, where it cracked and broke into many pieces.

Louhi and all the others despaired, for it seemed that the magnificent object was lost. But Väinämöinen saw that some of the pieces drifted toward Kalevala. He rejoiced that some of its magic would come to his people, and the land would be blessed after all. Louhi was even more enraged when she heard this. She threatened him, saying that she would bring ruin to him and his people, destroy their crops and herds, and bring frost to kill their crops. She would steal the moon and the sun and hide them deep within the Earth so that darkness would reign. She would raise up Otso the bear and also bring disease upon the people of Kalevala. But Väinämöinen disregarded her and said that he did not fear her or the powers of Pohjola at all.

Indeed, Louhi could feel her own power waning now that the Sampo was destroyed, so she caught hold of its lid and flew back to Pohjola, weeping bitterly.

True to his word, when Väinämöinen returned home, he

gathered up all the pieces of the Sampo that he could find. He spoke magic over them and scattered them into the ground that they might make the land even more fertile and bring happiness to everyone.

And yet, Väinämöinen himself was still devastated over the loss of his kantele. He wanted to search for it, but he knew that the goddess Vellamo now held it jealously and would not willingly let it go. Väinämöinen asked Ilmarinen to forge him a copper rake so that he could try to reach to the bottom of the ocean and bring it up. When he had the tool, he used magic to take his boat out to sea, but though he raked and searched, he could not find his beloved instrument.

He gave up and went home in sadness. One day soon after, he went out walking and heard a sorrowful cry coming from a birch tree. Väinämöinen asked it why it wept so, and it replied it was destined for a terrible fate. Its leaves would be used as whisks in saunas while its bark would be tapped for sap. Eventually, it would be cut down and burned.

Väinämöinen had an idea and said that soon the birch would weep with happiness. He began to work, using wood from the birch for a new project, a kantele that would be even finer than the one he had lost. The body came from the birch, while he used silver and gold for the pegs and the hair of a maiden to fashion strings.

And when he had finished, he sat himself down on a rock, tuned the instrument, and began to play. And once again, magic filled the air as the strings shimmered under his touch. Even the mountains danced. Trees swayed, and tree stumps jumped for joy. And all who heard the music, whether young or old, poor or rich, stopped and listened. Some wept, some laughed, but all were overcome with joy and contentment.

And the animals again reveled in these new sounds: the birds, the foxes, the fish in the rivers, and even worms in the ground. And Väinämöinen continued to make his wondrous music, playing outside, and indoors, delighting all who would hear: human and animal, wood and stone, earth and air. For two days he played the kantele, and the whole of Kalevala basked in the glory of his songs.

## THE NINE DISEASES, THE BEAR, THE THEFT OF THE MOON, SUN, AND FIRE, AND THEIR RESTORATION

*Runes XLV to XLIX*

Louhi was enraged over the loss of the Sampo, and that not only had it been destroyed, but that fragments of it were now bringing wealth, prosperity, and happiness to the people of Kalevala. She was determined to ruin their newfound joy by any means necessary. She devised a plan to unleash many horrid pestilences over the land. She prayed for a way to unleash her vengeance and one came to her: the blind goddess, Loviatar. She was the most evil daughter of the death goddess, Tuoni, and was loathsome in appearance and intent. She came forth and allowed herself to be impregnated by the wind, and when the time came for her to give birth, she did so in a sauna that Louhi had prepared for her.

There, Loviatar became the mother of nine creatures, representing nine awful diseases: consumption, colic, gout, rickets, ulcers, scabs, cancer, and one that remained unnamed, but whom Loviatar sent to cause harm in the marshes and lowlands.

Filled with her desire for revenge, Louhi sent all these diseases to Kalevala that they might afflict the people and cause great misery and death. And the afflictions took their toll. Stricken with sickness, many people soon lay dying under decaying blankets, while the floors beneath them began to rot.

Seeing this misery, Väinämöinen swore that he would save his people. He set to work, declaring war on Tuoni. He heated up a sauna and gathered wood for whisks. He threw water on the

hot rocks and began to intone his magic. He first called to Ukko for relief and asked for the magic and the strength to drive away these afflictions. He sought to lock them away in the rocks and stone, which could bear them far better than the people.

He then appealed to Kiputyttö, a goddess of pain and illness in Tuonela, who sat on Pain Mountain, to gather up the people's suffering and place it in a blue stone. He asked that she then roll the stone into the ocean and let it drop to the bottom of the sea, where it could never harm anyone again. He asked that she take the people's wounds and place them in a copper box and trap it in the depths of Pain Mountain itself. He asked that she take the people's anguish and set it into a pan the size of a thumb and cook it away. He asked that their pain be placed into a hole in a rock and shut away forever.

Then Väinämöinen traveled about and treated as many people as he could with his unguents and salves. He did whatever was possible, but he knew that he still needed help. So, he called again on Ukko, and the great god answered his prayers, bringing healing to the suffering people of Kalevala. At last, the diseases were banished from the land.

When Louhi learned what Väinämöinen had done, she was furious, and swore that she was not yet defeated. She resolved to call up the great bear, Otso, and send him to Kalevala to wreak havoc and bring death and destruction to livestock and people alike. Now Otso was a feared and wondrous creature, sometimes known as Honey Paw and the Apple of the Forest. He had been created by Mielikki, goddess of the forest. Väinämöinen knew that he would have to approach this animal with care and respect. He asked Ilmarinen to forge him a new spear that he might confront the beast. And so armed, he went with his dog to find Otso, singing hunting spells and again calling to the gods and spirits for help.

He appealed to Mielikki, wife of Tapio, that the forest might receive him with welcome and allow him to confront the bear. He asked that he might save Kalevala and its people. And uttering these prayers, he set off, guided by his dog. Väinämöinen found Otso, and engaging him, he killed the bear. But it was not enough to simply slay the animal, for its mighty spirit needed to be appeased and honored. Väinämöinen invited the animal's spirit to come with him back to his land, so that the bear's life could be celebrated properly.

And Väinämöinen was true to his word; the people held a great feast in honor of Otso. They ate of his body and preserved his fine pelt. Väinämöinen took out his kantele and sang a long song in honor of the bear, recounting how Mielikki had fashioned him from wool and hair cast down by Ukko, and how she had given him teeth and claws for protection, and how he loved honey. And he gave thanks to Mielikki and the other spirits of the forest for their great gift. He thanked Ukko for their deliverance and asked that the people of Kalevala would always be so lucky in their hunts.

So joyous was his music that it attracted the interest of the moon and the sun, and they came down to hear and see all that unfolded in the celebration. They sat atop trees and marveled at Väinämöinen's remarkable runes. But Louhi, her plans once again thwarted, lurked nearby, and she was determined yet to have victory. She snatched up both sun and moon and bore them off to Pohjola, where she locked them away so that they would never be seen again.

She hid the moon within a rock and the sun inside a mountain of steel. She swore that both would never shine as long as she held them captive. But not content with this crime, she returned to Pohjola and stole fire from the people, such that all light went out, all heat vanished, and misery came once again to Kalevala. Never-ending night fell not only over the land, but even the heavens.

The great god Ukko wondered what had caused this and searched for the moon and the sun, but even he could not find them. So, he resolved that he must create them again. With a sword he struck a flame to try to fashion a new moon and sun. He gave the spark he'd created to the maidens of the air to mind,

but it slipped from their fingers and fell to the Earth. It landed in Lake Alue and was so hot that the lake itself nearly caught fire. A fish swallowed the fire, but the flame burned it from the inside. A pike ate that fish, and it also began to burn.

Väinämöinen wondered at this strange sight, this flame falling from the sky, and went with Ilmarinen to the lake's shore. There, they fashioned a net to try to catch the pike and succeeded. Once they had it in hand, they searched and found the smaller fish in its stomach, and within that fish, the spark that had fallen. It was lively and hot, burning Väinämöinen's hand as it escaped. It burned a part of the forest and some of the land before Väinämöinen was able to recapture it and place it in a copper pot.

He brought fire back to Kalevala, but the moon and the sun were still nowhere to be seen. The loss of the sun meant that things no longer could grow and that the cold would not abate. Ilmarinen tried to create a new sun in his forge, but this was beyond even his considerable skills. Väinämöinen knew that magic was involved in the loss, and using his own magic, he discovered that both sun and moon were locked away in Pohjola. He knew at once who was responsible.

He transformed himself into a pike so that he could quickly swim to Pohjola. When he arrived, he changed back into a man, only to be met by a company of Louhi's best warriors. But Väinämöinen proved to be their equal and defeated them, cutting off the heads of many. He went to where the celestial lights were imprisoned, but try as he might, he could not weaken or open the locks that bound them. Despondent, Väinämöinen had no choice but to return home, his quest a failure. But Ilmarinen had set to work forging new keys that would open the locks. Louhi heard of this work. She feared that Ilmarinen was forging shackles and that they were coming for her. Realizing that they might capture her, or worse, she agreed to free the sun and moon and let them return to their rightful places in the sky.

Väinämöinen gave thanks to the gods for their return, and he asked the sun to shine in all its glory, bringing health and life to the people and the land. He wished the moon good health in its own journey across the sky and hailed them for lighting up the day and the night once more.

And so, the sun and moon were restored, fire was recovered, and Louhi's plans for revenge were thwarted.

## MARJATTA, THE NEW KING OF KALEVALA, AND VÄINÄMÖINEN'S DEPARTURE

*Rune L*

Marjatta was the youngest of her family and was raised in a high-born home. She had fine clothes to wear, and rings and other adornments, and yet she was holy and humble. She ate fine fish, but not eggs, or meat from a ewe that had been with a ram. She would not milk the cows, even when her mother asked her to, for they had been with bulls. Nor would she ride in a sleigh pulled by mares who had been with the stallions. Thus, she kept herself away from all male creatures and any boy or man, but she would herd sheep, so that she might spend time alone.

Once, she climbed a hill with her herd and she heard the call of a golden cuckoo. She sat beside a mound where lingonberries grew and asked the cuckoo to call for her again. She asked it if her fate was to remain a shepherdess for one summer, or even ten. She heard nothing in reply, nothing that would answer her question or satisfy her longing to be something more.

But it happened one day as she was out with the sheep that she again came to the mound with the lingonberries. She heard a voice call to her from one of these berries, asking her to come and find it, to pluck it before a slug or a worm might eat it. She searched for the source of this strange request, and at last spied the berry up the hill, on the heath. She grabbed a stick to retrieve it, and once she had done so, it bounded onto her lap and then up

to her chest, and then into her open mouth and onto her tongue. Before she knew what had happened, she had swallowed it.

And by this miraculous berry, she came to be with child, though the child had no father. And over the months that passed, she sought to hide her pregnancy from her parents, who only knew that she acted strangely and loosened her clothing. But at the end of nine months and into the tenth, she knew her time had come, and she asked her mother to prepare a birthing room. But her mother was furious, wanting to know what man had done the deed.

Marjatta swore that there had been no man, and that it had been a berry on the heath that had jumped into her mouth, but her mother did not believe her. Her father also would not hear her plea and told her to be gone from the house, for she had whored herself and now would have to face the consequences by giving birth alone out in the wilderness. But somehow, Marjatta knew that this child would be special, that he would grow to be a great king and would even outshine Väinämöinen himself.

She bid her maid Piltti to go to the nearby village and ask the sauna to prepare a space for her. Piltti did as she asked, but Herod, the owner of the sauna, refused. He and his wife had heard about Marjatta and would have no one like her bringing shame to their sauna. So Piltti went back to tell Marjatta the terrible news. Marjatta wept, for she knew she was truly alone in the world.

So she composed herself, and struggling with much pain, she set out for the forest to give birth. She prayed to Ukko for guidance and protection and soon found a small hut for shelter. And there, a gentle horse came to her and nuzzled her, and the steam from its breath warmed her belly and soothed her. In due course, she gave birth to a baby boy, and laid him in the straw near the horse. Wrapping him in warm cloth, she cared for him, and nursed him, but one day, as she held him, he simply vanished from her lap. She was distraught and searched long and far for her son. She asked the stars and the moon if they had seen him, and while they hadn't, they acknowledged him as their creator. Then she asked the sun, who also acknowledged that she had created the boy, and told Marjatta that she would find him in the swamp. And indeed, when she searched there, she found him and brought him back.

Marjatta cared for him, but he still had no name, though she called him her Little Flower. And yet, no priest would bless him, fearing that he might grow up to be a powerful sorcerer. Väinämöinen came to see this mysterious child who had been born of a berry from the heath, that he might assess him and pass judgment. And indeed, Väinämöinen thought that the boy was cursed. He declared that the baby must have come from some strange magic and thus should be returned to the swamp.

But the boy, still only two weeks old, spoke up and admonished Väinämöinen, calling him a wretched old man who was guilty of many crimes of his own, none of which had sent him to be abandoned in a swamp. Those who heard these words were struck with wonder, and they saw that the boy was not a cursed monster but might in fact grow up to be a great man. So, the priest blessed him and predicted that he would one day become king of Kalevala.

Väinämöinen was angry at these words, but he knew that his time as the protector of the people of Kalevala had come to an end. So, he went to the seashore and using his magic, he sang into existence a boat of copper and pushed it out into the water. As he sailed out into the ocean, leaving behind his land, he said that a time would come when his music and magic would be needed again, whether to craft a new Sampo, to create a new moon and sun, or simply to bring joy to the people. And then, he sailed in his boat toward the horizon, but he left behind his kantele that others might continue to rejoice in its beautiful music for generations to come.

# EPILOGUE

Now I end my singing,
And bid my weary tongue to keep silence,
Leave my songs to other singers.
Horses have their times of resting
After many hours of labor;
Even sickles will grow weary
When they have been reaping too long;
Waters seek a quiet haven
After running in rivers;
Fire subsides and sinks in slumber
At the dawning of the morning;
Therefore I should end my singing,
As my song is growing weary,
For the pleasure of the evening,
For the joy of morning arising.
Thus beginning, and thus ending,
I roll up all my legends,
Roll them into a ball for safety,
And arrange them in my memory,
So that they might not escape,
And my weary tongue is silent.
Only the forest will listen to me,
Sacred birches, sighing pine-trees,
Junipers endowed with kindness,
Alder-trees that love to bear me,
With the aspens and the willows.

Do not blame me for singing badly,
I have never had the teaching,
Never lived with ancient heroes,
Never learned the tongues of strangers,
Never claimed to know much wisdom.
Others have had language-masters,
Nature was my only teacher,
Woods and waters were my instructors.
Be this as it may, my people,
This may point the way to others,
To the singers better gifted,
For the good of future ages,
For the coming generations,
For the rising people of Suomi.

# Sámi Culture & Belief

The Sámi are a semi-nomadic people who inhabit the northern regions of Norway, Sweden, Finland, and Western Russia—an area properly known as Sápmi—and have limited autonomy from those nations. Previously, this territory was called Lapland, and the Sámi were called Lapps or the Laplanders. The word "Lapp" might come from the Old Norse word leppr ("rag" or "cloth"), or the Finnish word lappa (possibly "remote place"). But in recent decades, the Sámi have regarded it as derogatory and do not use it for themselves. Nor do they wish for others to use it. The Sámi are an indigenous culture of Europe (recognized as such by the European Union), and have inhabited their lands for thousands of years, surviving by hunting, fishing, and herding reindeer.

It's tempting to think that the world's remaining indigenous cultures have survived largely untouched and unchanged over the centuries, but of course, that's never the case, and certainly not for the Sámi. They have been in contact with numerous other cultures and peoples, including the Norse, the Finns, the Russians, and most devastatingly, Christian missionaries from Sweden, Norway, and Finland beginning in the seventeenth century. While Christianity (both Catholicism and Russian Orthodoxy) had been in the north since the Middle Ages, it was the Lutheran invaders who did everything they could to wipe out traditional Sámi beliefs and impose Christian beliefs. Missionary actions included censoring Sámi stories, outlawing their spiritual practices, making church attendance compulsory, banning their languages, and burning their sacred drums. Sadly, only a small number of these historic instruments survive and can now be found in museums.

Unfortunately, the Sámi suffered the same fate that many indigenous peoples have when encountering colonial powers, including the First Nations peoples of Canada, Native Americans, and the Aborigines of Australia. While all of these cultures have survived, they have been badly damaged, perhaps beyond repair. The Sámi have long since adopted elements of Swedish, Finnish, and Norwegian culture and spiritual beliefs, but enough of their original traditions survive that we can get some picture of how they might have lived in centuries past.

Sámi culture is in no way monolithic or monolingual, and there are differences between the various Sámi groups living in different northern regions, just as there are with any culture. Even with a population of probably no more than 100,000 people in Scandinavia and Russia, there are nine different Sámi languages. They also have different views on myth and tradition. The Sámi and their culture probably influenced their Norse and Finnish neighbors and were in turn influenced by them. The Norse peoples of the Viking Age seem to have regarded them as mysterious and potentially dangerous, steeped in powerful magic and mystery. The Sámi show up as background characters in various Icelandic sagas, such as *Egil's Saga* and the *Ynglinga Saga of Vanlandi*, among several others. In the Finnish myths, the dark land of Pohjola and its mysterious and sometimes hostile people might represent the Sámi, though scholarly opinions about this differ.

It's possible that certain Sámi gods and concepts found their way into Norse and Finnish beliefs, and vice versa. As we've seen, some scholars theorize that the story of the marriage of Skadi and Njord might represent the basic incompatibilities between the seafaring Vikings and their northerly, more landbound neighbors. The Sámi god Horagelles might have influenced both Ukko and Thor, or they were at least drawn from common traditions. The Sámi god Waralden Olmai has been linked to Freyr. And the spiritual practices of the Noaide might have some aspects in common with the Norse practitioners of Seidr, and perhaps the figures of Väinämöinen and Lem-minkäinen in Finnish belief.

Sámi culture is a living tradition. As such, it's best to let them speak for themselves, rather than trying to impose an outsider's interpretation of their ways. This section will not dive deeply into speculations about their ways of life, but it will discuss some of their beliefs and current practices from their own sources (books and websites), considering what might have been related to their ancient southern neighbors in the Nordic and Finnish lands.

## SÁMI COSMOLOGY

Traditional Sámi spirituality was based on animism, to-temism, and veneration for the ancestors. All things were believed to have souls, including rocks and trees. In fact, one Sámi traditional belief held that these inanimate objects had only recently (relatively speaking) lost their ability to speak, so it was necessary to continue to treat them with respect. Spirits also abounded in the natural landscape. A Sámi hunter might ask the Leib Olmai, the forest spirits, for help in obtaining a good catch, or seek advice from the meadow spirits, the Gieddegæš-galggo.

Other entities included the gods, such as the Father, Mother, Son, and Daughter (Radienacca, Radienacce, Radienkiedde, and Radienneida). Some scholars have proposed that three sister Sámi goddesses—Sarahkka, Juoksaahkka, and Uksaahkka—could have been the original form of the three Norns. We'll discuss some of these entities more in the following pages.

The Sámi's animist worldview also included belief in sacred objects, called seites or sieidi, which could be rock formations, trees, or even objects of wood or stone. The Sámi often built fences around seites to create a space called a passe, though not every passe had seites and vice versa. These locations and objects were contact points with the underworld and could be used as places of offering and sacrifice. Prayers might also be offered at a place called the Tarvopaike.

In rituals facilitated by holy people called the Naideh, the Sámi made offerings and sacrifices to specific deities or spirits, or sometimes for the dead and the ancestors. The similarly named Noaide would speak with the entities invoked to learn what they wanted and what was required.

Offerings made could include unusually shaped rocks, animal parts, bones and antlers, food, living animals, and according to some sources, humans. However, it's possible that Christian missionaries—and anyone else who wanted to tell a fearsome tale about the mysterious "others"—claimed that the Sámi practiced human sacrifice in an effort to slander them; there is little evidence for it.

People also kept personal seites in secret locations known only to a few, perhaps the Noaide and a few members of a given family, who would pass the secret down to their children. There might also have been communal seites that were honored by the whole group, but likewise, their locations were kept secret from outsiders.

The Sámi believed in Boahjenasti, the North Star, which was an axis or pole that the world turned around. Rituals, meditations, and sacrifices were needed to ensure that this pole stayed up and did not collapse, for such a calamity might bring about the end of all things.

They further believed in an underworld, Jabma Aimo, where the Jábmiid, the spirits of humanity, went after death. This was not a "heaven" exactly, but it wasn't a place of doom and gloom. Rather, it was a realm where the dead could recover from their harsh lives, a place free from worry about cold, dark, and starvation.

There was also the Saiwo (or Saivo) Aimo, a separate world filled with its own strange and mysterious beings. Some of these entities were beneficial, while some wanted to cause harm. Among the latter were the Stállo, dim-witted human-troll creatures who hated humanity and caused trouble. They liked nothing better than the chance to eat a tasty human being!

As with their Norse and Finnish counterparts, the Sámi saw little difference between the living and the dead. Indeed, the dead never truly left the living, they had just moved on, and the living could communicate with them under the right circumstances. However, Christian missionaries tried to convince the Sámi that the living couldn't (or shouldn't) contact the dead, and any efforts to do so were akin to doing the devil's work. The idea that speaking with the dead was an evil act was utterly foreign to the Sámi and became one major reason for the tensions between them and the missionaries who were trying to convert them.

While much lore has been lost to time and enforced Christianization, some myths and legends survive to tell how the Sámi came to be. These differed from region to region, but it seems that most Sámi at one time considered themselves to be children of the sun. One can imagine that living in the far north, the sun would take on an even more important role than for those who lived farther south. It would never be absent from the sky in the summer months, but in winter, it would be gone for weeks. Many cultures around the world traditionally celebrate the "return" of the sun, in either December in the northern hemisphere, or June in the southern. But for Arctic peoples, this return took on an even more meaningful role, so it's perhaps natural that some of them would develop a special relationship with the ultimate giver of light and warmth.

The Sámi did not consider their hardships as punishments. The fact that the sun disappears for a while each year is simply a fact of life to be endured; they didn't believe that the sun was angry with them or cursing them by being absent. They saw the world as simply being what it was, rather than trying to force it to do their bidding. The creatures of the world existed because they were created to be so. None were superior to any other, including the Sámi themselves. There were also unseen powers, spirits, and lesser deities that inhabited the landscape, who had their own roles and purposes, some well-known, some mysterious.

Two important works from oral tradition in Sámi belief describe the creation of the world and its early days: "The Death of the Sun's Daughter" and "The Son of the Sun's Courting in the Land of the Giants."

"The Death of the Sun's Daughter" survives only in a partial form. As the title implies, it tells the tale of the Sun's daughter, weak and on her deathbed. While her family watches her slip away, she begs her father to rise again and restore hope to the people, for they have been dwelling in darkness, with their herds declining and illness spreading among them. She wants the Sámi to thrive again. This myth speaks directly to the importance of the sun in Sámi culture and their connection to it.

The much longer epic, "The Son of the Sun's Courting in the Land of the Giants," tells of the origins of the Gállá-bártnit, or "the Hunting Sons," the original ancestors of the Sámi people. In the land of the Son of the Sun there are no women, or at least none that please the Son. So, he sets out on a quest to find a bride, traveling to a land that is west of the sun and moon and filled with treasures. He sails with his crew for about a year before finally arriving in the land of the giants. There he meets a fair maiden, a giant's daughter.

She asks him why he has come to her land, and he tells her that he seeks refuge from the travails of life. He is looking for a warm smile, support and comfort, companionship, and someone to have children with. She is very taken with his words, and he wins her over, but her old, blind father is not so well disposed, and it takes some time and trickery to convince him. But the Son finally does, and the two are wed, mixing their blood and tying knots in fabric to ward off bad luck. Then they consummate their marriage and she accepts his "key." Her father pays a generous dowry, and the two of them set off back to the land of the Sun.

But the maiden's brothers are not happy with this arrangement and decide to go after them. Using her magic to call up strong winds, the bride wards them off. When they behold the Sun's light, they turn to stone, allowing the young couple to escape. Once back at the Son's home, they have another marriage ceremony, and the bride is transformed into a human-sized woman. In time, she gives birth to the Gállá-bártnit, who eventually rise into the sky and take their rightful place in the heavens with their grandfather, but not before siring the Sámi people. They invent skis and are skilled elk hunters, and now they can be seen in the constellation of Orion, where they hunt still. And so, the myth explains why the Sámi have a special relationship with the Sun, for they are its descendants.

The Sun is the father of all life, while the Earth is its mother, and the two have brought about all things. But they did not create the land of the giants or the giants themselves, which implies that these beings were already there, or that they came from another, unnamed source. By mixing the blood of the Sun and of the giants together, a new people—the Sámi—are made.

The tale of the Son and his bride calls to mind some interesting imagery that we've already seen in Finnish myth: a journey to find a bride in a dark land, reluctant parents, angry siblings, long sea voyages with dangers and pursuits, using magic to manipulate the elements, settling down into a new life together, and links to the cosmic order.

The possible connections to Norse myths are even more interesting: the "giants" themselves, their mysterious origins as something "other" who live in a land of their own, the use of trickery to outwit them, and their vulnerability to the sun, which turns them to stone.

It's tempting to try to identify links between these various details and suggest that there must be cultural influences, in one direction or the other. These motifs might represent some shared ideas and myths that filtered into each culture over time and became their own unique things. Proving that, of course, is

very difficult. Did the Sámi hold to these ideas first and over time they were absorbed by the Finns and the Norse? It's possible, especially given that the Sámi are by far the oldest culture of the three. We know that they had somewhat regular contact with their more southerly neighbors (both friendly and otherwise), so perhaps some of these tales and ideas gradually seeped into the beliefs of the Norse and the Finns. But Finnish and Nordic accounts tended to portray the Sámi somewhat negatively, so to what extent Sámi beliefs would have influenced their neighbors is not clear. Or perhaps the process was reversed, and some myths evolved first in Nordic and Finnish lands and worked their way north over many centuries. But it might also be that these characters and plots come from an ancient, common tradition. We are at too great a distance in time now to ever know for sure.

In any case, the Sámi had variants of these stories, and many versions have probably been lost to time, along with several other stories about the early days of the Sámi people. But even if these epics vanished, Sámi holy men and women kept many important traditions alive, and it is to them we now turn.

## THE NOAIDE

The Noaides are the holy people of the Sámi. Known by different but similar names to different branches of the Sámi, anthropologists have often referred to them as "shamans." But this term is not quite accurate, as the word "shaman" comes from Central Asian origin and refers to the spiritual practices of various Siberian peoples. It is better to say that the Noaides represent the animistic spirituality of the Sámi and work with spirits in ways that resemble those of their Siberian Arctic counterparts. They communicate with the spirit world, make sacrifices to spirits and gods, perform healings, and offer advice to the people of the siida, the Sámi social unit of extended families who live in the same group. As mediators, they help maintain the balance between the human world and the spirit world.

The two most important "tools" in the Noaides' spiritual practice are drumming and joik, a unique form of vocalization that can take many forms. The Noaides combine joik and striking the drum to induce a trance state that the Sámi call jamal-gai, which allows them to call up the "free soul." The free soul can leave the body and travel to the realm of the spirits and communicate with unseen beings. This is different from the "body soul" that we all have, one that, as the name implies, cannot leave the body. It's possible that the Noaides might historically have enhanced their spiritual journeys with the use of psychoactive compounds, such as the fly agaric mushroom.

Once in the other world, they might seek out the advice and counsel of the spirits who live there. Each Noaide had access to their own saiwo-vuoign, a group of three spirit animals. The saiwo-vuoign usually included a bird called the saiwo-lodde, a fish (or sometimes a snake) known as the saiwo-guolle, and a reindeer called the saiwo-sarve. Traditionally, the greatest of the Noaides had reindeer bulls as their animal guides.

Beginning in the seventeenth century, the Noaides faced powerful human adversaries, in the form of Scandinavian Lutheran missionaries. The missionaries began an aggressive Christianization campaign in the far north and were determined to wipe out all traces of "sorcery" and "black magic," particularly the practices and knowledge of the Noaides. They considered the saiwo-vuoign to be demons, not benevolent spirit guides. Several Noaides were put on trial and executed for "witchcraft," with the support of both church and state. For better or for worse, some of what we know about the Noaides comes from these trials and court records, as well as missionary writings.

At this time, the official state religion in Sweden was Lutheran Christianity, and all others were outlawed. When the Sámi angrily and aggressively resisted attempts at conversion, they were charged with resisting the crown as much as believing in heresy or practicing "devil worship." It was a convenient fiction that allowed for land-grabs and the imposition of Swedish law. Some Sámi were executed, not just for engaging in "sorcery," but also for being a "danger" to the Swedish government and monarchy. Because of this institutional persecution, the Sámi lost many of their traditional ways, cultural practices, and material heritage.

From 1716 until 1727, a missionary named Thomas von Westen traveled throughout the north, attempting to convert the Sámi to Christianity. Von Westen had no real sympathy for traditional Sámi beliefs, but he did want to use their native languages to try to speak with them and persuade them of the superiority of his religion. His approach wasn't always popular among the Scandinavian authorities, as many wanted to "civilize" the Sámi by forcing them to adopt official Scandinavian languages. Unfortunately, Scandinavian countries (the Danish-Norwegian state in particular) enforced the policy of suppressing indigenous languages well into the twentieth century.

In his time, Von Westen tried to trick the Noaides into denouncing their own beliefs and practices. But the Sámi were far more clever than he gave them credit for. Since he did not know their languages as well as he thought he did, they would sometimes make useless or irrelevant condemnations, sending him away satisfied that he'd gotten to them, when in fact, they probably laughed at him! In some instances, he insisted that they burn their sacred drums, so they collected up old ones that were no longer used, or that were believed to no longer have power, and burned those instead. And then, they kept right on doing what they'd always done.

In 1726, as the "Age of Reason" began to take hold, the Norwegian government abolished the death penalty for those accused of sorcery and "witchcraft." But this didn't mean that the Sámi were now free to do whatever they wished. They were still subjected to harsh punishments and inhumane treatments if they did not accept the new religion, attend church services regularly, and accept all the other trappings of the religion imposed on them. Sámi children were forced to attend missionary schools, and the parents had no choice in the matter, a scenario played out in many instances around the world, where colonial powers try to indoctrinate the young.

Some of the Sámi simply refused to convert and tried to relocate farther north, out of the clutches of the missionaries, at least for a while. But it was only a matter of time before the forces of colonialism and religious rigidity caught up with them.

Indeed, many Sámi finally embraced Christianity in the nineteenth century, thanks in large part to the efforts of Lars Levi Læstadius (1800–1861), a man with Sámi ancestry who was a biologist and Lutheran pastor. He was determined to Christianize the Sámi once and for all, and he began a campaign to bring his message to them in plain, everyday language that seemed to understand their plights and offered solutions. He was ardently anti-alcohol and had seen the effects that alcoholism had had on Sámi communities (similar to what it has also done to Native American and Australian Aboriginal groups). He wanted to offer a way out that would bring genuine relief.

His efforts were successful, and greater numbers of Sámi converted. As they did, they began to adopt more of the ways of their Scandinavian neighbors, and their spiritual practices began to wane. Today most Sámi are, at least in name, part of the Lutheran Church, though the Skolt Sámi in Russia are mostly members of the Orthodox Church, even if they keep their own traditions in the home. Many Sámi believed that the last of the true Noaide died out in the mid-nineteenth century and that any others that persisted were either tawdry imitators or outright frauds, perhaps trying to play on people's superstitious beliefs and fears. There will always be "holy men" who will offer quack cures and wisdom for a price.

While most authentic Noaides were usually men, we know of at least a few women who became Noaides, most notably Ri kuo-Maja of Arvidsjaur (1661–1757) and Anna Greta Matsdotter of Vapsten (1794–1870). These women might have taken on the role of Noaide at a time when the old ways were being exterminated, perhaps due to an absence of suitable male candidates. There could well have been many more women Noaides in ages past, though their names are now long forgotten.

In addition to the Noaides, the elderly Gieddegeasgalgu were also renowned for their wisdom. These women of the North Sámi often lived at the edge of their communities. People would go to them when they wanted a practical or magical solution to any given problem. After Christianization, these women were often viewed with suspicion and even hostility. They were sometimes reduced in status to being nothing more than gossips, and even disparagingly called "chatter crones." The similarities between them and the images of witches and wise women in other cultures are obvious.

While today the so-called secular Scandinavian governments no longer actively persecute or attempt to convert the Sámi, the Sámi continue to face opposition and discrimination. The government of Norway, for instance, while recognizing Sámi animism, still tacitly favors the Lutheran church, which continues to speak out against other religions and tries to limit their influence. Obviously, a lot of people are unhappy with this behavior, and the hope is that this will change.

Today, the practices of the Noaide still exist in Sámi lands and culture, though in a greatly diminished form. Some Sámi are reviving animist ideas, beliefs, and practices, but most are certainly not engaged in spiritual activities to the extent that their ancestors were. Even while being at least nominally Christian, many incorporate some of the old ways into their lives, and this seems to indicate a growing interest in reclaiming a crucial part of their heritage.

One problem with researching or studying this kind of animist revival is that the Sámi are understandably reluctant to talk about their practices with outsiders, given the history of their oppression. Theirs is a closed system that they will only share if they see fit, and outsiders need to respect that.

All that said, here's an interesting side note about the potential for cultural influence far beyond their own territory. One fascinating theory suggests a link between the Noaides and ... Santa Claus. Seriously. Some anthropologists and folklorists think that these holy men would once visit temporary Sámi settlements, sometimes accompanied by a reindeer, and dressed in red and white, colors that might have represented the fly agaric mushroom, used by shamans and other spiritual navigators throughout the Arctic. The traditional Sámi dwelling (the *lávvu* or *goahti*) resembles the tipis of the Plains American Indians, and if these were snowed in, the only way to enter would have been through the smoke-hole in the top. Dressed in their colorful garb, the Noaide could bring the "gifts" of healing and counsel to each family through the tops of the dwellings, and in return they might receive some food and drink as a thank-you or payment. It's not all that different from leaving out milk and cookies for Santa when he drops down a chimney to bring presents to your house! Knowledge of this ancient practice might have found its way into American accounts of the Sámi written by Finnish immigrants and become intertwined with other Father Christmas legends.

Another Christmas origin theory concerns spirits known as the Juovlajohttit or "Christmas Travelers," whose roles changed on the arrival of Christianity. They were said to travel across the sky in sleds, some even pulled by reindeer. Others were believed to wear red.

While we can't determine for sure whether the Juovlajohttit or the Noaide theory are indeed part of the origin stories for contemporary Christmas imagery, it's not too far-fetched. Indeed, most of us associate Santa with the North Pole, or at least somewhere northern and snowy, like Finland. If you happen to visit northern Finland, you can spend a day or more in the famed Santa Claus Village in Rovaniemi, a very popular tourist desti-

nation. While the Sámi have survived despite centuries of persecution and forced assimilation, some of their ancient spiritual practices and folk beliefs might well live on in the commercialized Christmas holiday industry.

## JOIK

Sámi joik (or yoik) is far more than just singing or even "chanting." It is a form of vocalizing that has many layers and meanings and is one of the oldest vocal traditions in Europe. In any given joik, there are often few dajahusat, or words, and the sounds and melody take over in importance. Traditionally, a joik was chanted by the Noaide to help them enter a trance state and so that they could make the journey to one of the other worlds, via their free soul. They would then return with new knowledge, offering up another joik to describe any insights gained from the other world.

Noaides aren't the only ones who practice joik; anyone in the Sámi community can joik in order to call to mind another person, an animal, or a place. The chant is not about the person or beast. Rather the chant *becomes* that desired entity. One would not joik *about* the bear, for example, one would actually joik the bear itself. If a person were traveling without someone and missed them, they might joik their friend so that he or she could be with them on their journey.

There are many different kinds of joiks. There are joiks for animals, joiks for the natural world and its many sounds, joiks for people (friends, family, personal relationships, children), joiks for specific events and gatherings, joiks for places, ritual joiks, and even joiks that simply arise spontaneously for whatever reasons. The Sámi prefer to say that a joik comes to a person, rather than believing that they themselves created or composed it. The person joiking intends to offer the listener a sense of the subject, such that they can almost feel that place, animal, or person in the sound.

A joik about a person is never to be performed by that person, and no one would create a joik about themselves; this would be seen as bragging. The personal joik is something that others do for them. To receive a joik from another is a great honor. Indeed, joiks are even given as gifts of courtship or at weddings. Importantly, a joik belongs to the person who is joiked, not the person who created it. And if the one who envisioned that joik wants to perform it in public, they should always get permission from the person being joiked.

Some joiks imitate the sounds of nature, especially animals. When joiking a given animal, it makes sense to imitate that animal's sounds in the chant itself, or perhaps to use a joik to draw out an animal that one is hunting. Other joiks have overtone and throat-singing elements that might call to mind the sounds of Siberian, Mongolian, or even Tibetan chants, though these are a more recent stylistic development, rather than indicating an ancient practice or connection between joik and Central Asian throat-singing. Some joiks remind people of Native American chants, though this probably has less to do with any direct connection spanning thousands of miles and years and speaks more to a tendency for certain cultural and artistic practices to arise independently. Of course, we cannot completely rule out that the two chant traditions might have some long-lost, ancient common origin in Central Asia or Siberia, but we'll probably never know.

Joiks can also be a way of communicating hidden meanings to those who understand what they are listening to. Someone from outside the community might recognize one aspect of the joik, while those in the know would perceive other meanings. As you can imagine, this secrecy did not sit well with Christian missionaries, and joiking became one of their main bones of contention with Sámi culture. After all, who among them could know what the Sámi were *really* saying about them? Since the

Noaide were some of the main practitioners of joik, it was just one more reason to target them for elimination.

The Vuolle style of joik of the South Sámi was particularly disliked by missionaries, and many people in the community ceased practicing it altogether in the face of oppression. Meanwhile, the Luohti style of the North Sámi fared better and is the style more commonly heard today, in various forms. Happily, joiking was not wiped out, and it is experiencing a renaissance in popularity, especially since the 1990s.

Today many Sámi musicians are crafting new, updated joik styles and combining the traditional practice of solo voice with modern instruments, such as guitars and synthesizers, to create a whole new world-fusion art form, one that is growing in popularity among fans of folk music. Artists such as Mari Boine have received international acclaim for blending joik with rock and pop. Different types of joik are now being chanted by younger members of Sámi groups, to distinguish them from the more traditional and spiritual joiks of a community's older members.

## THE SÁMI DRUM

While joik was one crucial component of spiritual travel to other worlds, just as important was the *govada*, or drum. A Noaide would beat the drum in hypnotic, rhythmic patterns to help achieve dirran, a trance state. Traditional cultures all over the world practice techniques for achieving ecstatic or out-of-body states. The Sámi are no different, but their drums have a unique feature: they are maps for the Noaides to use in their spirit travels. These instruments feature hand-drawn representations of humans, animals, spirits, natural features, and other objects found in the otherworld. This artwork gives those making the journeys signposts to use when they are in the spirit realms. Makers of the drums traditionally used a dark-colored dye made from the bark of the alder tree, which resembles blood.

Historically, the Sámi made their drums with reindeer hide stretched over a wooden oval-shaped frame. They most often used birch wood, which still has significance to the Sámi, as it is a hardy tree that can survive the extreme cold temperatures of the north much better than many other trees, and so it was more available as a resource. The drums traditionally were hit with a beater made of reindeer antler or sometimes copper.

These drums could also be used for divination purposes, by putting an arpa, a small piece of bone or copper, on the drumhead, and then beating the drum and letting the vibrations move and bounce the *arpa* about. When the drumming stopped, the *arpa's* position would be interpreted by whatever place or figure on the drum it had come to rest near or on.

Unsurprisingly, the use in divination and other spiritual practices drew negative attention from Christians. The Finnish Lutheran parish priest Henric Forbus (1674–1737) vehemently declared that the Sámi drum was a tool of Satan, and that it contained images of devils and false gods. He insisted that each time a Noaide beat on it, it was a beat made by Satan in hell, foreshadowing when the Noaide's soul would finally be sent there. To him, the images on the drums were pure evil, literally portraying the demons that the Sámi allegedly worshiped.

On a less fire-and-brimstone note, the French playwright Jean-François Regnard (1655–1709) was perhaps the first "tourist" in the Scandinavian north in the early modern age. He went without a political or religious agenda, and he observed and recorded several interesting facts about the Sámi. Regarding the drums and their designs, he wrote:

"The top is covered with a reindeer skin, on which they paint a number of figures in red, and from which we see hanging several copper rings and a few pieces of reindeer bone. They usually paint the following figures: they first make, towards the middle of the drum, a line which goes transversely, above which they place the gods whom they have in greatest veneration, like Thor with his valets, and Seyta; and they draw another a little lower like the other, but which extends only to half the drum: there we see the image of Jesus Christ with two or three apostles.

"Above these lines are the moon, stars and birds; but the place of the sun is below these same lines, under which they put the bears and the serpents. These also represent animals, sometimes lakes and rivers. This is the shape of a drum; but they don't all put the same things on them, because there are some where herds of reindeer are painted, to know where they must find them, and when there is someone lost. There are figures that make known the place where they must go for fishing, others for hunting, some to know if the diseases they are suffering from must be fatal or not; as well as several other things of which they are in doubt."

It's noteworthy that he writes that the Sámi place images of Thor on their drums, but it's most likely a misrepresentation. The Norse gods and their myths were barely understood in mainland Europe at the time, so it is entirely possible that "Thor" was simply a name he'd heard of that could be used for any northern god. Still, it brings up the possibility once again of deeper connections between the Sámi and their Norse neighbors in times long past. But what was Jesus doing there? Again, this might be a misinterpretation, or perhaps he was witnessing a curious blend of two traditions as some Sámi tried to integrate the new god with their own beliefs. The Norse and the Finnish certainly had done the same, putting up altars to the old gods and the new, side-by-side.

Regnard also observed:

"They hold this instrument in such reverence that they always have it wrapped in a reindeer skin, or something; and they never let it into the house by the ordinary door through which women pass; but they take it either over the sheet which surrounds their hut, or through the hole which gives passage to the smoke.

"They usually use the drum for three main things: for hunting and fishing, for sacrifices, and to know the things that are done in the most distant countries; and when they want to know something about this, they take care first to bandage the skin of the drum by bringing it near the fire. Then a Lapp kneeling with all those present, he begins to beat in circles on his drum; and, redoubling the blows with the words that he utters like a possessed man, his face turns blue, his hair bristles, and he finally falls on his face without movement. He remains in this state as long as he is possessed by the devil, and for as long as his soul needs to bring back a sign that makes it known that he has been in the place where he was sent. Then, coming to himself, he tells what the devil has revealed to him, and shows the mark that was brought to him."

It's clear that Regnard was fascinated by Sámi drumming, but his mention of the "devil" reveals biases from his own French Christian culture. Indeed, he associates the spirits the Noaide contacts with the devil without hesitation.

To be sure, the missionaries who were in the northern region at the same time as Regnard's visit and beheld these ceremonies for themselves didn't think of them as harmless superstitious nonsense. They truly believed that the Noaides were in contact with diabolical powers that were using and deceiving the Sámi. Seeing these drums as a tool for communicating with demons and the devil, Christians sought to destroy as many of them as possible, a tragic loss for world culture. Today, skilled craftspersons are making beautiful new drums, but out of the thousands that once existed, only seventy-one known original Sámi drums survive intact.

# SÁMI IN THE OLD NORSE WORLD VIEW
# AND IN THE SAGAS

Old Norse sources often referred to the Sámi as finnar, which is not to be confused with the Finnish. As we've seen, the Sámi were mainly a nomadic people, whereas the Norse peoples were farmers and explorers, so their cultures were already quite different, perhaps even incompatible. And yet, they almost certainly had some influence on each other in culture, spirituality, daily life, and perhaps in other ways.

Though the Sámi lived in northern Scandinavia, there is archaeological evidence that they lived farther south, at least in Norway, where that evidence shows that they might have traveled not far from modern Oslo. While some of these migrations might have occurred after the Viking Age, chances are that the Sámi would have encountered the Norse people and their settlements in earlier centuries. There were no political borders to their lands, and it's possible that in some places the two groups coexisted, even if uneasily. The Norse probably encountered the Sámi fairly regularly, and were willing to co-exist with them, at least to the extent that there doesn't seem to have been attempts to try to subjugate them, conduct raids against them, or occupy their lands. For their part, the Sámi never tried to attack the Norse, as they were not war-like. And as far as we know, there were never any attempts to try to force religion or spirituality on each other; that simply wasn't a thing before monotheism. The Norse actually knew of some Sámi spiritual and cultural practices.

Indeed, knowledge of the Sámi extended to a famous Norse oath, which says that there will be peace as long as the falcon flies, as long as the pine grows, as long as the rivers flow into the sea, as long as children will cry for their mothers, and as long as the Sámi go skiing. In other words, there would be peace forever. So obviously, the Norse knew that the Sámi were skilled in skiing, and that this was a regular part of their culture and of their life, along with their nomadic and animist ways.

Connections between the Sámi and the Norse people appear in Norse mythology, particularly in the story of the goddess Skadi. Skadi is a skilled skier and huntress, associated with winter and wintertime activities. And as we've seen, it's possible that Skadi was originally a Sámi goddess or even a god. We've noted that her name is what's called a "soft masculine name." Names ending with the letter "i" tend to be masculine, and we've already pondered about her original sex (male or female?). She might have, at least in part, been based on a Sámi deity, since she lived and hunted in the wintry mountains and only came to the Aesir and Vanir gods after they had chosen to end their war and make peace. While it's possible that the story of her marriage to the sea god Njord shows the relative incompatibility of the two cultures, there may be even more to it and to her.

Some scholars think that Skadi was actually modeled on the Sámi themselves, for not only does she engage in skiing and hunting, activities reserved for men (in both the Norse and Sámi view), she takes on a masculine role when she comes to avenge the death of her father, Thiazi. In Norse myth, Skadi plays a role typically associated with men, particularly when she comes to Asgard. The gods offer her the option of marrying one of them, but when choosing, she can only see their feet.

Historically, however, these roles would be reversed. In northern Scandinavian cultures, a chieftain or other ruler might offer a visiting man the option of marrying a daughter (or choosing, if he had more than one) in exchange for some kind of alliance or peace agreement. While this was not fair to the woman involved, it was a common Norse practice that the Sámi probably also have engaged in. But in the myth, the gods (not the goddesses) are on offer and are concealed from the woman, just as the faces of Norse or Sámi brides might have been veiled for men.

So, the Norse gods receive and treat Skadi—a woman and a goddess—in essentially the same way as they would a man. They offer her a marriage contract to end a potential blood feud

between them. She gets to choose her husband, an option that would have rarely been afforded to women in real life. So is Skadi's story a gender-bent tale about a marriage alliance meant to bring an end to a potential deadly conflict modeled on a possible real-life exchange between the two cultures? Possibly.

Of course, it's also possible that this scene was merely meant to be humorous, since it's followed by the story of Loki, the goat, and Loki's poor testicles. But some scholars propose that the pain Loki experiences indicates something of a wounded masculinity for the gods, who are now on offer. Whatever the original intention, Skadi takes on roles usually reserved for men, and in this way, she could have possibly represented the Sámi themselves.

The Norse also seemed to have regarded the Sámi as masters of magic, and some scholars have speculated that there might be a connection between the animist practices of the Sámi Noiade and the magic of Norse Seidr. It's not at all impossible that Sámi animist traditions had some influence on Seidr magic, which might explain why the Norse often viewed Seidr with suspicion, even if both Freya and Odin practiced it. The two cultures probably influenced each other's myths and gods to a greater extent than we will ever know.

In some accounts in the sagas and elsewhere, the Sámi are referred to not only as finnar, but also jötnar, meaning that they might actually be the "giants" of Norse imagination. The Norse seemed to have seen the Sámi as masters of natural magic, including the ability to control the weather, to cause storms, and possibly to transform themselves into animals, much like the jötnar could. Are the Sámi the original model for the jötnar, a group of strange people from outside the realm of the familiar? The Sámi of the sagas are clearly humans, so the term might have been meant to be insulting, or to show that the Norse were looking down on them. But it might also simply have meant that the writers of the sagas saw the Sámi as strange and unknowable beings that lived a nomadic existence far beyond the confines of Norse culture and civilization, especially during the Christian era.

The Norse trader and adventurer Ohthere of Hålogaland traveled extensively in the far north, and visited the court of King Alfred of Wessex (the Great) in England in about 890. He spoke of the people that lived in those northern regions, recorded in Anglo-Saxon accounts as the Finnas (Sámi), the Cwenas, and the Beormas. Scholars debate who exactly the second and third sets of peoples he named were, but it's possible they were different groups of Sámi.

Clearly, the Sámi were fascinating to their southern neighbors. The Norse thought that the Sámi had the power to both heal and kill with their magic, and would have feared and respected these abilities, probably being careful when dealing with any Sámi in their own lands. For their part, the Sámi do not seem to have been overly aggressive or hostile, but no doubt the Norse would have wanted to stay on their good side, and especially would have avoided angering a testy practitioner of ancient and powerful magic!

Despite this fear, the Sámi are also described in the sagas as "trolls," which calls to mind images of grotesque creatures who live under bridges and turn to stone in sunlight. Trolls are indeed a staple of later Nordic folklore, but the sagas' designation doesn't mean that the Norse saw the Sámi as misshapen monsters. It simply meant that they were outsiders, from somewhere strange, and perhaps there was an implication that they would never truly fit in.

If "troll" referred to some kind of outsider, then it's also possible that some Sámi even immigrated to Iceland. This is a hotly debated topic, however, and not everyone is convinced that any Sámi ever did make such a voyage. That said, such a thing wouldn't be impossible, given how many Irish also moved to Iceland (often against their will), as did people from Norway and Scotland. Perhaps some Sámi individuals, and maybe even whole families, did make the long journey to Iceland. If so, they probably would have been held in lower esteem than their Norse counterparts and faced suspicion and even discrimination. It's interesting to think that some Sámi left their homelands and sailed across the northern Atlantic in the hopes of taking up a new life in a new land, far from their traditional ways.

In another connection between the mythic and the mundane, Norse poems and histories sometimes link the Norse line of kings with the Sámi, much in the same way that earlier kings claimed to be descended from the gods and the jötnar, such as Odin and Rig (Heimdall), and in Sweden with Freyr and Gerd. Even during the Christian era, it seems that in some instances, kings wanted to trace their lineage back to a Norse ancestor who had married a Sámi woman. Here, the Sámi seem to stand in for the jötnar, perhaps representing something strange, magical, and powerful. These claims might have been useful for Norse kings who wished to exercise sovereignty over Sámi territory in the far north (or those living closer to their own realms), because if such kings could show that they were descended from the Sámi, then of course they had the right to rule over them. Even more importantly, they could impose taxes and extract tributes from them, which could bring substantial wealth. This very action is described in various writings, such as in *Egil's Saga*. From those mythic unions, whether of gods or humans, came lines of kings that would later claim sovereignty over various lands. Both lineage myths served their purposes.

We find another interesting parallel in the Norse myths, in that we hear of Norse gods marrying or mating with jötnar and kings marrying Sámi women, but not the reverse. No Norse goddesses ever took jötnar as husbands. Indeed, the jötnar are usually seen as leering and repulsive, such as the times when Freya has to fend off more than one would-be jötunn lover and master. And in the mortal world, we read of Norse kings taking Sámi women as wives, but not of Norse men joining Sámi families by marrying one of their powerful and high-standing women. It might have been done from time to time, but there are no records of it. So we can assume that there must have been prohibitions on such actions, and that the Norse peoples enforced a double-standard, at least some of the time.

In any case, such unions could be dangerous. A story about the fear of Sámi magic and the intermarriage of two cultures intertwined is found in the *Ynglinga Saga of Vanlandi*. The Swedish King Vanlandi travels to the lands of the Sámi, and there he makes an agreement with the Sámi leader Drift that he will marry Drift's daughter at some point in the next three years. But Vanlandi doesn't keep his end of the bargain, and after ten years, Drift decides to take action. He visits a Sámi sorcerer and asks him to put a spell on Vanlandi that will force him to either return to Drift and keep his promise, or kill him if he refuses. The magic works, and Vanlandi soon has a desire to return to the Sámi chieftain and keep his word. But before he can leave, his friends persuade him to change his mind, and when he does, he dies. Clearly, while marrying a Sámi woman could bring prestige and new blood to a royal line, there was also danger in doing so, and kings needed to be careful not to cross angry fathers!

It's worth noting that while there are various references to the Sámi in the sagas, they are not main characters, and the view of them is entirely from the outside. We don't have any written accounts from the Sámi telling us about themselves. Rather, we only have accounts of how the Norse perceived them, mostly from Christian Norse writers. Of course, their views are colored with suspicion and often portray the Sámi as workers of black magic, just as they were during the later Lutheran persecutions. The Sámi are primarily seen as practitioners of witchcraft, and that has a negative connotation for them, for they might spread these "wicked" activities to others. As such, it's difficult to know exactly what is historical and what is fanciful in the saga literature.

Some surviving accounts tell stories of people who learned magic and other traditions from the Sámi, such as the semi-historical Nordic Queen Gunnhildr (c. 910–c. 980). She was said to have studied magic with the sorcerers in Finnmark (Sápmi). This accusation was clearly meant to imply that because she studied and learned Sámi traditions, she returned home knowing a great deal of evil magic and how to use it to her advantage. These powers made her a topic of suspicion among later writers, though they insisted that she actually converted to Christianity before her death, perhaps as a way of making her royal status more palatable to Christian audiences.

The images of the Sámi in the Norse sagas and other literature have to be considered semi-mythical, but they give us a glimpse into a possible relationship between these two ancient cultures. We can't make many definite conclusions about their interactions, but we can entertain theories, and we know that the Sámi certainly had contact with the Norse and even the Vikings for long periods of time.

## GODS AND GODDESSES

There are many attje and akkas—Sámi gods and goddesses—across the various regions and groups of Sápmi. This entry is far from a comprehensive or definitive description of them, partially because few written accounts exist outside of the Sámi languages, and there are far too many deities to list in detail. A good number of them are likely forgotten.

If you happen upon the names of these deities in other books, you might notice that there are multiple spellings for each deity's name, depending on the Sámi language and region one is researching. The spellings here aren't meant to be definitive; they're some of the more commonly used ones.

All that said, let's look at some of the better known and most important gods.

HORAGELLES ("Thunder Hero") is a god of weather and thunder who carries two hammers. He fights against trolls and other monsters, with the intent of keeping things in balance and defeating evil. His similarity to Thor is obvious, but whether this god influenced ideas about Thor or if they derive from a common ancestor is not clear. Since a version of Thor originated in Germanic lands, it's possible that these two gods share a deep ancestry.

DIERMMES is another god of thunder (or perhaps the same god as Horagelles in a different form) who holds a rainbow in one hand and a bow that shoots lightning in the other. The imagery calls to mind the Norse Bifrost Bridge. But Diermmes seems less inclined to do good, for he chases after a reindeer called Meandas-pyyrre (or Golle Coarveheargi in some traditions) who has golden antlers, a black head, a silver coat, and glowing eyes. This hunt, called Sarvvabivdu, is said to be on display every night in the stars of the constellations of Gemini and Castor and Pollux. Rather like the wolves that chase the sun and moon in Norse myth, Diermmes pursues the animal with the intent of killing it. He has struck it once with an arrow, which has brought droughts, deserts, and lack of rain to parts of the world. His second arrow will melt the ice and bring fire (which seems very similar to Icelandic visions of erupting volcanoes). And when he finally gets close enough to stab the animal, the moon and the sun will darken, and the world will end. This imagery is strikingly similar to the Norse Ragnarök, and might be a later addition to the mythology, or it might even show some Christian influence.

AKKA is said to be Horagalles' wife, a goddess associated with creation. She was worshiped in remote places, like caves or rocky outcroppings. Unlike Thor's wife, Sif, Akka is said to be an old crone; no lustrous golden locks for her! She is not to be confused with the broader term akka, used for goddesses and spirits, but she is probably related to the creator goddess Mattarahkka/Maderakka, detailed next. Akka is also the name of Ukko's wife in Finnish mythology, and it is said that when they have sex, thunder is the result!

MATTARAHKKA is the "Great Grandmother," a goddess of the Earth, and is the first mother of the people. She not only gives humans their forms, but also oversees all women and girls. She

watches over boys, too, until they are old enough to be named as men. She receives souls from above and helps them to integrate into human bodies. Sámi women looked to her for protection and inspiration. She is the mother of three important goddesses: Sarahkka, Uksahkka, and Juksahkka, and she might be related to another Earth goddess, Eanan.

It's possible that Sarahkka, Uksahkka, and Juksahkka, having such control over life and even death, might have been a source of inspiration for the Norns, or at least come from a common source.

SARAHKKA helps to shape an unborn child's form so that it fits neatly around its soul. She is associated with fertility, sexuality, pregnancy, childbirth, and menstruation. She assists women in giving birth and having their periods. After giving birth, a Sámi woman would traditionally eat a special porridge dedicated to her and offer up drinks in her honor. In some traditions, she is a house goddess who lives in or near the hearth, which is the center of the home. There is a modern Sámi organization dedicated to women's rights named for her.

UKSAHKKA, or "Door Wife," is a midwife goddess who also determines the sex of a fetus before the baby is born. She protects newborn infants and children from dangers such as illness and violence and even simple trials such as learning to walk. Traditionally, she dwelled at a home's door (hence her name) and would help to protect the home from all harm if the family invoked and honored her.

Curiously, JUKSAHKKA is a goddess of both children and hunting, said to dwell behind the fireplace of the *lávvu*, the traditional tipi-like home for many nomadic Sámi. She is more associated with boys and is said to be able to transform an unborn child into a boy if she chooses. Thus, a family hoping for a son might pray to her for this transformation. Boys learning to hunt might also pray to her for inspiration and skill, for she was said to instruct them. She might be related to the goddess Boazuáhkku, a goddess of reindeer and good luck in hunting.

She might also have some relation to the Norse Skadi and the Finnish Mielikki. It's especially interesting that, as we've seen, Skadi might once have been a male god who changed over time into a female, while Juksahkka is able to change the sex of a baby to a male. This could be nothing more than a curious co-incidence, but there might be a hint of some kind of gender or sex-swapping hunting god/goddess from a common northern tradition that found its expression in different myths for the Norse and the Sámi.

Speaking of hunting gods, LEIBOLMMAI, the "Alder Wood Man," is a god of forests and the hunt. He also looks after wild animals and accepts sacrifices and offerings from hunters for protection and successful hunts. In this, he bears a strong re-semblance to the Finnish god Tapio, the Celtic Cernunnos, and perhaps even to the Norse god Freyr. Because of his asso-ciation with the alder wood tree, the Sámi used the juice from its red blood-like bark to paint their drums. In some regions, Sámi women would also spit this juice on bear hunters return-ing from the hunt, perhaps in honor of a successful catch. This juice, called *liejpie* in the south Sámi language, also represented menstrual blood.

JABEMEAHKKA is the goddess of death and the underworld, the realm known as Jabma Aimo or Jábmiidáibmu. She presides over the land of the dead, possibly in a manner similar to the Norse Hel, and is perhaps related to the original version of Lovi-atar from pagan Finnish belief.

BEAIVI is the goddess of the sun, though in some traditions, the sun is honored as a male with the name BEAIVVAS. As we've seen, veneration of the sun was a central part of traditional Sámi belief, given that they relied so heavily on it for their daily life, and that it disappears for weeks at a time in the Arctic winter. At the winter solstice, the Sámi would sacrifice a white reindeer to her, an offering to ensure her return. Sometimes they'd put the meat onto sticks, which they bent into the shape of rings and adorned with ribbons. The people would also place butter or fat at the entrances to homes as a sacrifice to the goddess after the return of the light. As it melted in the low sun, it was seen as a source of nourishment that helped her to regain her strength after being away and allowed her to climb higher into the sky with each passing day.

The Sámi would also offer up prayers to her for anyone afflicted with mental health issues, as they thought that these were caused by the long dark of the winter. In this, they were not completely wrong, since we know that Seasonal Affective Disorder is very real for millions of people. It certainly must have been an issue for at least some in the siidi going back thousands of years.

The sun has a daughter, or perhaps more than one, or they might all be aspects of the sun goddess herself. BEAIVI-NIEIDA travels with her mother through the sky in a vehicle made of antlers and bones, while AKNIDI was said to have lived among the Sámi for a time, teaching them sewing skills, singing, and stories. Some members of the community were jealous of her beauty and abilities, and they smashed her with a large rock, but she simply returned to the sky.

There were also three goddesses associated with spring. SALA NIEJTA was responsible for bringing winter to an end and ushering in spring. SERVGE EDNI was a goddess who brought new life at the end of winter. Finally, there was RADIENNEIDA or RANA NIEJTA, who made things grow.

RADIENACCA, RADIENACCE, RADIENKIEDDE, and RADIENNEIDA are four different gods and goddesses, whose names have many different spellings in different Sámi languages. Their identities and functions might seem a bit confusing at first, but they are effectively a father, mother, son, and daughter. Radienacca is something like the supreme god, the highest of all and a god of the sky. From him come the souls that then move on to Mattarahkka and her daughters to be born into the world, though in some traditions, it is his wife, also known as Sierg-Edne or Serge-edni, who sends these souls down.

Their children are a creator god and a fertility goddess. The daughter, Radienneida, makes all things grow green in the spring and brings the new reindeer each year so that the herds can continue. In some traditions, it's possible that the father and son are the same, a god called Ibmil, or that at least, the father works through the son. However, this construct is suspiciously Christian and might be a later addition. Indeed, Christian missionaries used the name Ibmil to refer to their own god during their attempts at conversion.

MANNO/MANNU/ASKE is a goddess and personification of the moon, who seems to have been worshiped around the time of the new moon each month, as she would again begin to grow into her full radiance and power. Some saw the moon as masculine and as a deity to approach with caution. Either as a male or female, some were suspicious of the moon in general. Why did the moon only choose to come out at night? What was it up to? The dark, especially in winter, could be a time for evil spirits to wander about, possibly at the moon's direction. In some older traditions, the Sámi seem to have sacrificed hay and other feed to the moon, perhaps in the belief that a totem animal dwelled on it, or perhaps simply to get the beast to leave them alone! The similarity between Manno and the Norse Mani is clear.

Regardless of the moon's intentions, it is said to have a beautiful daughter, NIEKIJA, who has exquisite silver hair. In one story, the sun, in the form of the god Beaivvas, sent his son PEIVALKE to woo her on his behalf. But of course, Peivalke fell in love with her instead. The moon tried to hide Niekija away on a remote island, but there NAINNAS, the chief of the Northern Lights, saw her and also fell in love with her, and she with him. But they could not be together, and so now they gaze at each other across the northern night skies.

BIEGGOLMMAI carries a shovel (to scoop up ice and snow) and is a god of winds and storms. He decides which direction the wind will blow toward and from, which was important for the Sámi to know when traveling across the northern landscapes with their herds, or perhaps when venturing out onto boats. So, they would pray to him to learn the answer. Another name for the (presumably) same deity in the north and east Sámi territories is Ilmaris, who brings precipitation and winds. This name is obviously very similar to the Finnish Ilmarinen, and suggests an ancient connection. In yet another form, he is known as GEDDEKIS AKKO, a god who not only controls the weather but can grant wishes if he favors the one who asks.

There are many other gods in Sámi belief, including:

Barbmoáhkku, who watches over migrating birds to ensure that they return from the south.

Čahceolmmái, a god of lakes and water life.

Guolleipmil, a god for fish in lakes, rivers, and oceans. He seems to be separate from Čahceolmmái. Sacrificial stones near bodies of water were often called Guolleipmil.

Hálddit, a god of flora and fauna, who seems to be separate from Leibolmmai.

Mader Akko, a goddess who could restore lost senses, such as sight and hearing. She was also believed to offer help and guidance for those lost in the dark or the wilderness.

Rohttu/Ruottha, the god of sickness and death, separate from Jabemeahkka, but who dwells in a gloomy realm called Rohttuaibmu. One can see similarities between him and Loviatar (who brought deadly diseases to Kalevala), as well as Tuonela and Hel. And like the latter two, he seems to be confined to this underworld and cannot leave it.

## SPIRITS AND OTHER ENTITIES

Many other gods, demi-gods, and other powerful spirits inhabit the spiritual world of Sapmi. Some of these entities are benign, while others are quite evil, causing no end of trouble and torment to the unwary. Here are some of the more important ones.

Äppäräs: The ghost of a dead (often murdered) child who did not receive proper burial rites and who thus haunts the place where it died. This spirit is one of many types that could come back if its body was not treated according to established custom. One creepy Sámi folktale tells about a baby that suffered this fate and later took its revenge.

ARJA: A type of female gázzi, or spirit.

ARNE: Guardian spirits who watch over any buried treasures. They can be identified by the smoke they give off, allowing mortals to take the treasure if said mortals fulfill all of the conditions for taking it set by the one who originally buried it.

BOASSO-AHKKA: A guardian spirit or perhaps a goddess who dwells in the goahti (the home). She watches over the sacred spaces of men and their doings.

ČAHCERÁVGA: The "Water Man," who is a spirit living by a specific river, lake, or the sea. It can determine the success or failure of a fishing expedition and might also cause drownings. Parents might sometimes evoke the Water Man to scare small children, presumably to keep them away from bodies of water for their own safety.

ČAHKALAKKAT: Another group of water spirits who usually dwell by springs. They resemble small, naked humans and are said to have stomachs filled with silver. Their heads have healing powers, so if someone could trap and kill the Čahkalakkat, they could obtain both their money and healing.

GÁZZI: Also known as gáccit or gadze. These are helper spirits, especially for a Noaide. They usually appear in the form of an animal. A bird might guide the Noaide in journeys to the upper world (to the gods), while a four-legged animal would help with matters in the middle world (our own), and a lizard, snake, or fish would guide the Noaide in the lower world (that of the dead).

GUFIHTAR: These often beautiful beings live in the Earth. They can bring luck to those they favor, but one must have caution when dealing with them. If they invite a person to dine with them in their own world—called Gufihtarčohkka (the Gufitar Hills, also sometimes just called Saiwo)—that mortal might well become trapped there, never able to leave. In this way, they have clear parallels with the Celtic Sidhe (fairies) and can be both helpful and harmful. They are interested in trading with humans, and if they favor a certain mortal or group of mortals, they might give them gifts, such as magical animals.

One terrifying type of Gufihtar, the Ulda, carry away babies, making them similar to those disreputable Celtic fairies who abduct and replace mortal infants with changelings. It was said that if the baby wore a silver necklace or amulet, they would be protected. Here, silver—not iron as in Celtic tales—repels these magical intruders.

HALDI: Spirits especially common in the north of Finland. The word derives from the Finnish haltija, which itself comes from an old German word meaning "to protect" or "to control." Haldi are the essence or mother spirit of a particular animal or sometimes a place, and thus they have much in common with some traditional Finnish beliefs. And like Finnish belief, the spirit of the bear was especially highly prized among the Sámi. Places with their own Haldi were considered sacred, and people would leave offerings at them in honor of the spirit.

JEETANIS: Giants, who might or might not be hostile or dangerous. The similarity to the Old Norse "jötnar" is obvious, but which group came up with the word first?

NAAIDEGAZZI: Also known as the Noaidegadze or Saivogadze, these spirits are allies of the Noaide and Sámi people. One might well be the spirit of an ancestor of a particular Noaide and his or her family and can appear to them in brightly colored clothing. The Naaidegazzi often choose the next Noaide. If so, they will stay with the human in question and help to train them, and will also follow them on their spirit journeys. They might stay with the same family through several generations.

PADNAKJUNNE: These creatures are dangerous, dog-like humanoids with a taste for human flesh. They might have some relation to either werewolves or to other legends of dog-headed humans that are found surprisingly often in various mythologies around the world, dating back to ancient Egypt and Greece. Several medieval writers, including Marco Polo, claimed to have seen or heard about canine man-beasts on their travels.

RADIE: Known in Scandinavian folklore as Rå, these spirits are the guardians of a specific place or landmark or even of certain animals. It is important to cultivate a good relationship with them. If humans violate their places or creatures, or if they offend the Radie in any way, these spirits might take revenge against the ones foolish enough to transgress, bringing them bad luck or worse.

RAWGA: Known in Finnish as the Raukka, these are terrifying ghosts, often of those who drowned at sea. As with other similar spirits, these entities cannot rest because they never received proper funerals. The word might be related to the Old Norse *draugr*, restless and frightening spirits of the Viking undead.

RUÐOT: Another type of female gázzi.

SAIWO-NEIDAH: Much like sirens or mermaids, these beautiful female spirits are said to have green, linen-like hair and to sing with captivating voices, though they don't seem to be as dangerous as the more famous sirens that lure unwary sailors to their doom.

SÁIVU: This word can refer both to a sacred lake or mountain and to the spirit that inhabits it. Sáivu can also refer to another realm that can be accessed from one of these points, most commonly by a Noaide, and used to journey farther onward into other realms.

SILDE: These mischievous and sometimes malicious spirits can cause problems with travel, can scatter reindeer herds, and make general trouble if they are upset. They can bring ruin and death to those who anger them, but they have a benevolent side as well. They can grant gifts such as wealth and health to those mortals they favor.

STALLU/STÁLLO: These large, troll-like beings are dim-witted and like to fight. They have some of the characteristics of classic Nordic trolls and other such fairy-tale monsters. They are fond of human children in the sense that they find them tasty! They often carry large knives, but it is bad luck to take one of these away from them, much less keep it.

SUOLOGIEVRA: A wolf spirit that can travel between all the worlds. Its name means "the strong on the island," and might date from a time when the early Sámi thought that they lived on a large island in the middle of a sea. Recall that the word "Scandinavia" itself might originally have derived from "Skadi's Island," which once more raises questions about her relationship to the Sámi and their beliefs. Skadi also favors wolves.

TJATSE OLMAI: A water spirit that is found most often near river rapids. If one goes to such a place and offers this spirit a silver coin, it will respond with an answer to one's question or perhaps even assistance to a problem.

TONTA: A Stállo with only one eye that is especially protective of the area that it watches over. With just one eye, it is always attentive to its place.

TROLLKARINGA: The "troll women." These could also be Stállo or Jeetanis. Indeed, one of them, named Atsitje, was the wife of the first Stállo. They are generally evil, loathsome, and to be avoided.

VUORWO: A fearsome female spirit of the night who wanders from place to place, looking in on sleeping mortals in their bedchambers. If she finds that they have no water in the room, she will eat them. A gentle reminder to always sleep with some water nearby!

## FOLKTALES

Many sets of surviving folktales from different Sámi groups have been collected, mostly in the nineteenth century, though a good number have never been translated into English. They cover the whole range of stories from myths to fairy tales. Some of the more modern ones seem to be adaptations of stories compiled by the Brothers Grimm or from other such sources.

They often feature animals and explain how a particular creature or place came to be, just as we find in many fables and folktales around the world.

They don't usually have the same mythic or epic quality as the stories of the Norse and the Finnish. It's possible that such longer myths never existed, but it's more likely that many were lost forever before they could be written down, the sad fate of many oral traditions that meet with colonial or invading groups. Some Sámi folktales are undoubtedly very old, while others show signs of more modern settings and Christian influence, which simply shows that people will continue to tell and make up stories regardless of their circumstances.

Unfortunately, the folktales that do survive were often sanitized by the collectors to make them more acceptable to the sensibilities of nineteenth- and early twentieth-century European audiences. For example, a lot of the more ribald stories were not included in these collections, though thankfully, some slipped through (in lightly edited forms) or survived into modern times in oral tradition. As you might expect, these collections of written stories often show the Noaide in a negative light, continuing the long tradition of portraying them as suspicious wonder-workers at best, and evil sorcerers at worst. Some tales are suitably creepy, such as the story of a murdered infant who later comes back to life to stab the parents that cruelly killed it (it's a ready-made horror movie!), while others are humorous, or tell classic fairy tale–style narratives of rescuing princesses and going on adventures into unknown lands.

The "Further Reading" section at the end of the book lists a few recommended titles, should you wish to delve into this fascinating world of traditional Sámi stories more deeply.

# FURTHER READING

There is an absolute treasure trove of information about all of these myths, stories, and people. This list is long, but it's not at all the final word. These books, articles, authors, and websites are a great place to start if you want to delve more deeply into any subject from this book.

## NORSE MYTHOLOGY

*Books*

*The Poetic Edda*, trans. Carolyne Larrington. Oxford University Press, 2014.
Probably the best one-volume translation of the Eddic poems available.

*The Poetic Edda*, trans. Jackson Crawford. Hackett Publishing, 2015.
Another take on the poems, worth reading in comparison to Larrington's translation.

*The Prose Edda*, trans. Anthony Faulkes. Everyman, 1995.
The complete work.

*The Prose Edda*, trans. Jesse Byock. Penguin Classics, 2005.
An abridged version of the Prose Edda that is a great introduction.

*The Sagas of the Icelanders*, various translators. Penguin, 2000.
A selection of key sagas that will entertain and give the reader much more insight into the Norse mind and world.

Michael P. Barnes. *Runes: A Handbook*. Boydell Press, 2012.
A comprehensive history and study of runes and their use
from Roman times until the present. One of the best
introductions available.

Kevin Crossley-Holland. *The Norse Myths*. Pantheon Books, 1980.
A classic retelling of the key stories.

H. R. Ellis Davison. *Gods and Myths of Northern Europe*. Penguin,
1990.
A classic survey of the Norse gods and myths in a very
readable form.

Erik Evensen. *Gods of Asgard*. Evensen Creative, 2012.
A splendid graphic novel retelling key myths. A great introduction for younger readers or anyone who'd like visuals to these
timeless stories.

Neil Gaiman. *Norse Mythology*. W. W. Norton, 2018.
Gaiman offers a wonderful new spin on the old Norse myths in
his own unique story-telling style.

Genevieve Gornichec. *The Witch's Heart*. Ace, 2021.
This novel is a retelling of the story of Angrboda and Loki from
their point of view, and features many other Norse gods. Not a
traditional view of their story, but thought-provoking and
beautifully written.

John Lindow. *Norse Mythology: A Guide to Gods, Heroes, Rituals, and
Beliefs*. Oxford University Press, 2001.
Another classic study that covers just what the title says.

Neil Price. *Children of Ash and Elm: A History of the Vikings*. Basic
Books, 2022.
The best one-volume history of the Vikings available. A must-
read if you want to know more about the people who created
and held to these myths, and there is good information about
the gods and myths themselves.

Neil Price. *The Viking Way: Magic and Mind in Late Iron Age Scandinavia*. Oxbow, 2013.
A detailed study of Norse beliefs about magic, including Seidr and its possible relation to Sámi beliefs and practice.

Eleanor Rosamund Barraclough. *Beyond the Northlands: Viking Voyages and the Old Norse Sagas*. Oxford University Press, 2016.
A great introduction to the sagas and the many travels the Norse made both east and west.

## Articles

| | |
|---|---|
| Karen Bek-Pedersen | Henning Kure |
| Meghan Callaghan | Tommy Kuusela |
| Mads Dengsø Jessen | Emily Lyle |
| Amy May Franks | William P. Reaves |
| Juliette Friedlander | Lar Romsdal |
| Frog | Margaret Clunies Ross |
| Terry Gunnell | Laurie Sottilaro |
| Kurt Hohman | John Stephens |
| Joseph S. Hopkins | Aurelijus Vijūnas |

If you want to dive deeper into studying specific myths and concepts, here is a very small list of academic scholars whose articles make for great reading (and provided much useful information for this book). Many authors listed above have also written articles. Search **ACADEMIA.EDU** or **GOOGLE SCHOLAR** to find more of their work.

## Websites

Ocean Keltoi's Youtube page is a gold mine for information about all aspects of Norse mythology and spiritual practice:
**WWW.YOUTUBE.COM/@OCEANKELTOI**
A number of public domain versions of the *Eddas* and the sagas are also available online.

# FINNISH MYTHOLOGY

## Books

*The Kalevala*, trans. Keith Bosley. Oxford University Press, 1999, 2008.
The complete *Kalevala*, splendidly translated into modern English, while preserving the poetic form.

*The Kalevala*, trans. Eino Friberg. Penguin Classics, 2021.
Another excellent translation that preserves the poetic style and form.

*An Illustrated Kalevala*, retold by Kirsti Mäkinen. Floris Books, 2020.
A beautiful edition intended for younger readers that covers all the main stories accompanied by splendid illustrations by Pirkko-Liisa Surojegin.

Juha Y. Pentikäinen, trans. Ritva Poom. *Kalevala Mythology*. Indiana University Press, 1999.
A detailed academic look at the *Kalevala* and the story behind it, as well as the original poems and myths. He is the author of several other books.

Matti Sarmela. *Finnish Folklore Atlas*, trans. Annira Silver. Helsinki, 2009.
A huge book filled with information!

## Articles

Here are some authors of academic studies of specific stories and characters that offer in-depth studies of Finnish mythology and culture. Search **ACADEMIA.EDU** or **GOOGLE SCHOLAR** to find more of their work.

| Anssi Alhonen | Väinö Kaukonen |
|---|---|
| Pirkko Alhoniemi | Siria Kohonen |
| Pertti Anttonen | Matti Kuusi |
| Thomas DuBois | Eric Plourde |
| Lauri Honko | |

*Websites*

The *Kalevala* online: A nineteenth-century translation by John Martin Crawford, in public domain:
**HTTPS://STANDARDEBOOKS.ORG/EBOOKS/ELIAS-LONNROT/ THE-KALEVALA/JOHN-MARTIN-CRAWFORD**

## SÁMI CULTURE AND BELIEFS

*Books*

Thomas A. DuBois. *Sámi Media and Indigenous Agency in the Arctic North*. University of Washington Press, 2020.
A study of how contemporary Sámi are using all forms of media in both their native languages and others to create a sense of community and identity, and to educate the world about themselves and their goals, using music videos, film, and the internet.

Trude Fonneland, and Tiina Äikä, ed. *Sámi Religion: Religious Identities, Practices and Dynamics*. Mdpi AG, 2021.
As the title suggests, a collection of studies on Sámi religion, both traditional and modern, and how these beliefs exist and adapt in the modern world.

Emilie Demant Hatt, *By the Fire: Sámi Folktales and Legends*, trans. Barbara Sjoholm. University of Minnesota Press, 2019.
A short collection of Sámi folk tales, originally published

in 1922.

August V. Koskimies and Toivo I. Itkonen. *Inari Sámi Folklore: Stories from Aanaar*, tans. Tim Frandy. University of Wisconsin Press, 2019.
An extensive collection of tales, joiks, proverbs, and more, collected between 1886 and 1914.

Veli-Pekka Lehtola. *The Sámi People: Traditions in Transitions.* University of Alaska Press, 2005.
A short but useful introduction to Sámi history and culture, written by a North Sámi author.

Gabriel Kuhn. *Liberating Sápmi: Indigenous Resistance in Europe's Far North.* PM Press, 2020).
A collection of articles and interviews with Sámi from many different backgrounds, letting them speak for themselves on the situations that they face.

*Articles*

There are more useful articles and websites than books for the Sámi, so try searching for these authors on **ACADEMIA.EDU** or **GOOGLE SCHOLAR** to find more of their work.

Sirpa Aalto

Rein Amundsen

Stéphane Aubinet (had also written books on joik)

Andrew F. Besa

Merlyn Driver

Harald Gaski

Marko Jouste

Francis Joy

Else Mundal

Herman Pálson

Nicola Renzi

John Weinstock

*Websites*

The *Sami Culture* website has many excellent articles, grouped by topic:

Anthropology:
**LAITS.UTEXAS.EDU/SAMI/DIEDA/ANTHRO.HTM**

Religion (Christianity):
**LAITS.UTEXAS.EDU/SAMI/DIEHTU/SIIDA/CHRISTIANITY.HTM**

Religion (Traditional):
**LAITS.UTEXAS.EDU/SAMI/DIEHTU/SIIDA/SHAMAN.HTM**

Music:
**LAITS.UTEXAS.EDU/SAMI/DIEHTU/GIELLA/MUSIC.HTM**

Sami Culture in a New Era:
**LAITS.UTEXAS.EDU/SAMI/DIEHTU/NEWERA/NEWERA.HTM**

# ABOUT THE AUTHOR

**TIM RAYBORN** is a lifelong lover of myths, legends, history, and European cultures. He has written a huge number of books (about fifty at present!) and magazine articles (more than thirty!), especially in subjects such as music, the arts, general knowledge, the strange and bizarre, fantasy fiction, and history of all kinds.

He is planning to write more books, whether anyone wants him to or not. He lived in England for several years and studied at the University of Leeds for his PhD, which means he likes to pretend that he knows what he's talking about.

He's also an almost-famous musician who plays many medieval and traditional instruments that most people have never heard of and usually can't pronounce. He has appeared on more than forty recordings, and his musical wanderings and tours have taken him across the US, all over Europe, to Canada and Australia, and to such romantic locations as Umbrian medieval towns, Marrakech, Vienna, Renaissance chateaux, medieval churches, and high school gymnasiums.

He currently lives in Washington State with many books, recordings, and instruments. He's pretty enthusiastic about good wines and cooking excellent food.

**WWW.TIMRAYBORN.COM**

## ABOUT CIDER MILL PRESS
## BOOK PUBLISHERS

Good ideas ripen with time. From seed to harvest, Cider
Mill Press brings fine reading, information, and entertainment
together between the covers of its creatively crafted books.
Our Cider Mill bears fruit twice a year, publishing a new crop
of titles each spring and fall.

"Where Good Books Are Ready for Press"
501 Nelson Place
Nashville, Tennessee 37214

cidermillpress.com